HIDDEN TEACHINGS OF TIBET

HIDDEN TEACHINGS OF TIBET

An Explanation of the Terma Tradition of Tibetan Buddhism

TULKU THONDUP RINPOCHE

Edited by Harold Talbott

Wisdom Publications • Boston

Wisdom Publications
199 Elm Street
Somerville, MA 02144 USA
www.wisdompubs.org

Library of Congress Cataloging-in-Publication Data

Thondup, Tulku.
Hidden Teachings of Tibet: an explanation of the Terma tradition of Tibetan Buddhism / Tulku Thondup Rinpoche; edited by Harold Talbott.
p. cm.
Originally published: London: Wisdom Publications, 1986.
Includes index.
ISBN 0-86171-122-X (alk. paper)
1. Rñiṅ-ma-pa (Sect)—Sacred books—History. 2. Buddhist literature, Tibetan—History and criticism. 3. Padmasambhava, ca. 717–ca. 762. I. Talbott, Harold. II. Title.
BQ7662.2.T48 1997
294.3'923—dc21 96–51599

ISBN 0-8617-122-X

11 10 09 08 07
7 6 5 4 3

Cover Art: Padmasambhava, courtesy of Harold Talbott
Cover Photo: courtesy of John Cochran

Cover design: L·J·Sawlit

Wisdom Publications' books are printed on acid-free paper and meet the guidelines for the permanence and durability of the Committee on Production Guidelines for Book Longevity of the Council on Library Resources.

Printed in Singapore.

Contents

Acknowledgements

I am thankful to Harold Talbott for his energy and wisdom in editing this book. I am grateful to Michael Baldwin and the patrons of Buddhayana, under whose sponsorship I have been able to work on my scholarly projects for the past number of years. I am in debt to the kindness of Professor M. Nagatomi and the Department of Sanskrit and Indian Studies, Harvard University, under whose auspices I have done my academic work in recent years. I am highly grateful to the perpetual Refuges Dudjom Rinpoche, Dilgo Khyentse Rinpoche and Dodrup Chen Rinpoche for their precious clarifications of a number of difficult points that I encountered during my work on this book. I appreciate being able to have discussions with Lama Jig tshe of Golok, a real hidden yogi, whenever I need illumination and recharging while in the process of thinking, writing, and doing my research. Thanks are also due to Harry Winter and Vivian Kurz for preparing the index, to all those who provided the illustrations, and to John Cochran who kindly photographed the thangkas. Finally I wish to thank Lynn McDaid and Robina Courtin of Wisdom for their efforts in preparing and publishing this book.

Some Key Terms

Guru Padmasambhava (Lotus Born Master) or *Guru Rinpoche* (the Precious Master): one of the greatest Buddhist adepts, from India. He established Buddhism in Tibet in the ninth century and with his consort *Ye shey Tsho gyal* (*Ye Shes mTsho rGyal*) concealed numerous texts, relics and transmissions of teachings in Tibet. He is the founder of the Nyingma, the original Buddhist school in Tibet.

Ter, Terma, Tercho (*gTer, gTer Ma, gTer Ch'os*; Dharma Treasure, Hidden Treasure): treasures of texts, relics and the transmissions of teachings concealed by Guru Padmasambhava and Ye shey Tsho gyal.

Terton (*gTer sTon*; Dharma Treasure Discoverer): the reincarnations of the realized disciples of Guru Rinpoche who discovered Terma in the form of texts, relics and/or transmissions of teachings concealed by Guru Rinpoche and entrusted to them by him.

Note on Transliteration

I have capitalized the root-letters (*Ming gZhi*) of each word in the transliterated Tibetan in order to ensure a correct reading. When the root-letters are not capitalized, it is possible to confuse two entirely different words. For example, '*Gyang*' means 'wall,' while the meaning of '*gYang*' is 'luck.'

Publisher's Acknowledgment

The publisher gratefully acknowledges the generous help of the Hershey Family Foundation in sponsoring the production of this book.

Part One
Buddhism and the Terma Tradition

1 *Termas*

There have been many occasions in world history when scriptures and material objects have been discovered miraculously through the power of spirits, non-human beings and sometimes through psychic powers possessed by gifted human individuals. Termas are a kindred phenomenon. They are scriptures that have been deliberately concealed and discovered at successively appropriate times by realized masters through their enlightened power. Termas are teachings representing a most profound, authentic and powerful tantric form of Buddhist training. Hundreds of Tertons, the Discoverers of Dharma Treasures, have found thousands of volumes of scripture and sacred objects hidden in earth, water, sky, mountains, rocks and mind. By practicing these teachings, many of their followers have reached the state of full enlightenment, Buddhahood.

Various schools of Buddhism in Tibet have Termas but the Nyingma school has the richest tradition. This school was established in Tibet in the ninth century by Guru Padmasambhava, and it is through the power of the wisdom mind of this saint and his enlightened disciples that the transmission of these esoteric teachings takes place. Included in this book is a text written by the Third Dodrup Chen Rinpoche (1865–1926), one of the greatest scholars of the Nyingma school. This explains aspects and stages of the process of concealment and discovery of

Termas. It is a unique analysis of the transmission of wisdom represented by this type of sacred literature.

The Nyingma is the oldest, the mother school, of Tibetan Buddhism. Nyingma scriptures consist of the canon of sūtric and tantric teachings with their vast commentaries and the fascinating and popular scriptural tradition, the Terma teachings. There are thousands of volumes of Terma texts, which were discovered by hundreds of Tertons starting from the eleventh century and continuing to this day. The Terma tradition constitutes a major aspect of the teachings and practice of the Nyingma, therefore it is important for people who are interested in Buddhism, and specifically in the Nyingma lineage, to understand what Termas are.

The tradition of these discovered Dharma Treasures needs to be placed in the perspective of both sūtric and tantric Buddhism, so that a person who is new to it can understand exactly where they fit in and how they are used. Since this is the first work of its kind in English on the Terma tradition it will be helpful to give some background.

The teachings of the Buddha are usually classified into two: the Hīnayāna and the Mahāyāna, and also into three vehicles or *yānas:* (1) Srāvakayāna or the vehicle of Hearers or Disciples; (2) Pratyekabuddhayāna or the vehicle of Silent Buddhas or Self-Buddhas; and (3) Bodhisattvayāna, the vehicle of the seekers of enlightenment. Technically speaking the first two belong to Hīnayāna and the last one is Mahāyāna. Today, however, the most common meaning of the three vehicles is Hīnayāna, Mahāyāna and Vajrayāna or Tantrayāna, which are the esoteric or inner teachings of Mahāyāna Buddhism. These are discussed in the following chapters.

2 *Hīnayāna, Mahāyāna and Vajrayāna*

HĪNAYĀNA

The Hīnayāna path is characterized by the intention to liberate oneself. Its scriptural canon is known in Sanskrit as the Tripiṭaka, the Three Baskets: the Vinaya or code of moral discipline, essentially for monks and nuns; the Sūtras or discourses on various kinds of spiritual training; and the Abhidharma, the scripture on wisdom, philosophy and psychology. These texts focus on the way to attain Arhathood, the cessation of sorrow and its cause. They also include mental training in contemplation and wisdom, or insight. However, the primary emphasis is on forms of physical discipline and a solitary, isolated life to avoid circumstances that might generate emotional defilements. This physical distance protects the mind from falling into the lap of unvirtuous forces or negative energies.

In the Hīnayāna order there are two major schools of religious philosophy:

Hīnayāna

- Vaibhāṣika (18 schools)
- Sautrāntika

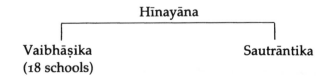

MAHĀYĀNA

The special characteristic of Mahāyāna is the intention, aspiration and practice to accomplish the happiness and liberation of others, not just oneself, which is a selfish attitude to be overcome. The Mahāyāna scriptures concerning the code of discipline and many other aspects of training are the same as those of the Hīnayāna, but they differ in interpretation. Apart from these common areas there are a vast number of canonical scriptures on mental contemplation and wisdom such as the Mahāyāna sūtras including the *Prajñāpāramitā*. In Mahāyāna training, whatever you are doing and wherever you are, the important aspect of training is the development of the compassionate aspiration for the well-being of others. So the main emphasis of Mahāyāna is on the mental attitude of cultivating beneficial thoughts for others; meditation, contemplation and wisdom, and physical discipline are treated as supports for sustaining this essential attitude. If your mind is filled with compassion towards others, you cannot do anything that might hurt them. Even if you are having a cup of tea, it won't be for the satisfaction of your greed but to sustain the body so that you can maintain it as a tool for serving others. This enlightened attitude is called bodhicitta. And if such an attitude is developed and does not decline or become destroyed, then you are a Bodhisattva, a being on the path to enlightenment. With this kind of mind, one can transmute one's day-to-day life into meritorious actions, the cause of enlightenment.

In the Mahāyāna vehicle, there are three major schools:

- Mahāyāna
  - Mādhyamika
    - Prāsaṅgika
    - Svātantrika
  - Cittamātrin (Yogācārin)
  - Vajrayāna
    - Six (Four) Tantras

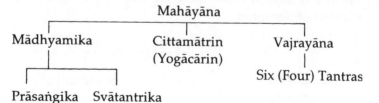

VAJRAYĀNA

The special characteristic of Vajrayāna is pure perception. Through an empowerment[1] transmitted by a tantric master, one sees and actualizes the world as a pure land and beings as enlightened ones. With the power or wisdom transmitted in the empowerment and with the extraordinary skillful means of the channels, energy, and essence of the vajra-body, tantrists generate the experience of the great union of bliss and emptiness, and this attainment brings the mind, by force, to the point of realization. In tantric practices there is nothing to be refrained from or destroyed, rather transmuted as the fuel of wisdom, the great union of bliss, clarity and emptiness itself. In common Mahāyāna the practitioners transmute daily life into spiritual training through right attitude, the thought of benefiting others. Thus day-to-day living is transmuted into meritorious practice, the cause of enlightenment. In tantra, however, one transmutes all into wisdom itself, which is the result or the goal of the path. In this way, Vajrayāna is known as the vehicle of result, for it takes the result itself as the path of training.

Although the three vehicles employ different methods of practice, their common purpose is to attain liberation from saṃsāra. As the result of Hīnayāna practice, one attains Arhathood, the state of having conquered the enemy or defilements. As the result of Mahāyāna and Vajrayāna practices, one attains Buddhahood, the fully enlightened state, which possesses the three bodies (see page 29) and five wisdoms.

According to the Nyingma tradition, within the Vajrayāna there are six major tantras (see pages 32–36).

- Vajrayāna
  - Three Outer Tantras
    - Kriyāyoga
    - Caryāyoga
    - Yogatantra
  - Three Inner Tantras
    - Mahāyoga
    - Anuyoga
    - Atiyoga

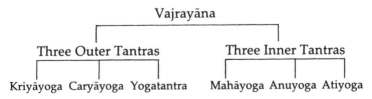

An example will illustrate the different characteristics distinguishing the methods of practice of the three vehicles.

The emotional defilements are like a poisonous tree. Hīnayāna followers are like those who protect themselves from the poisonous tree by avoiding it. Mahāyāna followers are like those who protect others as well as themselves from the poisonous tree by destroying it at the root. Vajrayāna followers are like those who, instead of wasting their energy and potential avoiding or destroying the poisonous tree, skilfully transform it into a medicinal tree and then use it.

These various ways of spiritual training are for liberation from saṃsāra, which is relative truth. Their purpose is to attain or to lead towards the attainment of the fully enlightened state, absolute truth.

The means used for liberation is interdependent causation. It is the Buddha's interpretation of karma, the law of cause and effect in actions, that produces the physical and ethical conditions in which living beings find themselves. By understanding and using the dynamic process of interdependent causation to free oneself from relative truth, the absolute truth, where karma is inoperative, can be attained.

Without using these conventional ways of spiritual training to free oneself from the causally interdependent factors operative in relative truth, it will not be possible to reach nirvāṇa, the cessation of sorrow, which is beyond relative truth. The relationship between the two truths is crucial for the possibility of enlightenment.

3 *Basic Philosophy of Sūtra*

The understanding of the basic philosophy of Buddhism is essential for comprehending the esoteric dimension of the religion, in which we find the philosophy, tradition, and even the cultural context of Terma. The following is a brief outline of Mahāyāna philosophy according to the Prāsaṇgika Mādhyamika school. Tibetan scholars and schools vary in their interpretations of the Prāsaṇgika view. The following is a summary of the standpoint of Long chen Rab jam (1308–1363), the greatest scholar of the Nyingma school, expounded in *Yid zhin dzod drel pe ma kar po*.[2] A full understanding of Prāsaṇgika philosophy requires familiarity with the original texts and the contrasting views of interpretive scholarship.

In Prāsaṇgika the proponents do not accept or present, as other schools do, any theory in any of the four modes, known as the four alternatives of existence: is, is not, both is and is not, neither is nor is not. Taking a position or presenting a theory that falls under one of the four modes is to commit oneself and to cling to a theory. This causes contradictory viewpoints; and it produces a theory that has the defect of needing to be defended. Prāsaṇgikas merely demolish and reject the theories of others. The principal theories to be demolished are those that uphold one or other of the extreme views of substantialism and nihilism. Substantialism asserts the existence of a universal entity that generates phenomena. Nihilism denies the existence of any such underlying substance. The method of Prāsaṇgikas is to expose the consequences of others' views without presenting any of their own.

Nāgārjuna said in his *Vigrahavyāvartanīkārikā*:[3]

> If I have presented any theory
> Then I am at fault.
> But I have not accepted any theory;
> I am totally free from any blame.

This philosophy is to be understood through the introduction of two categories: absolute nature and conventional level.

ABSOLUTE NATURE

In the absolute nature there is no division between relative and absolute truth. This division is only made on the relative or conventional level. On the absolute level there are not two truths. It can be said that there is only absolute truth. But relative and absolute just apply in relation to each other. So when the division is done away with, the truth is seen to be unqualifiable even as absolute. However, 'absolute' can also stand on its own, being used for the undifferentiated nature of truth. Absolute meaning is the meditative state of a realized person, the enlightened state of a Buddha, and the absolute nature of all existent phenomena.

Relative truth or the conventional aspect is reality perceived by the deluded mind. It is the object of an ordinary person's mind and senses. The absolute aspect is the realization of the wisdom of discriminating awareness. Neither aspect possesses any essential reality, for the objects of mind and senses are deluded perception, adventitious rather than essentially real, whereas the discriminating awareness of wisdom mind realizes the emptiness of beings and phenomena, their essential unreality. Both aspects of truth are said to be free from extremes of elaboration and judgement, because if there is elaboration into factors and qualifications, what is perceived becomes one of the extremes of existence—is, is not, both, and neither. In absolute meaning there is no arising, abiding or cessation of phenomena. From their very moment of arising, they are empty of essence or reality like the appearances in a reflection. There is neither existence nor non-existence in them and there is nothing to accept and no acceptor of any existence. Nothing is arisen or born from any of the four alternative possible causes of arising: from oneself, from others, from both, or from absence of a cause. Since there is no arising of phenomena, they do not cease, or abide in existence.

Nāgārjuna said in his *Mūlamadhyamakakārikā I*,[4]

> Phenomena do not arise from themselves,
> others,
> From both, or from absence of cause.
> Nothing, nowhere
> Ever arises.

The absolute nature is that of not existing in any form. Transcending the objects of dualistic mind, it is the indivisibility of the two truths and primordial freedom. Prāsaṅgikas, therefore, do not present any theory that discriminates.

CONVENTIONAL LEVEL

On the conventional level three aspects are distinguished in order to illustrate the philosophical view, the way and the goal of spiritual training: they are called ground, path, and result.

THE GROUND

The philosophical view of the two truths is the ground. In the philosophical view of the conventional level the phenomenal existents are divided into the two truths, the relative truth and absolute truth. Nāgārjuna said in *Mūlamadhyamakakārikā* XIV,[5]

> The teachings expounded by the Buddhas
> Are based on the two truths:
> The relative truth
> And the absolute truth.

Relative truth

Relative truth is the object of ordinary, that is, deluded mind and the sense faculties. Manifesting as an apparition, it has no essence or truth, but is true in so far as it fulfills a certain role for the deluded mind. Relative truth is the entire aspect of appearances before the mind along with the grasping of them as true. Since they have no essence, phenomena do not exist as true or false, as delusion or nondelusion, but because the mind has identified the objects, saying, this is a faculty, these are senses, and this is a house; and it discriminates and clings to them as subject and object. The objective aspect of this mental mode is called relative truth. Relative truth is characterized by phenomena that are circumscribed as mental objects and that do not stand up under analysis.

All existent phenomena are originated through interdependent causation. Phenomena that do not exist but which are presumed to exist or are falsely apprehended by the mind are contrasted with existent phenomena. The entities arise through interdependent causation. The nonentities arise through the operation of the mind, similar to the causal nexus of objective phenomena, known as interdependent postulation. Thoughts, ideas, and delusory perceptions—for example, the rope that is mistaken for a snake—are products of interdependent postulation.

Absolute truth

Absolute truth is the freedom from all elaborations and judgements, and is the object of self-awareness discriminating wisdom. This wisdom is the undeluded insight that transcends expression and conceptions. The Buddha said,[6]

> Transcendental wisdom is beyond conception
> and beyond expression,
> It is unarisen and unceasing as the nature of
> space,
> It is the object of self-awareness discriminating
> wisdom:
> Mother of the Buddhas of the three times, to you
> I pay homage.

This self-awareness is not the same as that of the Mind-only (*Cittamātrin*) school, who use it as a term for the ordinary mind.

Absolute truth is not an object of the mind. Śāntideva said in his *Bodhicaryāvatāra* IX:[7]

> Absolute truth is not an object of the mind;
> Mind is relative truth.

Absolute truth is the ultimate goal of spiritual training; and it is true as the path and result of spiritual training and achievement.

Absolute truth is the great peace, cessation, the nature of things, which transcends the objects of the mind. In their real sense the identities both of things and of the nature of things are equally pure, free and perfect, and they are beyond elaborations or judgements. They are remote from mental and characteristic references. People who realize the two truths perfect the path of dual accumulations and attain Buddhahood. Candrakīrti said in his *Madhyamakāvatāra* VI:[8]

> The kings of geese with well developed white
> Wings of relative and absolute truths,

Come into the presence of the geese, beings, and
with power of virtues
They fly beyond the ocean of virtues of the
Buddhas.

From the Buddhist standpoint, for something to be real, it must rely on nothing but itself for its existence. Its identity must not be dependent on the arising of anything else. Since phenomena have been demonstrated to arise through a process of interdependent causation, the conclusion is that things have no 'own-being.' This absence of real identity is their nature, and is called emptiness. The two truths are things and the nature of things. They are never found separately. They are emptiness because they are interdependent arising instead of being independently real. If they were real, there would be no arising and cessation. Phenomena are arising and functioning interdependently because they are emptiness. If they were not emptiness and unreal, nothing would arise or cease or function through interdependent origination. Nāgārjuna said in *Vigrahavyāvartanīkārikā*:[9]

The phenomena that have arisen
interdependently
Are designated as emptiness;
Whatever has arisen through interdependent
causation
Has no reality.

Both truths are free from reality. In *Madhyamakāvatāra* VI[10] it is said:

In both truths there is no essential reality,
So they are neither eternal nor nil.

Whoever understands the meaning of emptiness will understand the law of interdependent arising as, for example, the karmic principle. In the Middle Way the two truths are the same, and that truth is the teaching of the Buddha. In *Vigrahavyāvartanīkārikā*[11] it is said:

To whomever emptiness is possible
All meanings are possible.
To whomever emptiness is not possible
Nothing is possible.
The emptiness and interdependent arising
Are the same in the middle way.
To him who spoke this excellent speech,
The Buddha, I pay homage.

Without knowing the meaning of the two truths it is impossible to understand and realize Buddhist teachings. Without relying on the conventional level there is no way to express, understand and realize the absolute meaning in order to attain nirvāṇa. It is said in *Mūlamadhyamakakārikā* XXIV:[12]

Whoever does not know the two truths,
Does not know the profound suchness.
Without relying on convention
The absolute meaning cannot be taught or
discovered.
Without understanding the absolute meaning
Nirvāṇa cannot be attained.

In absolute truth, there is no distinction between affirmation or negation. However, these divisions are maintained in relative truth: when engaged either in debate or in contemplation on the ultimate nature one does not hold any thesis or present any view, since the ultimate nature is free from holding or presenting any view. When in an off-meditative period or when dealing with the conventional world, one should see, ponder upon, and teach others the details of the existent phenomena of relative truth as given in the scriptures, that is, that they are like a dream or apparition. This recognition of the dream-like nature of things will open one's eyes to the path of two accumulations, and then one shall attain the two bodies—the ultimate body and the form body—of the enlightened state, Buddhahood.

THE PATH

The path is the way of spiritual training in two accumulations. There are two processes of accumulation in order to attain the goal: the accumulation of merits and the accumulation of wisdom. It is necessary to complete the twofold accumulations in order to realize emptiness and then to achieve the twofold results, the two bodies of the Buddha. Nāgārjuna said in *Yuktiṣaṣtikākārikā:*[13]

> By the merits of [writing] this [text] may all
> beings
> Gain merits and wisdom, and
> May they achieve the twofold excellent bodies
> Which are generated through merit and wisdom.

Merit

Merit is spiritual training in skillful means based on the view of relative truth. It is the training in the six perfections, that is, generosity, discipline, patience, diligence, contemplation and wisdom.

Wisdom

Wisdom is the training based on the understanding of the view of absolute truth. It is the meditation on the insight of wisdom, free from elaboration, and cessation of the mind and mental events. The Buddha said in the *Aṣṭasāhasrikā:*[14] 'O Subhūti! Minds are luminescent in their nature.' In *Ratnāvalī*[15] it is said:

> The form body of the Buddhas
> Is produced by the accumulation of merits;
> The ultimate body, in brief,
> Is produced by the accumulation of supreme
> wisdom.

First one should reach the point of understanding freedom from conceptualizations through reasoning and seeing the absence of reality, which is the emptiness nature of existent phenomena.

Examine a flower for example: Try to find out and prove how the flower exists. Is the color of the flower the flower, or is the design? No, they are color and design but not flower. Are the different substances the flower? No. We will not discover the flower even if we reduce it to its smallest particles. If we cannot find it in the flower's parts, it cannot be found in the aggregation of those parts, including color, design and substances. So there is nothing in the flower that we can identify as its existence. Instead, what has been proved is the non-existence, no-self and emptiness of the flower in its real nature. The same method of examination is applicable to all forms of matter down to the smallest particles, and to the mind even in its shortest moment of duration. Therefore, form and the other constituents of existence are emptiness.

How do phenomena appear to be real and functioning? The basis is emptiness. Phenomena arise and function as real when perceived by ordinary people like ourselves. The process of emergence from emptiness into apparent reality takes place through the interdependence of the objective aspect, which is causes and conditions, and the subjective aspect, which is dualistic thought, defiled emotions, and the karmic process rooted in ignorance. Existent phenomena arise when the causal factors are complete. The example is given of a magician creating an illusion. When the mantras, substances, and meditation have been completed, the houses and trees created by magical power will appear as real. In the same way, emptiness is form and so on.

As a result of the dependent arising of phenomenal existence, phenomena are unreal and are emptiness in their true nature. And because they are emptiness they are capable of arising and functioning through dependent arising. Similarly, space enables the earth and beings to function. Although the phenomenal appearances are not true in their real nature, they appear and function as true at the relative level, which is falsehood. The extreme view of substantialism is avoided by understanding the appearances. For while appearing to have being, the flower is an emptiness, a non-existence. The extreme view of nihilism is avoided by understanding emptiness. For emptiness is able to arise as interdependent origination. The emptiness and interdependent origination are inseparable. Therefore, emptiness is not other than form and form is not other than emptiness. The *Heart Sūtra* says: 'Form is emptiness, emptiness is form, emptiness is not other than form, and form is not other than emptiness.'

When one trains in this contemplation of wisdom, first one shall ease one's mind and then one shall remain experientially in the state of freedom from thoughts, referred to as the view of absolute truth. Whilst one remains in that state the concepts of objects outside and mind within stop being generated. The duality of the objective and subjective is overcome. That is the freedom from dual conceptions and perceptions. At that time there is neither affirmation nor negation in the mind engaged in contemplation, and there is nothing but insight free from elaborations. It is the meditation on the luminescent wisdom of self-discriminating awareness.

Sāntideva said in *Bodhicaryāvatāra* IX:[16]

> Once neither things nor non-things
> Remain before the mind,
> There will not be anything—
> It is the great peace or cessation, freedom from
> conceptions.

The tendencies that are the first to cease through contemplation on the nature of phenomena are grasping at phenomena as real and affirmations and negations. Then later, even holding on to contemplation of the natural state of things will also cease. To begin with the realization of emptiness comes conceptually through inference and then in a total, non-dualistic direct insight. *Bodhicaryāvatāra* IX[17] says:

> By developing the experience of emptiness,
> Abandon the habit of apprehending phenomena
> as real.
> By developing the experience of nothing,
> That [holding on to emptiness] will also be
> abandoned.

Once grasping at the sense of self and at the reality of phenomena have ceased, the very concept of an antidote to these radical delusions will cease. It is the conception of the emptiness of phenomena itself. Once it has ceased, the meditator will attain transcendental wisdom. The Buddha said in *Āryaprajñāpāramitāsañcayagāthā:*[18]

> One who is free from various conceptions and
> enjoys the supreme peace
> Is enjoying the excellent perfection of
> transcendental wisdom.

Ignorance causes a person to be subject to the dependent origination of causes and conditions, the sphere of worldly experience that does not end until the attainment of the absolute state, Buddhahood. Before this realization of the great emptiness or absolute truth, the effects of karma are never transcended. The way to have a happier life and to make efforts leading to Buddhahood is to practice meritorious actions and meditation leading to wisdom. Faith, generosity, love, and proper conduct will pacify the negative forces within us and generate positive energy, leading us towards the perfect state. The practice of meritorious actions and wisdom is possible because of the dynamic pattern of interdependent causation.

RESULT

The result is the two bodies of the Buddhas. Through the process of training in the path, one's mind and mental events, the cause of saṃsāra, are dissolved into the ultimate sphere (*dharmadhātu*). At enlightenment, for oneself one attains the ultimate body (*dharmakāya*). For others the form bodies (*rūpakāya*) appear spontaneously, like the reflection of the moon in water, until saṃsāra is emptied. They appear in accordance with the aspirations one made when training on the path, and with the karmic connections of beings.

In *Madhyamakāvatāra* XI,[19] it is said:

> The cessation [which results from] the burning
> Down of the entire fuel of knowable entities
> Is the ultimate body of the victorious one.
> At that time there is neither birth nor death.

And

> The body of peace radiates like a wish-fulfilling
> gem.
> Until sentient beings are liberated, for the
> endowment of the world
> [The emanations of peace] appear eternally
> without conceptions.

In *Bodhicaryāvatāra* IX[20] it is said:

> Wish-fulfilling trees and wish-fulfilling gems
> Completely fulfill wishes:
> Likewise for disciples, because of aspirations,
> The body of the victorious ones appears.

Sāntideva further illustrates the principle of enlightened actions that fulfill the wishes of beings without mental concepts and effort but by the power of aspirations in the past. He tells the story of a Brāhmin named Śaṇku. This Brāhmin blessed a reliquary of Garuda, a deity in the form of a sacred bird. Even after the Brāhmin's death, for a long time this reliquary had been effective in neutralizing poisons. In *Bodhicaryāvatāra* IX[21] it is said:

For example, the Garuda reliquary that
[Śaṇku] consecrated, and [then he] died long
ago,
Yet it has been effective in neutralizing poison
and so on.
Similarly, by acting in accordance with the
actions of the Bodhisattvas,
One achieves the reliquary [the bodies] of the
Buddhas.
Although the Bodhisattva has now passed
beyond sorrow [the world],
He fulfills all the aims [the wishes of beings].

4 *Basic Philosophy of Tantra*

An understanding of the philosophical view of Mādhyamika makes it easy to comprehend the view, ritual, training and culture of the various levels of tantric scriptures that are taught in the Termas.

The training in the tantric teachings of Buddhism, the esoteric path known as Vajrayāna, does not rely on reasoning or on a wisdom produced by analysis. The ultimate body is achieved directly through the transmission of empowerment and the skillful means of the channels, energy and essence of the vajra body. By these means practitioners maintain their minds naturally in the transmitted realization. They see the true face of absolute nature. Then, through training, in a short period of time, they perfect that realization as the union of bliss and emptiness, a fully enlightened state. In sūtric training the practitioners follow the path of training in the two accumulations as the cause of achieving the final result, the two bodies of the Buddhas. In tantric teachings one views the two truths as equal, pure and indivisible. Long chen Rab jam says in his *Padma Kar po*:[22]

> The tantric [esoteric or ultimate] essence with all its virtues inheres spontaneously in all living beings and is the basis of purification, like the sun itself. The eight consciousnesses including the

> universal ground, which are the nature of saṃsāra, are that which is to be purified like clouds covering [the sun]. Empowerment and gradual training in the development and perfection stages purify [them] like clouds dissolving. To begin with they make the virtues arise, and as a result of that purification the absolute universal ground will be achieved like the sun shining brightly.

In *Tag nyee Tantra*[23] it is said:

> All living beings are the very Buddha
> But are obscured by adventitious defilements.
> If the obscurations are dispelled, they are the
> very Buddha.

Sūtric and tantric teachings are the same in that they both lead to the enlightened state, but the means used in their training are different.

Nyingma tantric scriptures classify the tantric teachings as three Outer Tantras and three Inner Tantras. In the view of the three Outer Tantras the distinction is made between the two means (skillful means and wisdom) as well as between the two truths (the absolute truth and relative truth), which are subsequent and separate.

OUTER TANTRAS

The basic views of the three Outer Tantras are:

Kriyāyoga

In absolute truth all existent phenomena are equal in the indivisible nature of the two truths, appearance and emptiness, but in relative truth the deities are viewed as lords and oneself as a devotee; the esoteric training of Kriyāyoga is pursued accordingly.

Caryāyoga

The view is the same as in Yogatantra, but in the method of training the deities are seen as equal to oneself.

Yogatantra

In absolute truth phenomena are viewed as the luminous nature free from elaborations, the wisdom of the realization of emptiness. Because of that realization, in relative truth the practitioners meditate themselves as the visualized deity and merge the wisdom deity into it 'as water into water' in order to become the deity themselves.

INNER TANTRAS

In the three Inner Tantras the practitioners view the two stages as well as the two truths as inseparable and simultaneous.

Mahāyoga

The two superior truths abide indivisibly as the superior ultimate body. The view of the two truths is that in superior relative truth all appearances, that is, all phenomena, are primordially the nature of the triple vajra—the vajra-body, vajra-speech, and vajra-mind of the Buddhas—while being empty in nature. In superior absolute truth all phenomena are the nature of non-existing emptiness, the inseparability of the bodies and wisdom of the Buddhas.

Anuyoga

All the phenomena of the two circles (maṇḍala) or truths abide equally in the indivisible nature as the Great Blissful Son, the circle of enlightened mind. The two circles are explained as follows: all appearing phenomena (relative truth) are Samantabhadra, the circle of spontaneous accomplishment. In their nature (absolute truth) they are emptiness, free from all the extremes. That emptiness is Samantabhadrī, the circle of suchness.

Atiyoga

In Atiyoga, or Mahāsandhi, a person of high intelligence and capacity is introduced directly to the ultimate nature of the mind, the Buddha nature. Then through meditative training he or she becomes fully enlightened in a very short time. Since the ultimate nature of the mind is the same enlightened nature or ultimate sphere of all aspects of phenomena, there is no need of meditation on or realization of different aspects of phenomena. In the view of Atiyoga all the existent phenomena of so-called saṃsāra and nirvāṇa have never strayed from the ultimate sphere or the ultimate nature of the mind. All phenomena remain in the nature of the great circle, the ultimate body, spontaneously arisen wisdom, effortlessly and changelessly. So the ultimate nature of saṃsāra and nirvāṇa is non-existence or emptiness. This ultimate sphere is described in terms of its three aspects: its essence is emptiness, which is the ultimate body (*dharmakāya*); its nature is clarity, which is the enjoyment body (*saṃbogakāya*); and its compassion or power is all-pervasive, which is the manifesting body (*nirmāṇakāya*). Kun khyen Jig med Ling pa said in his *Yon ten rin po che'i dzod:*[24]

> The phenomena of saṃsāra and nirvāṇa
> Have never strayed from the ultimate sphere,
> which is changeless.
> The non-existence of saṃsāra and nirvāṇa is the
> ultimate nature of the ground.
> It is also the perfection of essence, nature, and
> compassion.

Lo chen Dharmaśrī said in his *Sang dag zhal lung:*[25]

> In Mahāyoga one realizes all phenomena as the magical display of ultimate mind, the indivisi-

> bility of appearance and emptiness. In Anuyoga one realizes all phenomena as manifestive power of the ultimate mind, the indivisibility of the ultimate sphere and wisdom. In Atiyoga one realizes that all phenomena are self-appearances of the ultimate mind, the spontaneously arisen wisdom, which is primordially free from arising and cessation.

In the Mahāyāna view the Dharma teachings such as the Termas are the blessed expressions, sounds and words that have arisen spontaneously because of the aspirations made by Bodhisattvas when they were in the path of training. Because of the karmic connections of beings, the teachings will be heard and discovered as relative truth at the right time when the causes and conditions are complete. However, in absolute truth those teachings have never been expounded with conception by any enlightened being at any time. In the *Lankāvatārasūtra*[26] the Buddha said:

> In order to lead living beings to understanding
> I taught all the different yānas:
> But there was not any concept [of teachings in
> me].

Do de yong su kod pa[27] says:

> Without teaching anything
> The teachings pervasively appear for beings.
> When they desire gradual ways
> They receive them accordingly.
> For [those who desire] instant training
> The full teachings appear [in an instant].
> It is the greatness of the speech [of the Buddhas]
> Which fulfills the wishes [of beings].

5 *Nyingma School*

In Tibet, there are many different Buddhist schools or lineages of teaching and interpretation, but there are four major traditions, known in Tibetan as *Cho lug*.

From the seventh century when Buddhism first reached Tibet during the reign of King Srong tsen Gam po (617–698),[28] and then in the ninth century when Buddhism reached its peak during the reign of King Thri srong Deu tsen (790–858),[29] till the eleventh century when other schools emerged, there was only one tradition of Buddhism in Tibet. The tradition later became known as the Nyingma, the Ancient One, to distinguish it from other schools. In and after the eleventh century Tibetan Buddhist masters and Indian scholars brought many new teachings of Buddhism, especially of esoteric or tantric Buddhism, to Tibet. Over the course of time they established new lineages of practice and philosophical interpretation, and those lineages gradually strengthened into different schools.

The other schools are the Kagyud founded by the great translator Marpa (1012–1099), the Sakya founded by the revered sage Khon Kon chog Gyal po (1034–1102) and the Gelug founded by the celebrated scholar Je Tsong kha pa (1357–1419). In respect to scriptures and lineages of practice, the Nyingma school is the main body or the trunk of Buddhism in Tibet, and the other schools are the branches. However, at various times the other schools flourished more than the Nyingma. Many Buddhist scriptures belong to the earlier spread of Buddhism during the Nyingma period, and they remain vital today.

According to Buddhist scholars the whole of Buddhism can be categorized into two: the sūtras, the exoteric teachings, and the tantras, the esoteric teachings. Of the sūtric teachings there are two aspects: the sūtric scriptures of Hīnayāna or common teachings and the sūtric scriptures of Mahāyāna, the uncommon teachings. The original sūtric scriptures of both Mahāyāna and Hīnayāna are the teaching of Śākyamuni Buddha. Despite different interpretations and emphasis the four schools of Tibet have common scriptures that they study and practice.

The sūtric scriptures of Hīnayāna, which are the fundamental teachings of Buddhism, have three categories, known as the Tripiṭaka, the Three Baskets. As already mentioned, they are the scriptures of Vinaya, monastic discipline; of Sūtra, discourses of the Buddha on various subjects; and of Abhidharma, discourses on metaphysics. Most of the Vinaya and many sūtras were translated into Tibetan during the development of the Nyingma. The Vinaya lineage of the fully ordained monk in most of the other schools of Tibet also came from the Nyingma lineage. They were brought to Tibet By Śāntarakṣita. The full Abhidharma scriptures never reached Tibet. The texts written by Asaṅga and Vasubandhu are the main sources of Abhidharma for all schools. The Hīnayāna scriptures are the basic teachings on training: they emphasize physical training, such as observing strict monastic discipline, living in solitary places, poverty or simple living, and practice of tranquility (*śamatha*) and insight wisdom (*vipaśyanā*).

Tibetan scriptures are the richest source of sūtric material of the Mahāyāna, most of which came to Tibet during the development of the Nyingma teachings. Three of these are *Prajñāpāramitā*, *Ratnakūṭa* and *Avataṁsaka*, the teachings on training in generating bodhicitta, the enlightened mind, and the six perfections.

Tibetan Buddhism is the only living tradition in which one finds all levels of tantric scriptures and methods of practice. The tantric scriptures brought to Tibet during the Nyingma propagation are known as the Ancient Tantras and the ones brought to Tibet in and after the eleventh century are known as New Tantras. The Nyingma school follows the Ancient Tantras and the other schools follow the New Tantras. Some of the tantras, mostly New Tantras, are the teachings of Śākyamuni Buddha, but most of the Ancient Tantras are the teachings given directly by various Buddhas to different sages in their pure visions.

According to the Ancient Tantric tradition the tantric teachings are classified into six levels. They are Kriyāyoga, Caryāyoga and Yogatantra, the three Outer Tantras, and Mahāyoga, Anuyoga and Atiyoga or Mahāsandhi, the three Inner Tantras. According to the New Tantras the tantras are classified into four levels; Kriyāyoga, Caryāyoga, Yogatantra and Anuttarayoga. The inner tantric scriptures are the instructions on training in two stages, the development stage, the way of perceiving and actualizing phenomena as pure and perfect, and the perfection stage, the training in the method of attaining primordial wisdom, the union of bliss and emptiness. The scriptures of the three Inner Tantras of Nyingma did not appear or get retranslated during the later translation period; and most of the scriptures of Anuttaratantra of the New Tantras were not translated into Tibetan during the earlier period. Thus, there is a great difference between the tantric tradition of the Nyingma and of the other three schools in terms of scriptures, lineage and method of practice.

6 *Saṅgha*

In the Nyingma there are two categories of saṅgha or spiritual community; the communities of monks and nuns or renunciates, and the community of tantriks or the ascetic esoteric trainees. The renunciates emphasize the observance of celibacy, poverty, and a solitary life. Remaining physically away from worldly surroundings is a method to protect one's mind from falling under the influence of emotions so that spiritual practices can be maintained intact. Tantriks live a household life without renouncing mundane conditions. They do not enjoy sensory objects with attachment but use or transmute them as a means of practice through the power of their realized wisdom. Although they live with their families, they devote their lives to study and practice and transmute them as a support or means of practice, so they are totally different from the lay householders in the real quality of their lives.

In the tantric tradition the emphasis is on mental practices, seeing and taking all as pure, perfect, equanimity and the play of wisdom, without slipping under the control of external circumstances. Among Tibetan Buddhists there is no one who has not been initiated into tantric practices, so even monks and nuns are tantric in their inner and meditative practices. They are externally renunciates and internally tantriks. There are realized tantriks who have no emotional defilements and whose minds are not influenced by any external circumstances. Whatever discipline they adhere to, they are superior renunciates, free from all defilements. In its real sense, to maintain a tantric obligation is more difficult than to observe renunciate disciplines. The latter being physical, it is easy to notice and avoid mistakes. But the tantric disciplines are mental, and their scope is subtle and infinite.

Except in the Nyingma, there is no clerical community of non-renunciates among the Tibetan Buddhist schools. In the Sakya school there are certain individuals, such as the Throne-holder of Sakya, who are tantriks, but there is no non-renunciate saṅgha or community. In the Kagyud school too, except for some individual tantriks, there is no non-renunciate saṅgha. In the Gelug school, to be a renunciate is the first priority for becoming a member of the monastic community or saṅgha.

Nyingmapas are the least interested in organizational structures, hierarchical formalities and theoretical dialectics. They are more interested in devoting their lives to being simple and natural; and they stress the application to their own minds of whatever they have studied. The simplest but highest and deepest teaching and training in the Nyingma is the Great Perfection meditation, known in Tibetan as *Dzog chen*, a meditation for bringing the mind to the ultimate ease, the natural and undeluded state. It is the swiftest and most extraordinary means to dissolve the phenomena of mental fabrication into the absolute nature, Buddhahood. Great Perfection practitioners are remarkable for their attainment of the result: they train themselves through natural means to achieve the ultimate natural state in a short time. Those who are trained and perfected in this practice, in addition to being normal, simple and easy to be with, possess clairvoyance, miraculous power, and wisdom of united bliss and emptiness. Many who have attained the realization of this practice dissolve their mortal bodies at death without leaving behind any remains, which is a sign that they have attained the fully enlightened state, Buddhahood.

Part Two
Transmission of Esoteric Teachings

1 *Transmission*

In order to comprehend the Terma tradition it is important to understand the system of tantric transmission according to the Nyingma view. Tantra means the continuum or the continuity that connects or is the nature common to saṃsāra and nirvāṇa. Tantra is the Buddha nature of the ground, the union of the view and meditation of the path, and the bodies and wisdom resulting from spiritual practice and realization. Thus tantra actually means the ultimate nature of phenomenal existence, its esoteric meaning, which is Buddhahood. While the tantric teachings are the expressions of the ultimate state, dharmakāya, they are ordinarily apprehended through words, indications, and texts of esoteric practices. The transmission of teachings and the esoteric power that comes from the primordial Buddha through master to disciple is the basis of the tantric tradition. If the teachings are to be efficacious it is necessary that their accuracy be maintained through transmission from one generation to another. Thus all effective spiritual traditions pay great attention to the transmission, so that they do not become mere scriptural conventions for ordinary people or adulterated by so-called scholars without experience.

The tantric teachings of the Nyingmapa are transmitted through two major systems; the long transmission of the canon and the short transmission of the Termas. The canonical teachings were transmitted earlier through an unbroken lineage of teachers and disciples. The Tertons are the realized beings to whom the Termas were transmitted, mind-mandated and entrusted by Guru Padmasambhava.

LONG TRANSMISSION OF THE CANON

The tantric teachings of the Buddhas that have been transmitted through successive lineal masters to their disciples without bypassing any of the lineage members are known as the tantras of the long transmission of the canon.

The doctrine of the three bodies of the Buddha is important for all aspects of tantric teachings. The transmission comes from the ultimate body, the formless absolute, empty aspect of Buddhahood, the dharmakāya, to the body of enjoyment, the saṃbhogakāya. The latter is the first of the two form-bodies. Its radiant, transcendent form, endowed with the major and minor marks of buddhahood, can be perceived only by enlightened or highly attained beings. The Buddhas of the saṃbhogakāya level dwell in inconceivably vast pure lands or Buddha-fields, whereas the other expression of the form-body, the nirmāṇakāya, enters saṃsāra and manifests in various ways in order to free beings from suffering. The Tantra interprets the nature of mind and teaches methods of liberative meditation in terms of the three bodies of the Buddha, and through them the lineal transmissions of tantric teachings are effected.

Most of the scriptures of the Inner Tantra category of the Nyingma are the expression of the dharmakāya. Through the saṃbhogakāya, nirmāṇakāya and ordinary practitioners they are transmitted to ordinary beings. These transmissions took place in three stages: Mind, Indication and Aural Transmissions.

Mind Transmission

Samantabhadra, the dharmakāya, transmitted tantric teachings to the saṃbhogakāya Buddhas who are inseparable from him, through Mind Transmission without any verbal or physical expression. In reality the dharmakāya does not express anything, but for the saṃbhogakāya Buddhas the tantric transmission appears from the dharmakāya spontaneously. This is also known as the transmission between the Buddhas.

Indication Transmission

The saṃbhogakāya forms of Buddhas such as Vajrasattva transmit the teachings to the nirmāṇakāyas such as Prahevajra who in turn transmit them to other realized ones or to the knowledge-holders through Indication Transmission. This transmission takes place through symbolic expressions by verbal and physical indications. It is also known as the transmission between the knowledge-holders.

Aural Transmission

The nirmāṇakāyas such as Prahevajra, King Jha and Padmasambhava, after receiving the tantric teachings and transmissions from the saṃbhogakāya, transmit them to ordinary disciples through various means including aural transmission. This verbal communication is also known as the transmission between ordinary people.

The Aural Transmission of tantric teachings originated in Tibet with Guru Padmasambhava and his contemporaries and has continued till the present day. The Mind and Indication Transmission systems also exist among highly realized masters even today. In the tantric tradition the transmission is the most important aspect of practice. Without receiving it, tantric studies and meditation are dangerous and unbeneficial. Most of the extant scriptures of Ancient Tantra on the three Inner Tantras are preserved in a collection of texts in thirty-three volumes entitled *Nying ma gyud bum* and one in nine volumes entitled *Ka ma.*[30]

The Uncommon Tantras of the Nyingma are the scriptures of the three Inner Tantras, the Mahāyoga, Anuyoga and Atiyoga. They were brought to the human world and to Tibet in the following manner:

Mahāyoga: Vajrasattva transmitted the Mahāyoga tantras to King Jha of the Sahora country of India. This king also received those teachings from Vimalakīrti, who had received Mahāyoga teachings from Vajrapāṇi at the Malaya mountain (Śrīpāda?) in Śrīlaṅka. After they had passed through many teachers, Buddhaguhya received and transmitted them to Vimalamitra and Padmasambhava. They in turn transmitted the *Guhyagarbhamāyājālatantra* etc., the eighteen great tantras of Mahāyoga, to their Tibetan disciples Ma Rin chen Chog, Nyag Jñānakumāra and others.

Anuyoga: King Jha also received the teachings of Anuyoga tantra from Vajrasattva and Vimalakīrti. The king then transmitted them to Siddha Kukurāja, and they finally reached the great Tibetan tantrik Nub chen Sang gye Ye shey, who was one of the twenty-five chief disciples of Guru Padmasambhava. Nub chen taught Anuyoga tantras in Tibet, and the lineage has survived to the present day. There are about twenty-two tantras, for example the *Four Root Sūtras* of Anuyoga, in the *Nying ma gyud bum*.

Atiyoga: Vajrasattva transmitted the Atiyoga teachings to the nirmāṇakāya Prahevajra, who passed them on to lineages of teachers including Guru Padmasambhava, Vimalamitra and Vairocana. The Atiyoga tantras, also known as Mahāsandhi, have three divisions: the division of the Mind, the division of Great Expanse, and the division of Instructions. There are twenty-one extant texts of Mind-division and seven texts of Great Expanse, and they are in the *Nying ma gyud bum*.[31] These two divisions were brought to Tibet by Vimalamitra and Vairocana, the greatest Tibetan translator. The division of Instructions, also known as the

Instructions of the Innermost Essence, are the most profound tantric teachings of the Nyingma school. They were brought to Tibet by Vimalamitra and Guru Padmasambhava. There are many texts on the division of Instructions, mainly the seventeen tantras that are in the *Nying ma gyud bum.*[32]

SHORT TRANSMISSION OF TERMAS

This is the transmission of Termas which came through short lineage transmission. A disciple of Guru Padmasambhava who received transmission from him in the ninth century can transmit the empowerments and teachings to his disciples today. And if he is the Terton of that particular teaching in this life, he is second to Guru Padmasambhava in the lineage. The Termas are tantric scriptures, many from the Outer Tantras but the majority from the Inner Tantras. They came to the present-day disciples through six transmissions: the three Common Transmissions and the three Uncommon Transmissions. The three Common Transmissions have been discussed earlier—the Mind, Indication and Aural Transmissions. The three Uncommon Transmissions are the Aspirational Empowerment, Prophetic Authorization and Entrustment to Ḍākinīs. They are ways of transmission peculiar to the Termas of the Nyingma school.

2 *Guru Padmasambhava*

Guru Padmasambhava is the founder of Buddhism in Tibet and the source of the Terma tradition of the Nyingma. He is popularly known as Guru Rinpoche, the Precious Teacher. Nyingmapas respect him as the second Buddha—the one who is second to the Buddha.

Guru Padmasambhava is one of the most extraordinary beings in the history of Buddhist sages, a possessor of limitless enlightened power. He was a manifestation of the enlightened ones in the form of a great esoteric practitioner and master. He was not born from the womb of a woman but miraculously, in a lotus. He led an ascetic life of training and accomplishment in esoteric Buddhism, and for centuries he trained numerous followers in the esoteric approach to enlightenment, taking different forms at different places. He has achieved deathless attainment, maintaining the same body and becoming visible wherever and whenever it is appropriate for beings.

Guru Padmasambhava was born from a lotus in the Milk-Ocean in the country of Oḍḍiyāna, which modern scholars believe to be the Swat Valley of Pakistan. He took birth eight years after the passing away of the Buddha. He attained the deathless accomplishment through his esoteric practices; and in the ninth century, at the age of more than a thousand, he visited Tibet while still appearing to be in his youth. His followers believe that he is still in the same body in the Copper Colored Mountain, a manifested pure land in the center of the Cāmara sub-continent, and that he can be seen by realized people.

After Padmasambhava's lotus birth, King Indrabodhi of Oḍḍiyāna found him in the Milk-Ocean and brought him to his palace. The King, who had no heir, made him crown prince. Eventually he married Kha dro Od chang ma, but he asked the King to allow him to renounce the kingdom in order to lead the life of an ascetic. When the King refused, he performed a skillful means. The son of an evil minister was due to die because of the effects of his past karma. Padmasambhava could see this, so, while playing together, he killed the boy. In accordance with the law Padmasambhava was banished to a cemetery, where he finally was able to receive the esoteric teachings he had been wishing for, and practiced them. He was empowered by wisdom ḍākinīs, Kha dro Zhi wa tsho and Vajravarāhī. Then he visited various teachers with whom he studied medicine, astrology, logic and art. He was ordained as a monk by Ācārya Prabhahasti. He learned Vinaya from Ānanda, and tantras including Mahāsandhi from Prahevajra, Śrīsiṅha, Mañjuśrī, Nāgārjuna, Hūṁkāra, Vimalamitra and Buddhaguhya, all of whom were accomplished masters. Through the practice of these teachings he manifested as a fully accomplished sage.

Then Guru Padmasambhava visited the kingdom of Sahora. He went to the convent where Princess Mandārava and her ladies-in-waiting were living as renunciates, gave esoteric teachings, and accepted them as his disciples. The King, suspecting him of an illicit relationship with the princess, ordered Guru Padmasambhava to be burned to death as punishment, but instead of being burned by the fire, the Guru transformed it into a lotus lake. The King and his subjects became his devotees, and he accepted Princess Mandārava as his spiritual consort. Guru Padmasambhava went with Mandārava to Maratika cave, which is located in what is now called Nepāl, in order to do tantric practices.

Both of them achieved the attainment of control over life.

Then Guru Padmasambhava went with his consort to Oḍḍiyāna. There the wicked minister whose son he had killed recognized him. The King ordered Padmasambhava be burned alive. But he transformed the fire into a lake, and in the middle of it he and Mandārava were seen sitting in a huge lotus. The King and the whole country became his followers, and he remained there for thirteen years as the chaplain of the palace. He gave many profound esoteric teachings, including *Ka dü chö kyi gya tsho.*

From there he again went to Nepāl, and with the support of Princess Śākyadevi as a spiritual consort he achieved the supreme attainment through the profound practices of the sādhanas of the deities Yang dag (Vajraheruka) and Dor je Phur pa (Vajrakīla) at Yang le shöd cave, now known as Palphing.

At De ched Tseg pa stūpa, he met the eight great knowledge-holders. Each of the eight great knowledge-holders discovered one of the scriptures of the eight great deities, and Guru Padmasambhava discovered the text of condensed teachings of the eight great deities, known as *De sheg Du pa*. He also received the transmissions of the teachings on the eight great deities from the authorized discoverers of those teachings.

Guru Padmasambhava also visited many parts of the Indian subcontinent such as Hurmuja (a small island in Oḍḍiyāna), Sikodhara, Dhanakośa, Rukma, Tirāhuti, Kamaru, Tharu, Campa Khasya, Trilinga in south India, Kañchi, and Magadha in central India. He dispelled obstructions and gave teachings and transmissions to numerous disciples of human and non-human birth.

It is important to note that in *The History of Kha dro nying thig*[33] it is said: 'Then the great Master [Guru Padmasambhava] went to Tibet in the body of great transformation.'

Accomplished practitioners of Great Perfection can transform their bodies into a vajra-body called the body of great transformation by specific practices and will be able to remain as long as they wish without death. They will be visible to others as they wish or as it is appropriate. So Guru Padmasambhava lived for about a thousand years before he came to Tibet, and it was possible only because of his spiritual attainment. Thus, according to this text, *The History of Kha dro nying thig,* he came to Tibet in the body of great transformation.

In the ninth century King Thri srong Deu tsen became a very powerful ruler of Tibet. Under his rule Tibetan forces captured Ch'ang an, the capital of Tang dynasty China, and they also penetrated as far as Magadha in central India. The King was a powerful secular ruler who was also deeply devoted to Buddhism. He invited Śāntarakṣita, the abbot of Nālandā, to Tibet to build Sam ye monastery and establish Buddhism. But because of the influence of the King's evil ministers and because of the local spirits, it became impossible to carry out these Dharma projects. In accordance with the prophecy of Śāntarakṣita the king invited to Tibet Guru Padmasambhava, who was at that time renowned as the most powerful tantric Buddhist master in India. Through his enlightened power he quickly pacified and subdued all the forces opposed to the establishment of Buddhism and the construction of Sam ye. The monastery was composed of the main temple, twelve smaller temples, and four great stūpas surrounded by a high wall with 108 small stūpas. It was the center from which Buddhism spread to all parts of Tibet.

Guru Padmasambhava gave esoteric teachings and transmissions of Vajrayāna to hundreds of disciples including the 'twenty-five, King and subjects.' With his consort, Kha dro Ye shey Tsho gyal, he traveled by miraculous power throughout Tibet doing tantric practices, performing miracles, giving teachings and blessing hundreds of caves, mountains, lakes and temples as sacred places. He concealed thousands of Termas in many places for the benefit of future followers. Hundreds of Tibetans who received teachings from him became accomplished ones.

There are various accounts of the length of Guru Padmasambhava's visit to Tibet, but most Nyingma scholars agree that he stayed fifty-five years and six months, transforming Tibet into one of the richest lands of esoteric Buddhism. He finally departed during the reign of King Mu thri Tsen po for the Cāmara sub-continent in the year 864[34] with a wondrous display of miracles, riding a horse through the air at a place called the Kong thang Pass in the presence of the King, ministers and thousands of people who had gathered to see him off.

Part Three
Termas: Purpose, Concealment and Discovery

1 *Termas: Purpose and Transmission*

COMMON BUDDHIST TERMAS

In both the Mahāyāna sūtras and tantras there is the tradition of concealment and rediscovery of teachings through the enlightened power of realized beings. The tradition has two aspects. First, appropriate teachings can be discovered by realized beings, or they will appear for them from the sky, mountains, lakes, trees and beings spontaneously according to their wishes and mental abilities. Second, they can conceal the teachings in books and other forms and entrust them to gods, nāgas and other powerful beings to protect and hand over to the right person at the proper time. Other realized persons will rediscover these teachings in the future.

From the philosophical point of view, in the ultimate nature, or absolute truth, there is no difference between teacher and disciple, or between the effects of teaching and listening. Only in the relative truth, whenever the appropriate causes and conditions have been completed, conventional phenomena appear as the Dharma for the relevant people. Dharma is the realization, the source of the medium of realization, and the means to maintain and develop the realization. The Dharma may appear or be discovered in the form of thought, from indications or dialogues between teachers and disciples, conditioned by the nature and ability of the person involved. Thus, the Buddha did not give any teachings, yet for beings teachings appeared. The Dharma appears in the manner that accords with the perceptions of beings and with their karmic causation and circumstantial conditions. Dharma can be perceived in the form of teachings from a teacher through mental, indicative or aural communications. It can occur as forms, sounds, letters or thoughts. It comes from realized or ordinary beings, trees, water, sky, mountain, earth, rocks, or mind, according to the karma and conditions of the receiver. For a highly realized person all phenomena can be a source of Dharma, for many people only limited sources, and for some only the scriptures and the aural instructions. And for many nothing is a source of Dharma. In *Yon ten kod pa*[35] it is said:

> Without anything being said by me,
> [Dharma] appears pervasively for beings.
> When [people] aspire in a gradual way,
> For them it appears accordingly;
> For people who seek an instant approach,
> All the aspects of the Dharma appear completely [in an instant].
> It is the greatness of the speech [of the Buddhas]
> Which fulfills all the wishes [of beings].

The *Guhyagarbhamāyājālatantra*[36] says:

> At that time, various [manifestations]
> Appear for different beings according to their natures.
> [The Buddha] has not moved from the suchness state,
> [But] owing to beings' karma he appears differently.
> Like the reflections of a mirror and the moon in water.

While the Bodhisattvas are on the path of practice, they

make aspirations in order that when they become Buddhas, manifestations of the power of Buddhas to serve living beings will occur. As it is said in the Dedication Chapter, the tenth of the *Bodhicaryāvatāra:*

> May all embodied beings hear
> The sound of Dharma without cessation
> From birds, trees
> And from the lights and sky.

Many Mahāyāna sūtras including the *Prajñāpāramitā in One Hundred Thousand Verses,* and tantras including the *Kālacakra,* have been concealed in different places or taken to different realms of beings for a particular period through the miraculous powers of the Buddha and the sages, and at the right time have been brought back to the human world, the Jambu continent.

In the *Āryasāgaranāgarājaparipṛccha-sūtra,*[37] four characteristics of the Termas are described: maintaining the doctrine of the Buddha in the world, developing realization in the minds of beings, satisfying the minds of beings, and being as vast as the sky.

In the sūtras there are descriptions of the manner in which concealment and discovery take place. *Ārya-sarva-puṇyasamuccayasamādhi-nama*[38] says:

> O Dri ma Med pa'i Zi jid! For the great Bodhisattvas who wish for Dharma, the Dharma Treasures have been concealed in mountains, at the base of mountains, and in trees. The means of Dharma and dhāraṇīs will come into their hands in the form of volumes.

And

> For those whose minds are perfected, even if the Buddha is not present, the Dharma will appear from the sky, walls and trees.

The Precious Garland of Lapis Lazuli[39] says:

> Most of the Piṭakas [baskets of scriptures] of Mahāyāna went to different lands such as the realms of gods and nāgas and disappeared [from the Jambu continent]. The tantras were brought together by Vajradharas [sages] and ḍākinīs and concealed in the Dharmagañjo of Oḍḍiyāna etc. and protected. Later on when the time came the masters of the Mind-only school [Cittamātrin] received those Mahāyāna sūtras from Bodhisattvas such as Drib pa Nam sel. The *Prajñāpāramitā in One Hundred Thousand Verses* was brought back from the Nāga realm by Nāgārjuna. The sages who have achieved the supreme attainment such as Mahāsiddha Saraha, Ta chog, Tsho kyey, Lu yi pa and Tsi lu pa brought [back to the Jambu continent] tantras including *Guhyagarbha, Cakrasaṁvara, Hevajra* and *Kālacakra*. So they are all Termas.

In reality all the Dharmas of the triple body, the dharmakāya, saṃbhogakāya and nirmāṇakāya, that came through the Mind, Indication, and Aural Transmissions are in the form of Termas, the Dharma teachings that were discovered from the sacred treasure of the Buddhas or Buddhahood. *The Precious Garland of Lapis Lazuli*[40] says:

> In fact the entire doctrine of the Buddha is Mind, Indication, and Aural Transmissions, and they are not different from the Termas.

THE SPECIAL CHARACTERISTIC OF TERMAS OF THE NYINGMA TRADITION

The source of Dharma Treasure, the person who established the Terma system of the Nyingma, is Guru Padmasambhava, assisted by his consort Ye shey Tsho gyal. There are also teachings that were concealed or reconcealed by his disciples, such as Vairocana, and their reincarnations, and also by Vimalamitra, a great Indian scholar and sage of the ninth century.

The Termas are tantric scriptures, notably of the three Inner Tantras. There are two types of concealment of the Nyingma Termas. The first is Earth Terma, the concealment and discovery of the Terma using symbolic scripts as the key. Symbolic scripts written on scrolls of paper are concealed in rocks, lakes and temples. It is called Earth Terma because symbolic scripts on scrolls of paper are used as the key to awaken the recollection of the teaching that has been concealed in the essential nature of minds. Sometimes the whole text of the teaching is discovered at the concealment place. All the sacred objects discovered as Termas are also Earth Termas.

The second is Mind Terma. In most cases of this type, the discoverers find the symbolic scripts in their minds first, then the symbolic scripts become the key to the discovery of the teachings. In many cases there are no symbolic scripts for discovering the Mind Termas. In any case, in this system the symbolic scripts are not discovered by means of external objects, so they are called Mind rather than Earth Terma. The significant characteristic of the Nyingma Terma system is that Guru Padmasambhava concealed the teachings in the essential nature of the minds of his realized disciples through his Mind-mandate Transmission power. So, Nyingma Termas are not scriptures that are concealed in another realm or place as books and then rediscovered or brought back as the same physical text. Rather, they are discovered through the awakening of the teachings from the nature of the minds of the realized disciples of Guru Padmasambhava and others.

Another type of Terma in the Nyingma tradition is Pure Vision teachings, although all Pure Vision teachings are not necessarily Nyingma Termas. Teachings received in pure visions from deities and masters, for example, are not Nyingma Termas, whereas those concealed through Mind-mandate Transmission in the essential nature of the minds of disciples and then awakened by pure vision are Termas. There are also miraculously discovered esoteric teachings that are based on the tantras and instructions given by Guru Padmasambhava and other great sages of the Nyingma. They are called Termas because of their merit. A complete list of the Termas would number in the thousands. *Rinpoche ter kyi dzöd* is a sixty-volume edition of the Termas of major Tertons collected by Kong tul Yon ten Gya tsho.[41]

THE PURPOSE OF TERMAS

In *Trol thig wang chog*[42] by Kun khyen Jig med Ling pa (1729–1798) four reasons are given for the concealment and discovery of the Termas:

> [The Termas are concealed] with four intentions, namely that the doctrine shall not disappear, the instructions not be adulterated, the blessings not fade, and that the lineage of the transmission be shortened.

Firstly, many of the teachings given in ancient times have disappeared but the reappearance of the teachings as Termas again and again in a time like the present is helpful for maintaining them and making them available to people. Secondly, a fresh teaching coming from the source 'with warm breath' without going through the hands of different kinds of people in a lineage maintains the authenticity of the instructions. Thirdly, maintaining the purity and authenticity of the teachings helps to keep their blessings intact. Fourthly, within the lineage there is no one between Guru Padmasambhava in the ninth century and a Terton today, since the Terton received the teachings from Guru Padmasambhava then as his disciple. So discovery of Termas shortens the lineage.

In *Gong du nam shed* Kun khyen Jig med Ling pa said:[43]

> The purpose [of the Terma tradition] is as ex-

plained in the *Lung ten ka gya ma* of *La ma gong dü:* When the canonical teachings are adulterated like milk at a fair, and are on the point of disappearing, [then the Terma teachings] will spread. For the Termas are unadulterated and are the swift path of practice. Their many excellent qualities include being powerful and being an easier way to achieve accomplishments. That is why the Termas are important.

It is beneficial for various types of Terma to be discovered at different periods to suit the mental desires, needs and capacities of people born in those times.

TRANSMISSION OF TERMAS

The Termas of the Nyingmapas were concealed by various teachers, the majority by Guru Padmasambhava. An explanation of the Earth Terma concealed by Guru Padmasambhava will make the other types of concealment easy to understand.

First, how the Termas are transmitted and concealed: *Kha dro nying thig lo gyu*[44] lists six transmissions, three common transmissions of canonical tantras and three uncommon transmissions of Terma. The three common transmissions are Mind, Indication and Aural, as mentioned earlier. The three uncommon transmissions of Terma are:

The Prophetic Authorization or Prophetic Empowerment

At the time of transmission of a particular teaching to a disciple, Guru Padmasambhava prophesied that at a specific future time the disciple would take rebirth as a Terton and would discover it. Guru Rinpoche transmitted the Terma teaching to the Terton for the benefit of the beings of that future time. He also prophesied the time and place of discovery of the Terma. His prophecies were not mere predictions; his enlightened power actually caused what he foretold to occur. *Kha dro nying thig lo gyu*[45] refers to the Transmission of Compassionate Blessing: it is the transmission of the blessing of Guru Padmasambhava to the discoverers of the Termas so that in future they discover the introduction to the awareness state of mind just by seeing the teachings.

The Transmission of Aspirational Empowerment or the Mind-mandate Transmission

This is the heart of the concealment of Terma according to *Wonder Ocean* and many other texts. Concentrating his enlightened mind, Guru Padmasambhava concealed the teachings, by the power of aspirations, in the essential nature of the minds of his disciples, or in the expanse of their awareness state. If the teachings had been concealed in an external object or in the ordinary state of mind, they might be affected by changing circumstances. Concealed in the natural state of the mind, which is pure and changeless, they will remain stable until the time of discovery. *Kha dro nying thig lo gyu*[46] says:

> I, Guru Padma [sambhava], made the aspiration, 'May [these teachings] meet the fortunate person (so and so) in future.' Because of that aspiration the teachings will meet the fortunate person.

Wonder Ocean[47] says:

> The meaning of Mind-mandate Transmission is the mind transmission from the mind of Guru Padmasambhava to the mind of the realized disciple.... It is an actual transmission of realization which results in the minds of master and disciple becoming inseparable.

The Entrustment to Ḍākinīs

Guru Padmasambhava devised symbolic scripts for these

teachings, put them in caskets and concealed them in rocks, lakes, sky and so on. Then he entrusted them to the ḍākinīs and protectors.

They were instructed to protect them and to hand them over in future to the right person, the Terton. He also ordered them to protect the discovered teachings as well as the followers who practice them properly.

In *Gong dü Nam shed*[48] another system of clarification of the three uncommon transmissions of Termas is recorded. Here the Mind-mandate Transmission is explained as the transmission of the wisdom that is the meaning of symbolic teachings:

> (1) The Aspirational Empowerment [is the aspiration made by Guru Padmasambhava saying]: 'May the person who owns the particular Terma discover it.' (2) Prophetic Mind-mandate Transmission is the concealing of the meaning of the symbol, the ultimate wisdom, in the person who will discover the Terma, and the transmitting of it with mind-mandate through concentration of the enlightened mind of Guru Padmasambhava. (3) The verbal transmission of the yellow scroll is the symbolic script, which has been concealed in vajra-rocks, auspicious lakes and changeless caskets etc., made invisible [to others] and entrusted to various Terma owners [protectors].

All the Termas are transmitted to the Tertons through these six transmissions.

In *Gong dü nam shed*[49] Jig med Ling pa explains how the transmission for the concealment of *La ma gong dü* took place:

> Thinking of the numerous ocean-like disciples of the future, after giving the seal of the order of his prophecy of the three times to the assembled

> audience, he conferred the Mind-mandate Transmission of Aspirational Empowerment on the Prince-king and concealed the meaning of the symbolic indications or the instructions in the indestructible casket of the sphere of awareness of Prince Mu rum Tsen po. The symbolic scripts were concealed by Ye shey Tsho gyal, the manifestation of Saraswatī. . . and entrusted to the protectors of this Terma. . . .

Wonder Ocean uses the word *gTad rGya* for both the Mind-mandate Transmission of Aspirational Empowerment and of Entrustment to Ḍākinīs. In the case of Aspirational Empowerment I have translated *gTad rGya,* as Mind-mandate Transmission because this transmission actualizes the concealment of the teachings in the essential nature of the mind of the disciple through the power of the aspiration and concentration of the enlightened mind of Guru Padmasambhava and others. In the case of Entrustment to Ḍākinīs I have translated it simply as Entrustment since it is the act of entrusting the symbolic scripts or the objects to the ḍākinīs or the protectors to protect and to hand over to the discoverers in the future.

2 *Concealment of Termas*

The concealment of Termas has three aspects, comparable to the three uncommon transmission systems.

First, Guru Padmasambhava conferred numerous empowerments and teachings, mainly of the three Inner Tantras. Then he concealed most of those teachings in the natural state of the minds, or the expanse of awareness, of the assembly of realized disciples. Sometimes he concealed the same teachings in more than one person, but usually many teachings uniquely in each disciple. This process is known as the Aspirational Empowerment of the Mind-mandate concealment. Because of the concentration power of Guru Padmasambhava and the power of realization of the disciples, the teachings remain intact until the time of discovery. According to *Wonder Ocean*,[50] the one who concealed the Terma must have achieved the supreme attainment and the one in whom the Terma was concealed must at least have a realization of the perfection stage. The place of concealment is not the ordinary mind of the disciples since it is impure and changing in nature, whereas the expanse of the awareness state or the Buddha nature of the mind is pure and changeless.

Second, after the transmission of the esoteric teachings to his disciples, his consort Ye shey Tsho gyal compiled the teachings through the power of her unforgetting memory. Then according to the wishes and blessings of Guru

Padmasambhava, with the help of other realized calligraphers she wrote the teachings in symbolic scripts on yellow scrolls of paper, put them in caskets and concealed them in different places, so they would be discovered by the Tertons and used as keys to awaken the recollection of the words, meanings and realization of the Terma from their awakened state of mind. They also concealed the prophetic guides for the Tertons. This process is the Entrustment to Ḍākinīs or Terma protectors.

The nature of symbolic scripts, yellow scrolls, caskets, and concealment places is important and interesting. Sometimes Guru Padmasambhava and Ye shey Tsho gyal visited and blessed a place when concealing a Terma, but usually they concealed teachings from a great distance by their enlightened power. Sometimes Guru Padmasambhava summoned the non-human beings who were going to be the protectors and entrusted them with the teachings, along with blessings, to be kept and concealed in their own regions. The Termas of Guru Padmasambhava were not all concealed in the ninth century while he was visiting Tibet. If there is an important reason, he conceals or provides Termas today to be discovered for the benefit of beings. The transmission continues because of his enlightened power and not because of any limited cause and conditions.

Third, at the time of concealment, Guru Padmasambhava also gave the blessing prophecy of the future discovery of the teachings, including by whom, when, and where they will be discovered, who will be the supports or consorts of the Tertons, and who will be their doctrine-holders and main disciples. That is the Prophetic Authorization, which is not mere prediction of future happenings but has the power to make happen whatever has been said, owing to the power of the words of truth of Guru Padmasambhava. The prophecy also inspires the disciples to receive and practice the teachings and to make strong aspirations to discover the teachings in future.

CONCEALMENT PLACE

Symbolic scripts and religious objects are concealed in rocks, trees, mountains, temples, images, lakes, sky and so on through the miraculous manifestation of the enlightened power of Guru Padmasambhava. Because of the blessing power they become invisible to others and with the protection of the Terma protectors they are unable to be destroyed by the four elements. They remain in the place of concealment until the appropriate time comes centuries later. Sometimes, if the hiding place is being destroyed, the Terma will be moved and hidden elsewhere by the Terma protectors or by the limitless blessing power and action of Guru Padmasambhava.

SYMBOLIC SCRIPT

There are two types of symbolic script, the ḍākinī scripts and non-ḍākinī scripts. All the various ḍākinī scripts are illegible except to people who are highly realized or who have the transmission of the particular Terma. Non-ḍākinī scripts include Tibetan, Sanskrit, and other Indian scripts. Three kinds of symbolic script are distinguished by their content. Some are just a word or two, not necessarily a noun. Some give just a little indication of the subject, some history of the teaching or its title. Some give a little information about an event not directly related to the subject of the text but a contemporary occurrence that helps to awaken the hidden teachings. In some cases the complete text is concealed, and it seems that texts of this category are invariably in Tibetan. For example *Ka gyed de sheg du pa* in nine volumes discovered by Nyang Nyi ma Öd zer (1124–1192) is a complete-text discovery. His Holiness Dudjom Rinpoche (1904–1987) had one of the many parts of this text in his library.

The symbolic scripts are written by realized disciples of Guru Padmasambhava and sometimes by Guru Padmasambhava himself. They can write symbolic script one hundred times the length of *La ma Gong dü*, which has nine volumes, in the snap of a finger.

YELLOW SCROLL

Although they are known as yellow scrolls, the papers are of various colors, and the script is written in ink of various kinds and colors. A yellow scroll sixty feet in length, discovered by Thang tong Gyal po (1385–1509), is mentioned in *The Precious Garland of Lapis Lazuli*.[51] But this might be a complete text and not a coded script.

CASKET

The yellow scrolls are put in caskets made of precious gems, metals, wood, clay or stone. Sometimes symbolic scripts of many teachings are found in one casket and sometimes one teaching is divided among several caskets. But most frequently there is one teaching in a casket. The caskets are closed and show no sign of a lid or even a crack.

TERMA PROTECTORS

After the yellow scrolls were placed in caskets they were entrusted to Terma protectors such as Ekajaṭī, Vajrasādhu and Rāhu, who were to protect and hand over the Termas to the right discoverer, and to protect the followers and the tradition of the teaching. Those protectors come from classes of non-human beings or spirits such as gods, nāgas, yakṣas and rākṣasas. They are beings who have received teachings from Guru Padmasambhava and have taken a vow to protect the Dharma. Most of them are chiefs of their own classes of beings. Some protect many teachings, whereas other Termas have many protectors. Many protectors are Buddhas and Bodhisattvas manifesting as powerful spirits. Others are ordinary beings, but they are powerful by birth and realization owing to the teachings and blessings of Guru Padmasambhava.

3 *Discovery of Termas*

Nyingma Tertons are incarnations of realized disciples of Guru Padmasambhava. When the time for discovery comes, the accomplished disciples appear, each in their appropriate birth. They discover the concealed Termas and thus become Tertons.

There are more than one hundred Great Tertons and hundreds of Minor Tertons. According to *Wonder Ocean*[52] and other sources, if a Terton has discovered teachings of three types, he or she is a Great Terton. Without all three, he or she is a minor discoverer. The three categories are: teachings on Guru Padmasambhava, Avalokiteśvara and the Great Perfection. But Khyen tse'i Wang po said in *A Brief Account of the Throne Successors:*[53]

> Of the Earth Termas there are one hundred Great Tertons and one thousand minor ones. According to Ter dag Ling pa, a Terton who has discovered a complete system of teachings so that a person can achieve enlightenment [through his teachings alone] is a Great Terton. If a Discoverer has discovered only teachings on activities, he is a Minor Terton. An example of the first is Nyang [Nyi ma Öd Zer] and his disciples and of the second is Kal den Chi pa.

The Precious Garland of Lapis Lazuli provides brief lives or the names of 230 Tertons.[54] One hundred and eighty-nine are discoverers of Earth Terma and forty-one of Mind Terma and Pure Vision teachings. But among those 230, three are counted twice, as Earth and Mind Terma discoverers. A few others are named as Tertons, but it is not certain that their discovered teachings are of the Nyingma lineage or attributable to Guru Padmasambhava. They include Lha tsün Chang chub öd, Jo wo je, Zhang Dar ma Rin chen, Ge shey Dor je Kun trag and La ma Zang ri Re pa.

Sang gye Lama in the eleventh century was the first Terton of the Nyingma tradition. He was a reincarnation of King Thri srong Deu tsen, and discovered the texts of the sādhanas on Guru Padmasambhava and Avalokiteśvara and the teachings on the Great Perfection from a pillar of the Lo wo Ge kar temple in Nga ri province in Western Tibet. Among the Great Tertons, five are prominent and are known as the five kings of the Tertons. They are Nyang Nyi ma Öd zer, Guru Chö wang (1212–1270), Dor je Ling pa (1346–1405), Padma Ling pa (1450–?), and Khyen tse'i Wang po (1820–1892). There are hundreds of other famous Tertons who were contemporaries of Kong tul or who came after him who are not listed in his *The Precious Garland of Lapis Lazuli*.[55]

Most of the Tertons exhibit their special power from childhood. They take birth with wondrous signs, learn scriptures with little or no effort, display miracles at will and constantly receive visions and blessings of the Buddhas, deities and ḍākinīs. Some Tertons remain like ordinary people until later, usually when they discover their teachings.

PROPHETIC GUIDE

The prophetic guides are the prophecies and instructions to the Tertons before they discover the Termas. They inform them that they are Tertons, how, where, and when the treasures have been concealed and will be discovered, and who will be the support or consort, doctrine-holder and main disciples. They also indicate how and when to perform the preparatory practices, decode the symbolic scripts and practice and spread the teachings. Sometimes Tertons receive prophetic guides from manifestations of Guru Padmasambhava or of sages, from a ḍākinī or a Dharma protector in person or in a vision.

Ratna Ling pa (1403–1478) received his first prophetic guide from a manifestation of Guru Padmasambhava himself. In *The History of the Great Terma of Ratna Lingpa,*[56] he describes a visit from an impressive old ascetic wanderer whose whole attire from hat to shoes was made of yellow cloth. The ascetic gave him one of the three paper scrolls he kept in a cloth bag. After enjoying the meal Ratna Ling pa offered him, he gave instructions on how he should conduct himself in future in order to discover Termas, and then miraculously disappeared. The ascetic was a manifestation of Guru Padmasambhava.

The Precious Garland of Lapis Lazuli[57] tells how Sang gye Ling pa (1340–1396) received the prophetic guide from a Terma protector:

> While he was doing a retreat, one evening the great Tsen god, the Terma protector, presented him with three scrolls of paper, which were the prophetic guide for his Termas and the instructions on how to perform the preparatory practices.

Occasionally the prophetic guide is received from a ḍākinī. In the biography of Ter dag Ling pa (1646–1714), his brother Dharmaśrī writes of receiving the prophetic guide for the *Shin je shed Treg jom* from Yar lung Shel trag:[58]

> Early in the morning of the tenth day of the Nag pa month [third of Tibetan calendar], in a dream a celestial ḍākinī came to him in the form of a youthful, beautiful smiling lady attired in color-

ful silk with precious jewel ornaments. She began showing him the expression and indications of great bliss. By having union with her he was liberated into the expanse of freedom from elaborations, the nature of the experiences of exquisite great bliss. The ḍākinī said, 'The wisdom of great bliss is nothing else than this. Now you have accomplished the auspicious circumstances.' And she took off her precious ring and put it in his cup saying, 'Keep it as a sign of accomplishment.' Then she disappeared and he awoke. It wasn't dawn yet, so he couldn't see anything, but he felt a scroll of paper in his cup. He left it where it was. At dawn he took it to the window and found that it was the prophetic guide of a Terma. It was a light red scroll of paper with a script printed small in very thin letters as if written with a single hair. It began: 'E ma! the King Padma [sambhava], subduer of beings, now goes to subdue the Rākṣasas....'

Tertons may discover the prophetic guides in the places of concealment, or they may have to discover instructions that explain how to find them. In his biography Dud jom Ling pa (1835–1903) is quoted as saying[59] that he received the instructions from a ḍākinī and discovered in Ba ter rocky mountain, along with religious objects, the instructions on how and where he would find the prophetic guide. Following those instructions he withdrew the prophetic guide from Ngul god rocky mountain, enabling him to discover the Terma from Nga la Tag tse.

In addition to the general prophetic guides for discovery, there are usually specific prophetic guides for each major Terma of the same Terton. Many Tertons including Guru Chö wang and Ratna Ling pa have found Termas and along with them the prophetic guide to their next discovery. In the cases when there is no prophetic guide, the Tertons must find the Terma by their own spiritual insight.

There are three categories of prophetic guides: general, inner and innermost. Ratna Ling pa defines them in his *History of the Great Terma:*[60]

> A person who has been prophesied [as a Terton] should identify the valley [of concealment] by relying on the [general] prophetic guide; he should find the spot [concealment place] by measurements according to the inner prophetic guide; and he should open the door of the concealment place, make offerings to Terma Protectors and put in the substitutes for the Terma according to the innermost [prophetic guide].

Prophetic guides, oral and written, usually give full instructions on how to discover a Terma. In his autobiography,[61] Padma Ling pa says:

> When I was staying at Kun zang trag, in a dream three women in Tibetan dress came to me and said, 'Padma Ling pa, wake up!' When I suddenly awakened, before I could think, they told me, 'In the lower part of this valley, to the east of Thar ling at a place called Cha trag, there is a rocky mountain known as Dor je trag. Before the rocky mountain, there is a river, and on its bank an oak tree. Level with the top of the tree is a flat red rock like a mirror with a vermilion letter *Āh* in the middle of it. At a distance of one *dom;* [an arm-spread] to the right, the door of the Terma will be found in the design of a swastika. In the center of the swastika there is a hole the size of an egg, invisible from outside. If you put a wooden dagger in the hole and push upwards the door will open. Inside is a bronze image of Vajrasattva one and a half feet high and a four-inch scroll of

> the sādhana of Vajrasattva sealed by a letter *Āh*. You should discover them on the tenth of the sheep month [eleventh month of the Tibetan calendar].' And they disappeared.

PREPARATORY PRACTICES

Tertons perform preparatory practices before the discovery of a Terma if it is called for by the prophetic guide or if they see that it is necessary. The preparatory practices are sādhanas, the complete esoteric meditation and ritual performances of a deity. If the Tertons have previously discovered any sādhana texts, they will use them for this practice, otherwise they will use a sādhana discovered by another Terton. The practices might also be performed as a preparation and enforcement at various stages of the discovery: before opening the casket, before decoding the symbolic script, before transcribing it and before spreading it to others. The result will be peaceful and auspicious circumstances without any disturbances. In some cases, because of perfect auspicious circumstances, there is no need for preparatory practices.

Sang gye Ling pa described the signs he received when he performed the practices before the discovery of the La ma Gong dü cycle. In *The History of the Great Terma*[62] he says:

> I performed preparatory practices [in retreat] and on the tenth day the signs in sound, light and rays etc. appeared. I saw visions of gurus, tutelary deities, ḍākinīs and O gyen consorts [Guru Padmasambhava and Ye shey Tsho gyal] and received empowerments from them. On the fifteenth day I received the outer, inner and innermost signs [for the discovery of Terma], whereupon the retreat was over. Then I went to a feast offering ceremony held under the guidance of the Lama [i.e. Ch'os Kyi Blo Gros] and said to

> the assembly, 'I have received the prophecy of the O gyen Guru [Padmasambhava] and completed the signs of accomplishment of the preparatory practices. Now I am going to discover the Terma.'

DISCOVERY OF TERMAS

When the time of discovery arrives and the preparatory practices have been completed the Terton goes to the place of concealment. He or she withdraws the Terma from rocks, earth, lakes, temples, statues, trees, or sky, wherever it has been hidden by Guru Padmasambhava.

If it is a public discovery, people are invited to witness the miraculous event. If secret, only chosen people are present. Some discoveries take place unseen.

At the concealment place the Tertons perform a feast offering and prayers with their companions. The feast offering is a tantric ceremony for accumulating merits, purifying the effects of demeritorious actions and dispelling obstructions to the path of practice and discovery of the Terma. Usually the discovery takes place during the feast offering ceremony, sometimes later, and sometimes without any visible ceremony.

Tertons do not necessarily go to the concealment place, because the Terma protectors or the Dākinīs may bring the treasures to them, as often happened to Khyen tse'i Wang po.

Tertons' biographies and other sources include the following details:

Discovery from a rock

Sometimes the door of a concealment in rocks opens spontaneously when the Terton arrives or even at a gesture from him or her. In his autobiography Dud jom Ling pa recounts;[63]

> I received a prophecy [from a ḍākinī] saying, 'At Ba ter in Mar valley there is the rosary of [the great sage] Saraha, an image of Tārā made from red sand, and the prophetic guide of the Terma. Go there [and discover them] without delay.' Accordingly, on the tenth of the last month of summer [tenth month of the Tibetan calendar], I went to Ba ter rocky mountain, and just as I arrived a rock eight inches in diameter fell down from the mountain. In the place where the rock had been, I saw, in a heap of coal, an image of Tārā, a casket of sealing wax, and a beautiful old rosary. And I withdrew them.

Sometimes the discovery is fraught with hardships. On the other hand, Ter dag Ling pa miraculously discovered the *Shin je shed Treg jom* from Yar lung Shel trag. In his biography Dharmaśrī recounts:[64]

> As described in the prophetic guide, he saw the rock, the concealment place of the Terma, which had the design of a victory banner... when from a very narrow path in the middle of the rocky mountain he saw below his feet an abyss more than one hundred stories deep, and about four or five stories above him he saw rainbow lights in the design of a swastika, which was the mark of the place of concealment. But there was no way of reaching it. He could not even look at it because of his unbearable fear of the slope. In fact he became unconscious. Instantly he found himself on top of the rock. There he found a tent-like cave, with walls like crystal colored with bright frescoes. In that cave were a young and beautiful lady and a handsome man, both dressed in exquisite white clothing.... The lady gave him two scrolls and the man a three-cornered casket made of *se*. Then he turned back and

> found himself once more on the slope. Immediately he fainted again from fear of falling. When he regained consciousness he found himself on the narrow path.

Sometimes the discoverers climb the rocks with ladders and use hammers and chisels to dig out the Termas. In his autobiography[65] Dud jom Ling pa described how he withdrew his Terma from Nga la Tag tse in lower Ser valley:

> I climbed up the stone stairs for about five *dom*, with a feeling of bliss and comfort. Then I pounded the chisel into the semi-circular crack in the rock and opened the door. Inside I found many caskets covered with white birch and cedar bark in the middle of a heap of coal. . . . I put in the substitute for the Termas and closed the door as it had been. When I reached the foot of the rock I looked back and saw that the stairs had disappeared.

His Holiness Dud jom Rinpoche told me that when Yong ge Mi gyur Dor je was about to discover a Terma from a rock he asked a disciple to bring him a chisel. The disciple in fact brought nine chisels, and because of interdependent circumstances they had to dig out the rock until all nine became worn out.

Discovery in a lake

Padma Ling pa discovered his first Terma in a lake. In *The Precious Garland of Lapus Lazuli,*[66] Kong-tul summarizes the events:

> He [Padma Ling pa] discovered the cycle of Dzog chen long sal teachings in a lake called Me bar near Na ring rocky mountain. Before a huge gathering of people he jumped into the lake holding a lamp in his hand, and came up with

> the lamp still burning, holding under his arm a big Terma casket the size of a pot.

Discovery in statues and temples

In *The Great History of the Termas,*[67] Ratna Ling pa tells how he discovered two yellow scrolls of Thug drub teachings from the stūpa of Ge ri and Terma substances from the temple of Kho thing.[68] In *The Great History of the Termas of Guru Chö wang* the Terton describes withdrawals from the feet of a Hyagriva image in the Āryapalo temple of Samye monastery,[69] from the right hand thumb of the Vairocana image of Kho temple,[70] and from the seat of the Vairocana image in Bum thang, Bhutan.

Discovery of symbolic scripts on objects

Sometimes the symbolic scripts are found on rocks, images and ritual objects. In the biography of Khyen tse'i Wang po Kong tul said:[71]

> [Khyen tse'i Wang po] discovered a square-shaped rock, on which was the symbolic script from a rocky mountain known to be a sacred place. It was [the symbolic script for] the main text of *Tsa sum De sheg Du pa,* which he transcribed in fifty pages. Then he reconcealed the rock [with the symbolic script] at the same spot.

One Terton can depute another to discover Termas

Great Tertons can send another Terton to discover their share of Terma. According to Khyen tse'i Wang po's biography, Khyen tse sent Chog kyur Ling pa[72] and Kun trol Sang ba tsal[73] to discover his Termas.

Termas brought to the Terton

Termas and substances are brought to Great Tertons such

as Khyen tse'i Wang po by the ḍākinīs and protectors. During a ritual ceremony the Terma appears in front of him in the presence of many people and the Terton grasps it in his folded palms or wraps it in cloth. Sometimes it suddenly appears or descends upon the shrine table. In those cases the treasures are usually kept secret until the time of disclosure. It is hard to distinguish between Termas brought by the ḍākinīs and Termas discovered in the sky. In *Wonder Ocean*[74] Dodrup Chen suggests that most of them have been brought by the ḍākinīs or protectors:

> I haven't seen any teachings that had been discovered in the sky, although it is said that there are teachings that have been concealed there.

Transforming Earth Termas into Mind Termas

Tertons such as the First Dodrup Chen (1745–1821) and Khyen tse Ye shey Dor je (1800–?) were Earth Terma Tertons, but they transformed their Earth Termas into Mind Termas. Discovery of Earth Terma requires the right time, place, support, companion and materials in perfect order. If there is any imperfection in the arrangements discovery may be impossible, since Earth Terma discovery depends on external circumstances. But Mind Terma discovery is hardly influenced by external circumstances and is subject to fewer obstacles.

In his autobiography Khyen tse Ye shey Dor je explains why he transformed his Earth Termas into Mind Termas:[75]

> [The First Dodrup Chen] said, 'If you choose to, you will become a master of the Earth Termas of both Kham [eastern Tibet] and Wu [central Tibet].' But Earth Terma is very risky. There are all kinds of obstructions to perfectly favorable circumstances. Since the activity has to take place at a specific time, the right month of the right year, and with the appropriate companions, it is diffi-

> cult [to accomplish]. Furthermore, Terma objects are the gems of the land, and to remove them is very harmful to its richness. The best Termas are the Mind Termas. If like both Kun khyen Long chen Rab jam and the Refuge, the Knowledge-holder Jig med Ling pa, you transform Earth Terma into Mind Terma, the result will be superb. So keep this in mind. Your visions and prophecies indicate that you will be able to enjoy the secret treasures of the ḍākinīs.

The First Dodrup Chen himself, according to Kong tul, actually was an Earth Terton, but he chose to become a Mind Terton. Kong tul Yon ten Gya tsho says in *The Precious Garland of Lapis Lazuli:*[76]

> Because of the successive prophecies [about Dodrup Chen] it is certain that he was a master of Earth Terma, but he did not act [as one].

Support or consort

Most Tertons, except a very few such as Padma Wang gi Gyal po (1487–1542) and Ja tshon Nying po (1585–1656) who were celibate monks, have been followers of tantric discipline. They remained in the household life with consorts, children and possessions. For them the household life is a method of practice to transform every source of experience in life as the means of enlightened attainment. Its purpose is not the enjoyment of sensory objects.

The support of a consort has two purposes. First, through tantric training it helps to produce and maintain the wisdom of the union of great bliss and emptiness, by which the adept attains the ultimate state. Second, a realized person who has the requisite powerful aspirations takes birth as the consort of a Terton in order to fulfil the mission of discovering the profound esoteric teachings for the fortunate followers. For the Terma tradition a consort is a very important instrument. Through the auspicious circumstances of generating the wisdom of the union of bliss and emptiness or freedom in the Terton's mind, the consort causes him or her to awaken the realization as well as to discover the Termas. *Wonder Ocean* says:[77]

> ...by encountering the miraculous skill of a Vajradūta [consort] whose mind has been purified by empowerments and precepts, who has practiced the path of two stages, has been blessed by Guru Rinpoche himself to take birth in the future as a sacred support [consort], so that by the hook of spontaneously arisen bliss a Terton who has made appropriate aspirations may discover the Termas of the sphere of primordial wisdom.

Since the functioning of all existent phenomena depends on their positive causes and conditions, if the right consort cannot support the Terton, the discovery might become impossible or very difficult, like growing flowers without heat. Then even the Terton's life is threatened. For in most cases the purpose of a Terton's life is to discover the teachings for fortunate beings. The great Terton Padma Le drel tsal (1291?–1315?) did discover his Terma, but because he couldn't meet the right consort he died soon afterwards, before he could propagate it.

In his autobiography[78] Dud jom Ling pa said that he could not get the complete Terma from Nga la Tag tse because he didn't have a consort with him at the time.

Sometimes for the discovery of several major scriptures by the same person, the support of different consorts is required because of their specific aspirations for discoveries at the time of concealment. There was even a Terton who was young and who had to have the support of a woman who was in her eighties and was crippled. She had to be carried to the place of discovery to perform the ceremony since, owing to past karma and aspirations, her presence was essential. If the right person could not become the consort or be present, sometimes the gift of an ornament or a dress of the person can be a substitute. Because of interdependent causation, the substituted object becomes the support of the discovery, decoding of the symbolic script, and propagation of the teachings.

Substitute for Terma

The Terton puts a substitute in place of an Earth Terma. It can be religious objects, offering materials or any kind of auspicious substances as homage to please the protectors. The substitute helps to maintain the auspiciousness of the land provided by the Terma.

Casket

A casket is usually the first thing found in a concealment place. It contains the yellow scroll, papers in various colors, material and lengths. Sometimes there is no casket, only the yellow scrolls themselves or an object on which the symbolic scripts are written. Along with the casket and yellow scrolls there may be various kinds of Terma objects: images, stūpas, ritual objects and materials of wealth.

Sometimes in one casket there are many yellow scrolls or objects recording different teachings. Rig dzin God dem (1337–1408) withdrew from Ri wo Tra zang a huge square casket with five partitions. In each section there were different yellow scrolls and religious objects.

After the discovery of the casket, usually a preparatory practice is done again. Then a casket sometimes opens or cracks spontaneously like an egg, but other caskets have to be opened with ritual tools.

Symbolic scripts

Symbolic scripts are the keys to awaken the Mind-mandate

Transmission and the realization and teachings concealed in the essential nature of the Tertons' minds.

There are three kinds of symbolic script. The first, called Just Visible, is the shortest. It can be a syllable or two, and is not necessarily a noun. The second, Just an Indication, is of medium length. It can be a fragment of the history, an outline, the title of the text, or a phrase indicating directly or indirectly the events of the ancient age when Guru Padmasambhava transmitted the teachings. The third, Complete Text, is a symbolic script of the entire text. If the script is a Complete Text, there is no need for an awakening of the words of the text; so it is not a symbolic script in that sense. But it helps to awaken the meaning and especially the Mind-mandate Transmission and concealment in the Terton. So it has the effect of a symbolic script as do the first two kinds.

Decoding

Symbolic scripts in ḍākinīs' language behave in one of two ways while the discoverer reads and decodes them. In one type, as the discoverer reads the script, it changes frequently or appears unclear, or sometimes the meaning changes or is unclear. Sometimes both the script and the meaning change. Auspicious circumstances and preparatory practices help to make the reading stable and clear. Symbolic script that behaves in this way is called Illusory Miraculous Script.

In the other frequent type, Non-Illusory Miraculous Script, the words and meaning are clear and stable from the beginning. These variants are not caused by the symbolic scripts alone, but depend mainly upon different degrees of awakening of past experiences or habituations in Tertons' minds.

If the script is not in Tibetan there are three major decoding methods. In some cases in the casket along with the symbolic script is found a decoding key, a letter-by-letter equivalence between the symbolic script and the Tibetan alphabet. In other cases some unaccountable incident causes the ability to decode the script to awaken in the mind of the discoverer. In other cases, just by seeing the script the Terton instantly can read it, while in yet other cases the power comes by looking at the script again and again.

If the Terton cannot decode a symbolic script, another who has the Mind-mandate Transmission of the same teachings from Guru Padmasambhava may decode it for him. According to his biography,[79] Khyen tse'i Wang po decoded some symbolic scripts belonging to Chog kyur Ling pa (1829–1870). My teacher Kya la Khen po Chö chog (1893–1957) of Dodrup Chen monastery once told me that Le rab Ling pa (1856–1926) brought four symbolic scripts that he could not decode to the Third Dodrup Chen Rinpoche, who decoded two of them for him.

Transcription

Tertons transcribe the teachings themselves or dictate them to a scribe. If the symbolic script is in Complete Text form or is accompanied by an alphabetical equivalence, it can be transcribed by anyone. But if it is in an unknown language, or if it is in Just Visible or Just an Indication form, only the Terton or a person who has received the Mind-mandate Transmission from Guru Padmasambhava in the past, who is a Terton in this life, and who has permission from the Terton himself can decode and transcribe the text from the symbolic script.

After transcription some yellow scrolls must be reconcealed. Others will disappear: they are removed by the ḍākinīs and protectors. Others remain with the Tertons and their followers as objects of veneration.

When the transcription has been completed there is no additional text to discover and none can appear from the symbolic scripts, because the purpose of the aspirations and blessings made by Guru Padmasambhava when he concealed them have been fulfilled.

Secrecy

Secrecy is important in the discovery of Termas. It ensures peace and calm, and protects the teachings from obstructions and helps maintain auspicious circumstances.

Usually, Tertons keep the teachings secret at the time of discovery of the casket and whilst decoding the symbolic script—and for days, months and sometimes years afterwards. They wait for further spiritual guidance as to whether any more preparatory practices are needed to perfect the Terma and dispel negative forces. If the symbolic script is the Miraculous Illusory type, the discoverers must wait to confirm or to determine the real content of the symbolic script. After transcription, secrecy is maintained to ensure an auspicious beginning of the Terma practice. First they practice it themselves in order to generate the power to transmit it to others.

Reconcealment and rediscovery

There is only one copy of some symbolic scripts, even in the land of the ḍākinīs. Because of their extreme rarity, after transcription it is necessary to hide them as Reconcealed Termas. They do not have to be reconcealed in the places where they were discovered, but the protectors must be the same ones as before. Discovered teachings should be reconcealed if they are likely to benefit people in future.

Tertons reconceal the symbolic scripts to be rediscovered by future Tertons. For example, Khyen tse'i Wang po rediscovered many teachings, both Earth and Mind Termas. They include *Tsa sum dril drub* of Sang gye Ling pa and *Ka dü chö kyi gya tsho* of O gyen Ling pa (1323—?).

Doctrine-holders

Doctrine-holders are the principal receivers and holders of the transmission of a Terma. There are two kinds of doctrine-holders, special or root doctrine-holders and ordinary doctrine-holders. Both have received the Mind-mandate Transmission of a particular teaching from Guru Padmasambhava, but their way of receiving distinguishes them. Root doctrine-holders have received the Mind-mandate Transmissions and prophecies from Guru Padmasambhava in person together with the Terton in the ancient time. But ordinary doctrine-holders have not received the Mind-mandate Transmission from Guru Padmasambhava in person, and they may not even have been in his presence. Yet because of Guru Padmasambhava's aspirational and concentrative powers they have received the Mind-mandate Transmission through his concentration, which is the essence of the transmission.

A Terton may have many doctrine-holders for his various Termas, and one root doctrine-holder for them all. The First Dodrup Chen Rinpoche, for example, was the root doctrine-holder of the entire *Long chen nying thig* cycle, the Terma of Kun khyen Jig med Ling pa.

DISCOVERY OF MIND TERMA

Mind Terma are the teachings that have been concealed in and discovered from the awareness state of Tertons' minds. The awakening of the transmission does not rely on yellow scrolls of symbolic script. At the appropriate time, the transmission awakens from the awareness state of the Terton's mind. Sometimes its awakening is caused by visions of symbolic script, sounds of symbolic words or certain other means. What distinguishes Earth from Mind Terma is whether or not they rely on yellow scrolls. But they have three main similarities: first, they have been concealed in the indestructible nature of the Terton's mind by Guru Padmasambhava through his Mind-mandate Transmission; second, they remain in the natural state of the mind without change or decay; third, when the time comes they are discovered in the depths of realization of the awareness state of the Terton's mind with the sharp tools of luminous wisdom.

Some Mind Termas were transmitted and concealed by Guru Padmasambhava in the form of letters and others as sounds in the awareness state of the Tertons' minds. In Mind Terma the transmission of the Mind-mandate is itself the concealment. Thus concealment is instantaneous and does not require a series of actions.

The teachings will be discovered in the form in which they have been concealed, either letters or sounds, which appear in the Tertons' minds and awaken the teachings concealed in them. Because of the awakening process there is not necessarily any symbolic script at the beginning of Mind Terma texts.

The following is a summary of the account in *Daki'i sang tam chen mo*[80] of the discovery as a Mind Terma of the *Longchen nying thig* cycle by Kun khyen Jig med Ling pa.

Kun khyen Jig med Ling pa was in a three-year retreat at Pal ri monastery built by Threng po Ter chen She rab Öd zer (1518–1584). During the night of the twenty-fifth of the tenth month of the fire-ox year (1757) in a luminous meditative state he had a vision that he flew through the sky riding on a white lion and reached the circular road of Cha rung Kha shor (Boudha) stūpa in Nepal. There the wisdom ḍākinīs of the ultimate body gave him a wisdom casket in which he discovered five yellow scrolls and seven crystal beads. He opened two yellow scrolls. The first was the symbolic script of Avalokiteśvara in Tibetan script. The second was the prophetic guide, *Nad chang thug kyi drom bu*.[81] He ate all the yellow scrolls and crystal beads; and all the words and meaning of the Terma that were concealed in him were awakened in his mind as they have been printed. He kept them secret for years. In the earth-hare year (1759) he started another three-year retreat, at Chim phu near Sam ye monastery. During that retreat, because he was inspired by three successive pure visions of Kun khyen Long chen Rab jam (1308–1363), and was urged by repeated requests of dākinīs, he transcribed his Terma as the cycle of Long chen nying thig. On the tenth day of the sixth month (monkey month) of the monkey year (1764) he made his Terma public for the first time by conferring the transmission of empowerment and the instructions upon fifteen disciples.

PURE VISION DISCOVERY

There are two types of teachings discovered as Pure Visions: Common Pure Vision and Mind Terma discovered as Pure Vision teachings.

Common Pure Vision teachings are special and powerful, but they are not Termas according to the Nyingma tradition since they do not come through Mind-mandate Transmission and are not withdrawn from concealment. This type of teaching is received directly by highly realized Lamas in their pure visions, or in experiences or dreams from the Buddhas, Bodhisattvas, deities and sages.

The following is a quotation from the empowerment text, *The Immortal Celebration* written by Khyen tse'i Wang po for the sādhana entitled *Chi med dang ma chu dren* on the Long-life Buddha (Amitāyus) discovered by the Fifth Dalai Lama as a Pure Vision scripture:[82]

> There are three kinds of [discoveries in] Pure Vision, those directly received [from Buddhas, sages and deities], from experiences, and from dreams.

The Mind Termas discovered in the form of Pure Vision teachings are exemplified by *Rig dzin sog drub* discovered by Lha tsun Nam kha Jig med (1597–1650?). As mentioned in the history of this text,[83] Lha tsun discovered his teachings in the form of pure visions when he received the blessing of Vajravarāhī, and transcribed them as Pure

Vision teachings. But actually it was a Mind Terma of Guru Padmasambhava that had been awakened by means of symbolic scripts and pure visions of the Wisdom Ḍākinī. The powerful means of the visions awakened the transmission in him, but was not the real source of the teachings. What is the difference between Mind Terma and Pure Vision? Mind Terma are teachings discovered in Guru Padmasambhava's concealments. Pure Vision teachings are received in pure visions as special teachings. *Wonder Ocean* says:[84]

> If the symbolic script is not dissolved [concealed] in the mind and sealed in advance, there is no Terma aspect and there is nothing to be discovered. So if the first aspect [that is, awareness state] is present but not the second [that is, concealment], then the discovered teaching belongs to the category of Pure Vision.

In the biography of Khyen tse'i Wang po Kong tul describes[85] how Khyen tse received one of his teachings as Pure Vision:

> At the age of fifteen, when he was doing a strict recitation and practice retreat on longevity, at dawn on the tenth day of the Gyal month [12th] of the male wood-horse year [1834], he heard the sound of a hand-drum in the sky. There was an all-pervading fragrance and he saw a red light descend to the sādhana substances. From it in the form of Caṇḍālī, the long-life consort, immortal Mandārava, appeared. She gave him the teachings, instructions and empowerments on the male consort, the Infinite Life Deity [Amitāyus Buddha], and [they were the texts of] *The Cycle of the Single Hri* and Caṇḍālī, the long-life female consort. Finally, he saw a rain of red flowers when Caṇḍālī recited the prayers for auspiciousness.

REAL AND FALSE TERMAS

There are false Termas too, because of negative influences and aspirations and the evil karma of the people. Furthermore, an ordinary person does not find it easy to distinguish them. The author of *Wonder Ocean*[86] discusses two traditional ways of examining the authenticity of Termas: first, to receive clarification from one's tutelary deity; second, to examine by scriptural and intellectual reasoning. But he points out that nowadays it is rare that we have people who can check with their own tutelary deity directly, and there is no certainty that one will not make mistakes by reasoning. So both of these methods are of little help. He emphasizes that a true Terton must be a realized meditator of the Great Perfection, and a realized person cannot discover false teachings. He also advised checking whether or not a new discovered teaching is similar to the teachings of the authentic Termas. There will be differences in words and style, but if the meaning or the essence of a new Terma are similar to the traditional scriptures, they should be accepted as authentic. Further, he said that it is not proper to judge the Tertons by their style of life but by their teachings, as *Prajñāpāramitā* says:

> Whether or not a Bodhisattva is a Non-returner
> Can be known by his utterance of the Dharma.

UNITY OF DIFFERENT INTERPRETATIONS

Many Nyingma texts describe the discovery of Termas as taking place through the symbolic scripts, and they do not indicate that the Mind-mandate Transmission is the main source or medium of the concealment and discovery. However, the Third Dodrup Chen Rinpoche repeatedly emphasized that the Mind-mandate Transmission is the main aspect of the concealment and discovery of both Earth and Mind Termas of Guru Padmasambhava. The yellow scrolls of symbolic script of Earth Termas and the visions and sounds of symbolic words of Mind Termas are just keys to awaken the transmission from the awareness state of the Terton, but are not the place where the teachings have actually been concealed. The Third Dodrup Chen Rinpoche also quoted sūtras describing how Bodhisattvas discover teachings, but he indicated that theirs may not be of the same nature of discovery as the Terma teachings of Guru Padmasambhava, since there is no indication of Mind-mandate Transmission in them. For example, he quoted as follows from the *Aryadharmasaṁgīti Sūtra*: 'The Bodhisattvas whose minds are pure receive teachings and instructions just by wishing with their minds.'

It seems that the interpretation given in general Nyingma texts indicating that the Termas were concealed and discovered from the symbolic scripts is the outer interpretation. For common people it is apparent that the Termas are discovered by receiving and reading the symbolic scripts.

The interpretation given in *Wonder Ocean*, based on *Ka gyad sang ba yong dzog* by Guru Chö Wang and *Ka gyad rang chung rang shar* by Rig dzin God dem and other sources, emphasizes that the actual concealment and discovery of these teachings occurred in and from the awareness state of the minds of discoverers — that is, the inner interpretation. The actual transmission of words and meanings of this esoteric teaching and attainment must have taken place in the minds of the recipients, for even a transmission of an empowerment has to take place from the enlightened mind of the master to the mind of the disciple. The discovery of Terma is the awakening of the words and meanings as well as the realizations that have been received in ancient times. The symbolic scripts, visions and sounds are just a support or key to awaken the concealed transmission of the teachings.

Part Four
The Text of *Wonder Ocean*
An Explanation of the Dharma Treasure Tradition
gTer Gyi rNam bShad
by the Third Dodrup Chen Rinpoche

The Author of Wonder Ocean

The Third Dodrup Chen Rinpoche, Jig med Ten pa'i Nyi ma (1865–1926) is one of the greatest writers in Nyingma history. He was recognized as a reincarnation of, among others, Prince Mu rum Tsen po (823?–845?), the second son of King Thri srong Deu tsen (790–858), and of the great Terton Sang gye Ling pa (1340–1396). He was the throne-holder of the Dodrup Chen lineage.

The First Dodrup Chen, Jig med Thrin le Od zer, also known as Chang chub Dor je and Kun zang Zhen phen (1745–1821), was the chief disciple of Kun khyen Jig med Ling pa (1729–1798) and the Root Doctrine-holder (*rTsa Ba'i Ch'os bDag*) of Long chen Nying thig, the Terma discovered by Jig med Ling pa. He discovered his own Terma known as Dam chö de chen lam chog (*Dam Ch'os bDe Ch'en Lam mCh'og*) as a Mind Terma. His many famous disciples included Do Khyen tse Ye shey Dor je (1800–?), the reincarnation of Jig med Ling pa, Mi gyur Nam kha'i Dor je (1793–?), the Fourth Dzog Chen Rinpoche, Chö ying Tob den Dor je, Re pa Dam tshig Dor je, Do la Jig med Kal zang (or Chö kyi Lo dro), Gyal se Zhen phen Tha ye (1800–?), Ka thog Ge tse Mahāpaṇḍita, Chö gyal Ngag gi Wang po, a king of the Kokonor Mongols, and Ten tar Lha ram pa, a celebrated Gelug scholar.

In his autobiography,[87] Khyen tse Ye shey Dor je describes his last visit to Dodrup Chen before he left for Amdo:

> The Precious Lord, Dharma King [First Dodrup Chen] was in better health than before. Sometimes he would suddenly sing yogic songs, but we did not have the opportunity to write them down. Occasionally, he would describe his visions of pure lands of the saṃbhogakāya as well as the circumstances of the beings of the six realms. He also gave sudden prophecies of the future of the Dharma tradition and of individuals. Some of us kept seeing his body in different forms. Sometimes we saw him in saṃbhogakāya form. He kept displaying various forms, and sometimes there was no body but only his clothes. There were endless wonders, so that whenever we remembered any question we had on crucial points of instruction, he would answer spontaneously without our needing to ask him.

At the age of seventy-five he died at Yar lung Pe ma köd monastery in Ser valley in Golok leaving miraculous relics as the sign of his high accomplishment and as objects of homage for his disciples. Ten tar Lha ram pa in his commentary on *Yon ten dzöd*[88] has recounted the death of the First Dodrup Chen to illustrate one of the four main miraculous ways of dying by highly accomplished sages:

> Even someone who has the power of the view and of meditation to dissolve [his body into a rainbow body etc.] as I explained before, if he has still not exhausted his karmic air [energy process] because of turning a wheel of activities for the Dharma, or if the remains (*gDung* and *Ring bSrel*) are beneficial for living beings, then he will exhibit the attainment of the state of Knowledge-holder with Residue. It is like [the

> manner of death of] our precious refuge, the glorious Jig med Thrin le Od zer, the illusory manifestation of Samantabhadra, the primordial Buddha arisen in the perceptions of trainable beings as the lord of the sages and the embodiment of the hundred [Buddha] families.

Kong tul Yon ten Gya tsho pays homage to Dodrup Chen in his prayer to Tertons:[89]

> To you who are known as the Radiance [Öd zer]
> of the east, the manifestation-body,
> With four [disciple] yogis, as prophesied by the
> Guru [Padmasambhava],
> Who acted for the benefit [of beings], the
> wisdom reincarnation of Mu rum [Tsen po],
> Chang chub Dor je, Lord of sages, I pray.

The Third Dodrup Chen was a son of Dud jom Ling pa (1835–1903), the First Dudjom Rinpoche. The fame of his intellectual brilliance began at the age of seven or eight when he gave a discourse on the *Bodhicaryāvatāra* to a huge audience in the presence of his teacher Pal tul Rinpoche (1808–1887), the great scholar and writer.

He taught both sūtra and tantra for years. He taught the *Bodhicaryāvatāra* more than a hundred times, as he had promised Pal tul Rinpoche, and the *Guhyagarbhamāyājālatantra* more than forty times. Because of ill health he spent most of the last half of his life in retreat at a hermitage called Ge phel Ri throd (Hermitage of Virtues) near Dodrup Chen monastery.

In addition to being engaged all the time in meditation and reading, he wrote some unprecedented texts. Some of them are: *Explanation of the Recollection Power of Bodhisattvas (Byang Ch'ub Sems dPa'i gZungs Kyi rNam bShad)*, *Outline Commentary of Guhyagarbhamāyājālatantra* (*rGyud gSang Ba sNying Po'i sPyi Don*), and *Wonder Ocean, an Explanation of the Dharma Treasure Tradition* (*gTer Gyi rNam bShad) of the Nyingma School.*

In a prayer to himself that he wrote for his devotees he unfolds his true identity:

> From the primordial sphere of the ground, the
> pure dharmakāya,
> Various displays of saṃbhogakāya appear in the
> ten quarters;
> The ceaseless nirmāṇakāya serves the aim of
> beings:
> Jig med Ten pa'i Nyi ma, to you I pray:
> Please grant us all whatever accomplishments
> we wish.

WONDER OCEAN

Wonder Ocean is an explanation of the way in which the esoteric teachings have been concealed and rediscovered through the enlightened power of Guru Padmasambhava and his highly realized disciples. There are many texts which explain the Terma system. Some concern the tradition in general and others a specific Terma. The uniqueness of this text is that it provides a complete outline of the entire Terma system in detail. So this is the best text for studying the whole Terma tradition of the Nyingmapa.

The text includes extracts from and interpretation of many important sources: many sūtras, and the Termas discovered by Nyang Nyi ma Öd zer, Guru Chö wang, Rig dzin God dem, Padma Le drel tsal, Long chen Rab jam, Ter dag Ling pa, Jig med Ling pa and Le rab Ling pa. The interpretations are also heavily based on the oral teachings on this subject given by Kyen tse'i Wang po and on discussions the author had with Le rab Ling pa, as he says in the text and in the colophon.

1 *Authenticity and Transmission*

Homage to the great blissful and glorious teacher, Padmasambhava.[90]

In the Ancient Buddhist Tantric[91] tradition of Tibet known as the *Nyingma*[92] there are three main transmissions (*Babs So*). They are the transmissions of Canonical Teachings[93] (*bKa 'Ma*), of Terma (*gTer Ma*)[94] and of Pure Vision[95] teachings (*Dag sNang*). In this text I am going to explain briefly the supremely powerful teachings and renowned tradition, the Process of Terma. This initial explanation can serve as a seed for a detailed analysis.

1 AUTHENTICITY OF THE SOURCE OF TRANSMISSION AND CONTINUITY OF THE STREAM OF EMPOWERMENT OF TERMA

It is easy to understand how the teachings were transmitted uninterruptedly from Samantabhadra[96] and Vajrasattva[97] down to the great master Padmasambhava by means of Mind[98] (*dGongs brGyud*), Indication[99] (*brDa brGyud*) and Hearing or Aural[100] (*sNyan brGyud*) Transmission, and how they were transmitted by the Tertons[101] (*gTer sTon*) to the Doctrine-holders[102] (*ch'os bDag*). (But what is required is an explanation of how the teachings were transmitted from Guru Padmasambhava to the Tertons.)

2 THE TRANSMISSION OF THE TEACHINGS FROM THE GREAT MASTER [PADMASAMBHAVA] TO TERTONS

Of the texts of the Eight Great *Maṇḍalas*[103] (*bKa'brGyad*) both *Sang dzog*[104] (*gSang rDzogs*) and *Rang shar*[105] (*Rang Shar*) present an identical account of the transmission of the stream of empowerment.[106] They say:

> Thus all the aspects of the stream of empowerment were transmitted to me, Padmasambhava of Oḍḍiyāna.[107] I opened the door of the empowerment of *Zhi wa dor je ying* (*Zhi Ba rDo rJe dByings*) at Yang le shöd[108] in Nepāl, and transmitted it to Vimalamitra.[109] I bestowed the eight different empowerments of the divinities of the Eight Great Maṇḍalas on the Eight Fortunate People[110] at eight different sacred places in Tibet. At the summit [i.e. main temple] of Sam ye monastery[111] I conferred the great empowerment of De sheg du pa[112] (*bDe gShegs a'Dus Pa*) on the Lord[113] [King] and his Subjects,[114] the twenty-five chief disciples. Now, as I am transmitting the complete empowerment of Sang wa yong dzog (*gSang Ba Yongs rDzogs* or *gSang rDzogs*) to you, the Lord [King], the Subject[115] [i.e. Vairocana], and the Friend[116] [i.e. Ye Shes mTsho rGyal] and to the rest, the Nine Heart-sons,[117] I proclaim to you that the stream of empowerment is an unbroken transmission.
>
> Now I shall give the prophecy of the future course of the unbroken stream of empowerment. The future Tertons, Bodhisattvas[118] who are my Heart-sons, will be yourselves, the fortunate ones, to whom the stream of empowerment is being transmitted at this time. At the time when you, the fortunate ones, come upon these Termas of mine, your recollection of the transmission of

> empowerment which I, Oḍḍiyāna [Padmasambhava], have given you today will be awakened. These Termas and other precious instructions given by me exclusively to the King, Vairocana, and Ye shey Tsho gyal will also be discovered. Make sure that no doubt about the authenticity of the stream of empowerment arises in the minds of future followers.

Guru Rinpoche gave different teachings and conferred their empowerments on the King and his subjects in Tibet. Among those disciples the most fortunate were those whose flowers fell on the central[119] deity of the *maṇḍala* when the empowerments were conferred.[120] To them he gave the Mind-mandate Transmission[121] (*gTad rGya*) of the teachings and recognized them as his own regents and blessed them to tame the beings of the end-age.[122] The unbroken continuity of the stream of that empowerment and the mind-mandate up to the present is the characteristic of the Tertons' endowment with the extraordinary Transmission of Empowerment (*dBang*), Instruction[123] (*Khrid*), and Recitation[124] (*bKa' Lung*). It is because they possess such a transmission that at the appropriate time they discover, from the hands of the ḍākinīs,[125] the casket[126] of tantric teachings. It is not at all like the chance finding of a piece of coral on a riverbank. The Tertons already possess the transmission of the teachings even before their discovery. It is not the case that they receive the transmission when they discover the yellow scrolls (*Shog Ser*).[127] In a prophetic text[128] discovered by Dri med Kun ga[129] it is said:

> Tertons will appear in groups and groups.
> Tertons will come as suddenly as mushrooms.
> They are not fruitless.
> They are remembrances of me [the one from] the
> Oḍḍiyāna land [i.e. Padmasambhava].

Thus, not only the transmission of the teachings but also

the Tertons appear as proof of the true, infallible words of the Precious Master [i.e. Padmasambhava], as his compassionate protection of the people of Tibet. So the Tertons appear solely because of the power of the aspiration of the Master as the memorial of Guru Rinpoche for the sake of the people of Tibet. Therefore Tertons do not take birth or die as ordinary people do. There is need for a more detailed analysis of this matter.

3 BRIEF CLASSIFICATION OF THE TRANSMISSION OF THE TERMAS

The Transmission of the Prophetic Authorization (bKa' Babs Lung bsTan)

The Nine Heart-sons, for example, are authorized disciples of Guru Rinpoche who have perfected the performing of dual benefits (for self and others) by means of the particular teachings conferred on them. Guru Rinpoche gave the prophecy concerning them, which included various indications of place and time in which they shall serve the followers in the end-age by means of those particular teachings.

The Transmission of Aspirational Empowerment (sMon Lam dBang bsKur)

Guru Rinpoche gave his disciples the empowerment of aspiration with concentration, saying, 'In the future at the appropriate time may there arise clearly in your heart the instructions and empowerments which I am bestowing upon you now.' The King and his subjects also made those aspirations simultaneously and perfected them.

The Transmission Entrusting the Teachings to the Ḍākinīs

Guru Rinpoche entrusted the Terma teachings to Ma mos and ḍākinīs in order to ensure that they would come into the hands of the Tertons at the appropriate time, in order to spread them among fortunate beings; to make the followers of the lineage prosper; to keep the teachings secret from improper people; and to make them become powerful.

These are the three special transmissions of the Terma tradition, and together with three traditions of transmission which are common to the Canonical and Terma traditions, there is a total of six transmissions.

The Transmission of Prophetic Authorization in Detail

When it is prophesied of a disciple that he is going to be the authoritative master of certain teachings at a future time, this transmission of Prophetic Authorization creates highly auspicious circumstances in which he can become the Terton of those esoteric teachings. For example the prophecy given by the Master when conferring the empowerment generates the power for one to become a Buddha renowned throughout the three realms[130] (*Sa gSum*) of the world as indicated by the meaning of the [prophetic] mantra '*Bhur-buva. . . .*'[131] So this Terma prophecy is not comparable to other prophecies.

An Alternate Way of Classifying the Special Transmission of Termas

With the help of the writings of Ter dag Ling pa[132] (*gTer bDag Gling Pa*, 1646–1714) and others it needs to be determined whether it is correct to say that the Transmission of Aspirational Empowerment, the concealment of the meaning[133] of instructions in the hearts of the disciples of sublime fortune, is the past cause of the discovery of the Termas, and whether the entrustment of the text[134] through the symbolic scripts of the Termas to ḍākinīs and vow-holders[135] who possess foreknowledge is the present condition for the discovery of the Termas; and whether the prophecies concerning either the Doctrine-holder or the masters who hold the lineal transmission and maintain it by meditating, practicing, teaching, and propagating is the means for making the discovery of the Terma teachings beneficial.

The Aspirational Empowerment, the Main Transmission

Of the three [special] transmissions the Transmission of Aspirational Empowerment is the main one. The Terma scripts, the yellow scrolls, are only a sign for recollection. The real meaning of mind-mandate is just the transmission of the enlightened mind, that is to say, the transmission of teachings from the enlightened mind-stream of the Guru [Padmasambhava] to the minds of his disciples. Guru Rinpoche bestowed and stabilized the accomplishment or power of those teachings (*Ch'os Kyi dNgos Grub*) by integrating them with the luminous natural awareness (*A'od gSal gNyug Ma'i Rig Pa*) or the indestructible essence (*Mi Shigs Pa'i Thig Le*) of the minds of the disciples so that nothing can destroy them. Whereas, if the teachings were to have been concealed in [the ordinary state of] minds whose activities are conditioned by karmic energy (*Las rLung*), since that basis has a changeable nature, it would be difficult for the disciples to face up to any of the developing and diminishing circumstances which occur while they are passing through many deaths and births during the age of dregs. It is an extraordinary transmission, a transmission of actualization of ultimate meaning through direct transference of the wisdom of vajra speech of the vajra teacher [i.e. Padmasambhava] into the minds of the disciples through the power of concentration of his mind, so that the minds of teacher and disciple become inseparable.

Clearly, in order for that actual mind-mandate to take place, the teacher mandating the Termas has to have achieved the supreme attainment (*mCh'og Gi dNgos Grub*), and the disciple receiving the mind-mandate must be a person who at least has achieved an adequate realization (*Las Su Rung Ba*) of the perfection stage[136] (*rDzogs Rim*).

The reason why the yellow scrolls are indispensable in order for the teachings to be transcribed (*gTan La Pheb Pa*) is, I think, that it is through the yellow scrolls that Tertons have received the mind-mandate. And since in the past the yellow scrolls have stood symbolically (*mTshan Ma*) for the teachings, when they are seen now they help arouse in the minds of the Tertons the recollection of the entire teachings.

Furthermore, in order to arouse the accomplishment from their depths, the teachings which have been concealed in the natural sphere of the luminous state (*A'od gSal Gyi Khams*) [of their minds], it is also necessary to have the spontaneously arisen bliss (*Lhan sKyes Kyi dGa' Ba*) which can be produced by a special consort who has made the appropriate aspirations in the past, and who is to become the key to accomplishment. That is one of the reasons why all Tertons happen to have consorts.

Reception of the Three Common Transmissions in a Single Lifetime by the Tertons

From the comparative study of the Mother[137] [root] and Son [commentaries] texts of Kha dro nying thig [of Nying thig][138] and the view of Rig dzin Jig med Ling pa[139] the transmission of the Terma can, I think, be interpreted as follows: the Tertons receive the three common transmissions in the lifetime in which they discover the teachings. The direct awakening of the luminous vision (*A'od gSal Gyi dGongs Pa*) of Guru Rinpoche in the hearts [of the disciples] is the Mind Transmission. By receiving the symbolic scripts they awaken the experience of obtaining the authorization from Guru Rinpoche by his saying, 'In future you may confer empowerment on your disciples in this way.' That is the Indication Transmission. The decoding of the symbolic scripts[140] of the yellow scrolls is the Hearing Transmission. The reason for categorizing the last named as the Hearing Transmission is that Hearing Transmission means to receive the understanding of the words and meanings of the teachings from a teacher who possesses the lineal transmission. The yellow scrolls are without speech or sound, but in their ability to convey understanding of the words and meanings of the teachings, they are not merely equal to general Hearing Transmissions but far superior. In fact, the extraordinary transmissions of blessing (*Byin rLabs*) can be received from the yellow scrolls as from a teacher. For if the transmission of blessing could not be received, there would be no way of understanding (*brDa a'Phrod*) the words and meanings of the miraculous scripts[141] (*a 'Phrul Yig*) and so on (which will be discussed later). Also the symbolic scripts, which have no alphabetical key,[142] would not be able to be read.

Thus, the power gained by their receiving the Mind Transmission enables the Tertons to transfer the wisdom of actual transmission (*Don brGyud*) to their disciples by directing their concentration to those disciples; because of their insight into the essential points conveyed by the symbols through Indication Transmission, they can confer empowerments through symbolic substances, mantras, and gestures (*rDzas sNgags Phyag rGya*); and because of Hearing Transmission they can give instructional teachings (*gDams Khrid*), clarifications (*Zhal Shes*), and rubrics[143] (*Phyag bZhes*) without any errors, in accordance with their visions of Guru Rinpoche. These are much more extraordinary virtues than those of ordinary tantric teachers (*Vajrācārya*).

This type of perfecting of the three [common] transmissions without any effort in the very lifetime of a Terton happens through the integration of two factors: the karmic process of his receiving the first three [common] transmissions, and the ripening of the blessing of Guru Rinpoche's consideration of the future.

Reception of the Three Common Transmissions in the Ancient Time

The Tertons have received the first three [common] transmissions. It is not only that in Guru Rinpoche the three transmissions are gathered, but that the King and his subjects have received the Mind Transmission of integrating their minds with that of the master [Padmasambhava], the Indication Transmission of full empowerment and of the powers of the symbolic scripts, and the Hearing Transmission of receiving the detailed instructional teaching before the mind-mandate.

In the *Kha dro nying thig*, for the Three Later [special] Transmissions, instead of 'Prophetic Authorization' the expression is 'Transmission of Compassionate Blessing' (*Thugs rJe Byin rLabs*). This signifies the attainment of the power of serving beings by means of the Terma teachings in the age of dregs, and the capacity to bless the follower in order to make him or her capable of benefiting others because of having received the blessings of Guru Rinpoche. So, its meaning is similar to the transmission of Prophetic Authorization discussed earlier. The entrustment of the teachings to the ḍākinīs is the same as discussed earlier. The Transmission of Aspirational Empowerment is also similar to the earlier one, which is to say that Guru Rinpoche, the embodiment of the Buddhas of the three times, while concentrating upon the specific fortunate disciple, uttered this aspiration: 'In the future may this teaching meet up with the person who has a karmic connection with it.'

4 TERMAS IN THE FORM OF TEACHINGS

Among the Termas, there are various kinds of material including precious blessed substances, images and sacred objects. But here we are talking mainly about Terma in the form of teachings.

In *Phag pa da tar zhug pa'i ting nge dzin gyi do*[144] it is said that many great Bodhisattvas such as Bhadrapāla (*bZang sKyong*) received this sūtra[145] from the Buddha himself. Then they wrote it down, put it in caskets and handed it over to gods and nāgas who lived in stūpas, mountains, and rocks, whereupon the Bodhisattvas went off to pure lands. Later on they reappeared in this world and taught this sūtra.

That system is somewhat similar to this tradition. Also in *Sod nam tham chad du pa'i ting nge dzin gyi do*[146] and *Chö yang dag par dud pa,*[147] and so forth, it is said that the Bodhisattvas whose minds are pure and who desire teachings will discover Termas from the earth, trees, and rocks. But I think it is difficult to say for all of them that there is any proof that those teachings came through a Mind-mandate Transmission. What I am presenting here concerns the activities of the vajra speech of Padmasambhava about the concealed Termas of Vajrayāna[148] in this land at the time for the taming of the disciples. So this particular tradition should not be employed for making generalizations about all the various Terma systems.

2 *Script, Concealment and Protection*

5 THE SCRIPT OF TERMAS

There are Terma scripts written by human calligraphers such as Leg chin Nyi ma (*Legs Byin Nyi Ma*), supreme among the most excellent calligraphers, Den ma Tse mang (*lDan Ma rTse Mang*), supreme among the fastest calligraphers, and Ācārya Ye shey Yang (*A Tsa Ra Ye Shes dByangs*), supreme among the most accurate calligraphers. There are scripts written by non-human ḍākinīs and also those written by Guru Rinpoche himself. It is said that different calligraphers have different calligraphic designs or styles. Guru Rinpoche's handwriting is beautiful and thin, Ācārya Ye shey's big, thick and smooth, and Vairocana's correct and pliant or flowing (*mNyen lChug*).

In ordinary circumstances the writing speed of Den ma Tse mang and other calligraphers is the same as that of ordinary scribes. But when they write Terma scripts, through their enlightened miraculous power they can write texts such as *La ma gong dü* [in thirteen volumes] a hundred times in the snap of a finger. This is because their power of realization shines forth on account of their yogic[149] experiences, since they are great yogis,[150] and because of the blessings of Guru Rinpoche. There were many different kinds of calligraphers, human and non-human. Guru Rinpoche taught measureless tantras, sādhanas,[151] instructions, and rubrics in a single moment, and so endless Termas occur.

It is said that if there is some great significance about a teaching, in that it is very profound, or if there are no appropriate disciples in the human world for that particular teaching, or if the ḍākinīs and the Dharma protectors pay it more than usual respect and worship it because it is so rare, then Guru Rinpoche gives the order, 'It is not permitted to make more than one copy of this'; thus there are texts that have only one copy, even in the land of the ḍākinīs.

All the Terma scripts are blessed by Guru Rinpoche himself and possess the greatness of granting liberation-by-seeing[152] (*mThong Grol*). It is also said that because of the past karmic and aspirational power of the Tertons the yellow scrolls may appear suddenly at appropriate places: in snow mountains, rocks, lakes and so on, as the Spirit Lake[153] (*Bla mTsho*) at Drag da (*sBrag mDa'*) sprang out spontaneously when Lady Ye shey Tsho gyal was born. The power of dependent causation is inconceivably enormous.

6 THE MANNER OF CONCEALING THE TERMAS IN DIFFERENT PLACES

At the time of Guru Rinpoche's departure [in 864 AD] for Cāmaradvīpa,[154] he summoned the local spirits[155] from all over the central and outlying regions of Tibet. He entrusted to them the various Termas and instructed them, saying, 'You conceal this much at your place.' He also explained to them which Tertons would own which Termas and what benefits would be rendered by the various teachings in different circumstances, and he told them not to mix them up.

Accordingly, after the departure of the Second Buddha [i.e. Padmasambhava] for Rākṣasa Land, the great custodian of the concerns of Guru Rinpoche, the Great Blissful One, Tsho gyal, concluded the concealment of the Termas.

I am explaining only a part of this tradition, but it is

impossible to comprehend the whole of it in detail. For example, even in the manner of reconcealment (*a'Dab gTer*) there are many different methods (which will be briefly discussed later). After the concealment until the time of discovery arrives, the Termas will not be discovered by anybody, no matter how intensively they are searched for, because the Treasures will remain in the far depths of the place of concealment. At the time of discovery they come forth at the mouth of the place of concealment. The discovery of the treasures will become easier to the extent that the auspicious or favorable circumstances[156] are perfected. If the place of concealment of the Termas itself faces any changes they will be transferred to other places. Many Termas disappear like camphor if they cannot be discovered in time. The Omniscient Lord[157] has said that the occurrence of the Termas is conditional upon the presence or disappearance of the people [Tertons and disciples] who have made aspirations for those teachings. It may also be possible for the changes to occur on account of the Terma protectors,[158] but that is not in accordance with the traditional interpretation by the lineage; and so the matter depends not on any other factors, but solely upon the aspiration powers of Guru Rinpoche.

No specific text of this tradition has come to my notice that has been discovered from space, but in the texts it is said that there are Termas concealed in space. This is not astonishing since Guru Rinpoche concealed those particular Termas in the sky through his miraculous power, so they are free from destruction by any of the four elements,[159] and they are invisible to human and non-human beings and so on. It is also said that except for the particular protector of a specific Terma, no other ordinary ḍākas or ḍākinīs will be able to see them.

Also it is not necessary that all the concealed Termas are destined for discovery. For it is said that there are some that were concealed for the protection of the doctrine, for the auspiciousness of the land, and for the protection of the generations of the Dharma kings, and these are not for discovery.

7 THE TERMA PROTECTORS

There are two categories of Terma protectors; the protectors of Terma in general and those who take the responsibility of handing them to Tertons. As to the latter, sometimes there will be one protector for many Termas and sometimes one Terma will be entrusted to many protectors. There are not only those great protectors such as Ekajaṭī, who is the protectress of the tantras and the Great Mistress of the Desire Realm (*a'Dod Khams dBang Mo*) and so on, but also the ones who are appointed as the protectors from the various classes (*Rigs*) of beings such as Gyal po (*rGyal Po*), Tsen (*bTsen*) and Theu rang (*Theu Rang*), who are the chiefs among their own types of spirits. All of these protectors are related to Guru Rinpoche by aspirations, eager to fulfill the activities of the Triple Gem.[160] They have received empowerments into the tantric maṇḍalas, are observing the obligations[161] [valuing the samaya] as their own lives, and especially they have fulfilled the mind-mandate of a particular Terma by achieving the power of realization of it. They belong to the category of ḍākas and ḍākinīs who possess the inconceivable miraculous power over infinitely various activities such as elimination [of negative forces] and protection [of practitioners] through the practice of yoga, mantras,[162] and actions.[163] One of the other purposes in making these spirits the Terma protectors comes from the fact that the evil forces that cause obstructions to Dharma practitioners are the retinues of those chiefs among their spirit classes, so that by appointing their chiefs as the protectors, their subjects won't be able to transgress the orders.

3 *Terma Texts and Scripts*

8 THE VARIOUS TERMA SCRIPTURES

A brief account of some categories of Terma cycles occurs in various Thang yigs,[164] in *The Great Prophecy of Gong dü*[165] (*dGongs a'Dus*), and so forth. There are categories of discovered scriptures (resembling the various aspects of a tree) such as:

a. The Eastern Terma[166] cycle, which can be likened to ripened fruit,
b. The cyle of Southern Terma,[167] which is like the circular trunk,
c. The cycle of Western Terma[168] resembling the bright flowers,
d. The cycle of Northern Terma[169] resembling spreading branches,
e. The cycle of Central Terma[170] like the penetrating roots of a tree, and so on.

Roughly speaking, among the Termas there are texts of sūtras and of Outer Tantras but mostly of Anuttarayoga.[171] As I shall explain later, the purpose is to enhance the power of the transmission of the Anuttaratantra.

The yogas are the exceptionally concealed instructions that are intended for Tibetans and are prepared and arranged in order that people of lesser intelligence may find them easy to understand.[172] They are classified in three main categories: Root: the instructional teachings on Guru, tutelary deities (*Yi Dam*), and ḍākinīs; Branch: aspects of various activities and their associated divisions; and Heart or Essence: Teachings on Guru Sādhana,[173] Atiyoga[174] and Avalokiteśvara.[175]

A. *Root: the Instructional Teachings on the Cycle of Guru, Tutelary Deities and Ḍākinīs*

i. *The Cycle of Guru*

a. *General Textual Categories (sPyi bsDus)*

Tsa sum Ka du[176] (*rTsa gSum bKa'a'Dus*)
Chi pung[177] (*sPyi sPungs*)
Ne gyur[178] (*gNas bsGyur*)
Tso du[179] (*gTso bsDus*)
Chig dril gyi Drub lug[180] (*gChig Dril Gyi sGrub Lugs*) and so on.

b. *Specific Textual Categories (So Sor Phye Ba'i sKor)*

Categorization by manner of practice
Outer practice based on prayers
Inner practice based on sādhanas

Categorization by the deities
Peaceful Guru:[181]
Guru in single form
Guru with many retinue deities
Sādhanas of specific root and minor deities, and so on.

Wrathful Guru:[182]
Guru in single form
Guru with many retinue deities
Sādhanas of specific root and minor deities, and so on.

ii. *The Cycle of Tutelary Deities*[183] *(Yi Dam)*

It is said that among Dharma Treasures there are many scriptures of, for example, Cakrasaṁvara and Hevajra,[184] but the main ones are:

a. *The scriptures on peaceful and wrathful deities*[185]
Independent scriptures
Scriptures incorporated with other scriptures
b. *The scriptures of the Eight Great Maṇḍalas*
Individual or specific sādhanas
General sādhanas.

Other categories of scriptures associated with the tutelary deities cycle are:

a. *Tantras (rGyud), root esoteric scriptures*
b. *Āgama (Lung), esoteric teachings*
c. *Upadeśa (Man Ngag), esoteric instructions*
Meditational instructions (*sGom Khog*)
Explanations of deities (*Lha Khrid*)
Instructions on essential aspects (*gNad Yig*)
Answers to questions (*Zhus Lan*), and so on.
d. *Main texts of sādhana (sGrub gZhung)*
Elaborated sādhana (*sGrub gZhung rGyas Pa*)
Middle length sādhana (*sGrub gZhung a'Bring*)
Brief sādhana (*sGrub gZhung bsDus Pa*)
Heart sādhana (*sGrub gZhung sNying po*)

There are many scriptures for longevity, on Avalokiteśvara, Vajrakīla, and Yamarāja. Also there are texts of Hyagriva in each of the three root cycles.

iii *The Cycle of Ḍākinīs*

The most popular texts are of:

a. Vajravārāhī (*Phag Mo*)
b. Krodhī (*Khros Ma*)
c. Siṅhamukhā (*Seng gDong Ma*)

Also there are many texts on:

a. Guhyajñāna (*gSang Ba Ye Shes*)
b. Tārā (*sGrol Ma)*
c. Jñānasāgarā (*Ye Shes mTsho rGyal*) and so on.

There are numerous scriptures on the above mentioned

tantras on the Perfection Stage (*rDzogs Rim*): using one's own or another's body as the means of practice. In particular there are the cycles of instructions of Dzog chen:

a. Nying thig (*sNying Thig*) teachings of [or transmitted into Tibet through] Padmasambhava
b. Nying thig teachings of [or transmitted through] Vimalamitra
c. Nying thig teachings of [or transmitted through] Vairocana
d. Combined Nying thig teachings of all three masters.

There are many lengthy and detailed Dzog chen teachings and many short ones. Some are independent and some are incorporated with other teachings.

Also among them are endless sādhana cycles of Dharma protectors, from those of minor spirits up to the Great Beings such as:

a. Mainly of Lord (*nātha*) Ma ning, and
b. The Four-Armed Lord
c. The Lord Who Holds a Curved Blade
d. The Tiger-Riding Lord, and so on.

But the sādhanas of Dharma protectors have been included in those of the *Three Categories of Worldly Deities*[186] (*a'Jigs rTen Pa'i sDe gSum*) *of the Eight Great Maṇḍalas*, and so it is not incorrect if they have not been counted separately.

In brief, this vast land has been filled with known and unknown, named and unnamed Termas comparable to [a heap of] mustard seeds. Most of the teachings came accompanied by sacred substances, images, and instruments (*Phyag mTshan*) and with prophecies for the future.

B. *Branch: Aspects of Various Activities and Their Associated Divisions*

There are Termas of substances and instructions on the

accomplishment of the eight siddhis[187] or attainments, but mainly these are the numerous tantras on the Four Actions. They are on:

a. Medicine and treatment (*sMan Dang mKhyud dPyad*)
b. Extraction of nutrients[188] (*bChud Len*)
c. Charm wheel (*a'Khor Lo*)
d. Divination (*rNo mThong*)
e. Cross thread ceremony (*mDos gTo*)
f. Prospering of wealth (*Nor sGrub*)
g. Welfare of crops (*Lo Tog Phan Byed*)
h. Various protective means (*Srung Ba sNa Tshogs*)
i. Collection of mantras (*sNgags a'Bum*)
j. Various (minor) actions (*Las sNa Tshogs*)
k. Various miraculous actions (*sNa Tshogs rDzu a'Phrul*) and so on.

There are in particular a great number of exhorting mantras (*Drag sNgags*) in the Termas, the purpose of which is to protect the doctrine and the doctrine-holders in this utmost end-age when the power of evil forces is increasing. It has happened that just by the discovery of the Terma of wrathful deities and actions, some evil spirits who had taken birth as leaders in order to impoverish (*Phongs*) Tibet have been eliminated.

C. *Heart: Teachings on Guru Sādhana, Atiyoga and Avalokiteśvara*

This is the largest category of Terma. It is known that if a Terton has no Termas of these three kinds among his discovered teachings, then he is not considered a Great Terton. All the Great Tertons have discovered teachings on all three. It seems that even among the Minor Tertons there are none who have not discovered teachings of at least one of these three.

According to some sources the three divisions of the Heart Cycle are: the texts on (a) the peaceful and wrathful forms of Guru [Padmasambhava], (b) the mind-sādhana (*Thugs sGrub*), the practice on tutelary deities, and (c) the cycles on the perfecting stage. But according to earlier teachers and also the Reverend Spiritual Father, the Omniscient Lama (*mKhyen brTse'i dBang Po*), the cycles are:

a. Sādhana cycle on Guru [Padmasambhava] such as Sang dü,[189] and Gong dü (*Bla Ma dGongs a'Dus*),
b. Sādhana cycle on Avalokiteśvara such as Chö gyal ka bum,[190] and Yang nying dü pa,[191] and
c. Teaching cycle on Atiyoga [or Mahāsandhi] such as Kha dro nying thig and Gong pa zang thal.[192]

a. *Sādhana of Guru [Padmasambhava]*

The reason that there are many sādhana texts on Guru Rinpoche himself is that the manifestations of the Enlightened Ones have appeared in the form of knowledge-holding[193] teachers as messengers between ordinary beings and the deities. So it is much easier to accomplish the attainments if one practices through them.

In respect to Guru Rinpoche the quotation applies:

> The heritage of the Guru for Tibetans is the Guru
> [Padmasambhava] himself,
> The heritage of the deity is Avalokiteśvara.

The second Buddha of Oḍḍiyāna [Padmasambhava] was invited to Tibet by King Thri srong Deu tsen (790–858) in accordance with their past aspirations for the protection of the entire Himalayan region. Since Thri srong Deu tsen was the king of all Tibet, he made his requests not only on behalf of the whole race of Tibetans but on behalf of the animals also. For example, wherever the leader of the cows goes, the others will follow. Because of the favorable circumstances of the past, the blessings of Guru Rinpoche are much swifter for Tibetans than for others.

Guru Rinpoche is most gracious to Tibetans. He tamed the entire land, both central Tibet and its outskirts. It was the land of demons and rākṣasas but he blessed it as a source of the Dharma and a noble land. Guru Rinpoche turned most parts of the land of Tibet into meditation places and blessed them to have qualities equal to those of vajra-sacred places (of India). As proof he left behind rocks in the form of Hūṁ-letters,[194] foot-prints on four rocky mountains,[195] hand-prints on four lakes[196] and so on, which can still be seen. Guru Rinpoche, through his miraculous power, brought many tantric scriptures from the land of ḍākinīs that did not exist in the human world. He gave numerous discourses on tantra at Sam ye monastery and other places and introduced the King and twenty-five subjects, the chief disciples and so on to the supreme accomplishment. He established the foundation, the source of a succession of siddhas or accomplished ones. By appointing the twelve local spirits of Tibet, known as Ten mas,[197] a manifested form of the four yoginīs and eight door protectors of the Cakrasaṁvara maṇḍala, as the mistresses of Tibet, he ensured that the tantric doctrine would remain in Tibet, and he blocked the way for heretics to enter Tibet. Also, until the end of the age comes, because of ceaseless efforts of those such as the Tertons, Termas, both of teachings and materials, and detailed and appropriate prophecies will appear in time to protect Tibet from foreign invasions, internal fighting, disease, famine and so on.

Vajradhara Pal tul Rinpoche[198] (1808–1887) said:

> Here in this part of the land all men and women have devotion to the tantras of Mahāyāna and they have great desire to receive a tantric empowerment. They have high regard for receiving an empowerment even if it is just the form, or like the reflection of an empowerment. All of these are signs that Guru Rinpoche has blessed all men in Tibet as ḍākas and all women as ḍākinīs. It is not the case in other countries. The

merits obtained by just once having a feeling of devotion to the Vajrayāna caused by conformity to others may not be obtained through training in other paths even for a prolonged period.

Even at present, Guru Rinpoche remains in the same body in which he came to Tibet in an extraordinary land of knowledge-holders near the Jambu[199] continent. Furthermore, he has promised that on the tenth days of the Monkey months[200] he will make visits all over Tibet through his miraculous power and protect the people from suffering. So this is an important point to know—that it will be easier to attain whatever common or uncommon accomplishments if one practices accordingly.

b. *Sādhana on Avalokiteśvara*

Similarly the reason for having many teachings on Avalokiteśvara in the Termas can be understood from the above given quotation. I will briefly discuss this point on the basis of the teachings of the Lord Atīśa[201] (982–1054) and of the Termas discovered by Drub thob Ngö drub.[202]

The Buddha, the King of the Śākyas, has entrusted Tibet to Avalokiteśvara[203] as the land to tame. Likewise, the human race emerged from the noble monkey meditator,[204] a manifestation of Avalokiteśvara. The material wealth of Tibet began with the seeds of seven kinds of crops[205] scattered upon Tibet from the Potala[206] Pure Land by Avalokiteśvara. The spiritual wealth began in Tibet with the arrival of the Do de Za ma tog.[207] According to *Ka dam Leg pam Rinpoche,*[208] most of the earlier Dharma kings of Tibet were incarnations of Lord Avalokiteśvara. The coming of the two precious images of the Lord Śākyamuni[209] from China and India [Nepāl] to central Tibet and the construction of Ra sa'i Tsug lag khang[210] happened because of the kindness of King Srong tsen Gam po (617–698) and the self-arisen image of Avalokiteśvara.[211] Also the composition of the script and grammar for the Tibetan language by the minister Thon mi Sambhoṭa,[212] the proclamation of the law of the Ten Virtues,[213] the blessing of the land by the building of the Thrul nang [i.e. Ra'Sa'i gTsug Lag Khang], Tha dul, Yang dul and Ru non temples,[214] and the gathering in central Tibet of various arts and riches from all corners of the earth were some of the accomplishments of King Srong tsen Gam po, a manifestation of Avalokiteśvara.

In this country [Tibet] many things have happened [which confirm the role of Avalokiteśvara]. Even among lay people who do not know Dharma and have never had any experience of Dharma, when the thought of the next life arises in their minds, or when they see their life-partner die and so on, they spontaneously remember the Maṇi mantra [*oṃ maṇi padme hūṃ*][215] and recite it hundreds, thousands, tens of thousands or hundreds of thousands of times, as when a child is afraid and starts calling for his mother. By just reciting the Maṇi mantra many benefits occur, such as: in this lifetime the force of one's unvirtuous actions will decrease; one will have a long life and will face less harmful circumstances; blind people will start to see; people will be released from harmful spirits; they will have generations of auspicious descendents and will see manifestations of Avalokiteśvara in dreams. At the time of death the consciousness will be transferred to the pure lands by the sound of the six-syllable or Maṇi mantra. So, of course, whoever does practice on Avalokiteśvara properly will achieve the accomplishments. In Tibet there are children who, before being able to say their mother's name, clearly pronounce the Maṇi mantra. So, for many reasons it is clear that for Tibetans there is a more special connection with Avalokiteśvara than with any other Buddhas or Bodhisattvas. That is why there are many Dharma Treasure teachings on Avalokiteśvara. Although the root of happiness for Tibetans is the Treasure of Compassion [i.e. Avalokiteśvara], the excellent noble one, and the six-syllable mantra, the excellent Dharma, Tibetans appreciate new acquaintances, they forget the teachings quickly and they don't think of the significance of the teachings. So, because of the kindness of Guru Rinpoche, Termas on the Sādhana of Avalokiteśvara are discovered continually in order to remind and inspire the followers of this practice. We should be aware of the kindness of Guru Rinpoche, and by knowing it, we should fulfill his wishes.

When Guru Rinpoche appears as a knowledge-holder, the Excellent Teacher in the form of a human being, he is known as Guru Padmasambhava. When he exhibits himself in the form of a tutelary deity, he is known as Avalokiteś-vara. The difference is the name; in reality there are no differences. Thus it is stated in many authentic Terma texts, but I am not going to quote them here. There is great significance in having two different means of sādhana or practice, although in reality they are inseparable. One should know this in detail, based on the above given brief explanation.

c. *Teaching on Atiyoga [or Mahāsandhi]*

In the Termas, among the teachings of the perfection stage particular emphasis is placed on the teachings of Dzog pa Chen po, the Great Perfection. The reason is that in the general perfection stage the practice is based on using the mind as the path or means of practice, and it is difficult to attain the primordial wisdom if one is not a person of utmost diligence. Another reason is that because of the present time [the dark age] it will not be easy to achieve the ultimate goal, as it was in ancient times. In this excellent yāna [i.e. *rDzogs Pa Ch'en Po*], the primordial wisdom itself is used as the means of practice: therein lies the difference.

If one should analyze the various points of the meaning of the following quotation from *Ka gyed kyi drub zhung*[216] [page 15a] of Long chen nying thig, then one would understand that crucial point:

> Sentient beings who are attached to the wrong
> view (of grasping phenomena as) real,

Are difficult to tame by any of the other yānas,
(those) of Causation.
Therefore, (Buddhas and deities,) please carry
out the activities required for realization of
the self-arisen primordial wisdom.[217]

This deeply sacred vajra essence has very important ramifications, which should be explained in detail, but this is not the right place, so I will not go into detail here. As I mentioned earlier, if one is a holder of the Terma lineage, one should practice on Guru Padmasambhava, Avalokiteś-vara, and Dzog pa Chen po as the main practice. This can be illustrated by the lives of Lord Nyang Nyi ma Od zer (1124–1192) and [Guru] Chö wang (1212–1270), but in the present context this is enough.

9 SYMBOLIC SCRIPTS, THE MAIN MEANS TO AWAKEN THE MIND-MANDATE TRANSMISSION

The symbolic scripts are the main instrument for awakening the Mind-mandate Transmission of the concealed Terma teachings. The definition of the symbolic scripts is letters in a symbolic, coded form which clearly awaken the Terton's mind to the teachings concealed in ancient times [by Padmasambhava] in the disciple's vision of luminous vast expanse.

There are many other details to be given about the symbolic scripts and signs, and these will be discussed later in connection with the discovering of the mind-mandate of concealed Terma teachings. For example, that the scripts can be read is their special quality, which images and stūpas do not have. Similarly, the real symbolic scripts that clearly indicate the correct meanings of various tantras, precepts, and instructions, by means of these symbolic scripts, are unique to the Terma tradition. They are the principal symbolic material and the rest[218] are secondary symbols.

4 *Classification and Transcription of Terma Scripts*

10 CLASSIFICATION OF TERMA SCRIPTS

A. *Classification based on Different Scripts*

i. *Ḍākinī Script*

There are various Terma scripts known by the ḍākas and ḍākinīs of the vajra lands, such as Thang yig (*Thang Yig*), Pung yig (*sPung Yig*), Shur yig (*bShur Yig*), Dem yig (*lDem Yig*), Be yig (*sBas Yig*), Khar tseg (*mKhar brTsegs*), Thig le'i Yi ge (*Thig Le'i yi Ge*), Khyil chen (*a'Khyil Ch'en*) and Khyil chung (*a'Khyil Ch'ung*). Even within each land of ḍākinīs there are many different kinds of scripts. So, if one were to think that the script that was discovered by a particular Terton is the only kind of ḍākinī script that exists, it would be like someone thinking that there is no water except in the rivers of the four ranges (*Ru bZhi*) of central Tibet.

ii. *Other Scripts*

There are many common and uncommon scripts other than the ḍākinī scripts, such as Lañca, Vartu[219] (for Sanskrit) and Dzab (rDzab) and Shur (gShur) etc. for Tibetan. Even among Tibetan scripts there are different scripts such as Tsheg med, Phur med (*a'Phur Med*), and Gyen med (*rGyan Med*) or Dog med (*a 'Dogs Med*).

B. *Classification based on Method of Introduction (Ngo sProd)*

i. *Introduction Through Keys (lDe Mig Chan)*

There are Termas that came written in alphabets directly corresponding to the Tibetan alphabet.

ii. *Introduction Through Various Circumstances (rKyen Las Nges)*

Some Terma scripts are not in alphabetical correspondence but the Terton will understand the symbolic script suddenly and spontaneously through the agency of indefinite circumstances or conditions of the external world or of beings (*brTan a'Gro'i Yul rKyen*).

iii. *Direct Introduction (Rang Shes Pa)*

Sometimes the Tertons will be able to read the symbolic scripts by themselves without relying on alphabets or circumstances. These instances are of two types. The first is understanding the meaning of the symbolic script by seeing it, and the second is that by looking at the symbolic script again and again the Terton will understand the meaning by becoming familiar with it. These are distinctions that apply only to ḍākinī scripts.

C. *Classification based on the Structure of the Symbolic Scripts*

i. *Just Visible (sNang Tsam)*

This is just a symbolic indication without any summary, explanation or synopsis of the text. It might be one or two syllables, and there will not necessarily be a noun or even a [whole] word.

ii. *Just an Indication (rTen Tsam)*

a. *Actual Indication:* There will be a single point in the symbolic script giving a fragment of the history, name or outline of the text, but not in detail. Just as a seed one quarter the size of a mustard seed is sufficient to produce a Nyagrodha [Indian fig tree], these last two systems [*Barely Visible* and *Just an Indication*] are adequate means of discovering the teachings; it is sufficient to have only a few bits of symbolic script as the seed or basis of the Terma text.

b. *Provoking the Memory:* This type has two categories. The first is the symbolic script in which there is nothing but a phrase unrelated to the subject of the text but which indicates an incident in the events of the ancient time when Guru Rinpoche gave the teachings. Because of that indication the recollection of the teaching, the place, the time, Guru Rinpoche and his disciples occurs in the mind of the Terton, and he will be able to transcribe the teachings. For example, by seeing a statement written on the yellow scroll saying:

> At the time of the first arrival of the cuckoo, in front of Guru Rinpoche, the King and his subjects who were staying in a silken tent at the Trag mar Tsho mo gül,[220] many birds including geese and cuckoos assembled and played every day. It was a great delight.

The Terton will recollect the complete teachings thinking, 'Oh, Guru Rinpoche gave such and such teachings to us, the King and the subjects, at that time.'

In the second case, there will be nothing concerning the ancient time, and it looks as if whatever crossed the mind was written down. But by seeing it the Terton remembers how and what teachings Guru Rinpoche gave him in the ancient time.

c. *Complete Text:* In the case of some Termas, the whole text is written from beginning to end [in symbolic script].

As previously mentioned, whether the discovered teaching is in the indicative or complete form it is not certain in what script the symbolic script may be written. Those symbolic scripts that contain nouns and words can be in a variety of languages such as Sanskrit, Tibetan and ḍākinī's symbolic language. It is one of the obligations [samaya] binding members of this tradition that the symbolic language of the teachings must not be taught to anyone but the Terton.

There are two kinds of ḍākinī script: Illusory Miraculous Script and Non-illusory Miraculous Script. For this reason four degrees of understanding of the symbolic scripts are referred to in *Do chang* (*mDo Byang*):[221] Tertons may read the symbolic script but not have the awakening of the Mind-Mandate Transmission, or they may not read the symbolic script but have the awakening of the Mind-Mandate Transmission, and so on [may read the symbolic script and have the awakening of the Mind-Mandate Transmission, and may not read the symbolic script and not have the awakening of the Mind-Mandate Transmission]. The script and the length of the text, and so on, will not change even a little from the way in which it was written at the beginning [by Guru Rinpoche].

11 TRANSCRIBING THE DISCOVERED TEACHINGS FROM THE SYMBOLIC SCRIPT

The Tertons concentrate on the symbolic script and reflect again and again on the words and meanings of the teachings that were mind-mandated to them by Guru Rinpoche, who is the Buddha of the three times, whereupon the recollection of the teachings awakens from the expanse of his or her awareness [primordial wisdom]. By concentrating thus, the teachings will be able to be discovered as the Terton wishes. There is a somewhat more detailed explanation of this matter in *Do chang* of *Ter sar* (*gTer gSar*).[222]

Arising of Miraculous Scripts from the Symbolic Scripts

By concentrating on the symbolic script the Terton perceives in his or her awareness state that the scripts are changing miraculously every moment into different forms. Also, because of the power of the symbolic scripts his or her power of awareness (*Rig Pa'i rTsal*) increases, and accordingly the words and the meanings of the Terma remain of the same nature but appear changing back and forth into various forms, and the actual text and its meaning are uncertain. There are three kinds of changes: sometimes the script changes but not the words and the meaning. Sometimes the words and meaning change but not the script. Sometimes both change. The last instance is very difficult to distinguish, since it is like matted hemp.[223]

The Discoverer must reach the identification of the true text, one word and one meaning, by achieving fully perfected power in decoding the symbolic script. This is accomplished through favorable conditions such as meeting with the Doctrine-holder of those Termas; being in the right place or being present at an important occasion; and most important, by encountering the miraculous skill of a Vajradūta [consort] whose mind has been purified by empowerments and precepts, who has practiced the path of two stages (*Rim gNyis*), who has been blessed by Guru Rinpoche himself in order to take the birth of an appropriate sacred support [consort] for the Terton in future to discover the Termas of the sphere of primordial wisdom (*Ye Shes dByings*) by means of the hook (*lChags Kyu*) of spontaneously arisen bliss, and who himself or herself has made the appropriate aspirations [in the past]. Because of those conditions the Terton will become certain about the real words and meanings of the texts, and other appearances will disappear.

The Omniscient Vajradhara Mañju (*mKhyen brTse'i dBang Po*) has said:

> If the Tertons transcribe the teachings before they achieve the insight into and full perfection of understanding of the symbolic scripts right to their depths (*Klong Tu Kyur*), then because of a lack of smoothness the composition will not be

> clear and the meaning will have been mixed up, and it won't be easy to understand. It will be like some of the Termas of Long sal nying po.[224] Transcribing after the achievement of the full perfection of understanding of the symbolic scripts will ensure glorious words and clear composition without any complex or obscured meaning. It will be like *The Seven Chaptered Prayer* (*gSol a'Debs Leu bDun Ma*) discovered by Rig dzin God dem [1337–1408].

He has also said,

> The appearances (*a'Ch'ar Ch'a*) when reading the symbolic scripts while having fully perfected understanding and not having it are different. They are comparable to the effects of meditative experience and the realization itself. So, between these two stages there is the big difference of being a changing or an unchanging nature, like fog and space.

With this in mind the Lord Lo drö Tha ye[225] has said,

> The concealed Termas are like the face, the Tertons are like the mirror, and the words and the meanings of the teachings are like the reflections. Although the face is the same, because of the difference between mirrors there will be clear and unclear and perfect and imperfect reflections.

Of those the first vision (*sNang Ch'a*) of the symbolic script is not real, whereas the later readings are reliable. Because, for example, smoke from two pieces of wood being rubbed together is a presage of fire, not similar to the smoke of an ant-hill. It has the aspect of fire, giving the feeling of heat but less than the power of red flame. Likewise, because of the power of the yellow scrolls, those visions or readings arise as a sign of the shaking forth (*gYo*

Ba) of the recollection of the teachings from the depths. But most of those visions are a special teaching because they have risen due to the power of the Mind-mandate Transmission. Hence, they are much more extraordinary than ordinary teachings, such as those that arise through psychic visions or experiences[226] and are discovered through the powers of gods and demons.[227] The difference is like the difference between the sky and the earth. At that time the recollection of the Mind-mandate Transmission has been awakened in the Terton's mind, but not fully, and when he has attained certainty of the symbolic scripts, then his recollection is fully awakened. Thereafter he will discover nakedly the complete words and the meanings of the Termas as he had received them in ancient times.

Responsibility of the Tertons for the Miraculous Symbolic Scripts

The distinction of whether the symbolic script is a miraculous script or not does not depend on the script alone but on the subject and the degree of awakening of the recollection (*Bag Ch'ag*) of the discoverers. So, sometimes when the same yellow scroll is discovered and rediscovered by two different Tertons, even if it is a miraculous script for the first one, for the second one it might not be.

Who Reads or Transcribes[228] the Symbolic Scripts?

If the Terma script is in Tibetan and is a Complete Text, then a person other than the Terton can transcribe it also. Furthermore, even if it is in ḍākinī script and is a Complete Text and if there is an alphabet with it, then again others can transcribe it. But if it is a Just Visible text or Just an Indication, then no one but the Terton can transcribe it. Also, in general, the Terton who inherits a particular text is the only one who is able to decode the symbolic script. However, if among the people who have received the entrustment from Guru Padmasambhava together with the

Terton [in their past lives], there is one who is a Terton in this present life who has obtained the blessings and permission[229] of the Terton of that particular Terma, then he or she also can decode the symbolic script.

What Kind of Mind-mandate Transmission is Necessary?

In every case it is necessary to have received the Mind-mandate Transmission of the particular teaching; it is not sufficient to have had a Mind-mandate Transmission of just any kind of teaching. For example, as mentioned in *The Confidential Prophecy* [of *La Ma Gong Dü*][230] the Lama gong dü teachings were transmitted to Prince Mu rum Tsen po,[231] but along with him many other disciples, the King and subjects, also received the teachings and the transmission of Lama gong dü. Among those who received the Mind-mandate Transmission were Ba yo Ch'o kyi Lo drö,[232] a reincarnation of Vairocana, but not a Terton in that lifetime and thus not able to decode the symbolic scripts. But Long po Chang chub Ling pa,[233] a reincarnation of Nam kha'i Nying po,[234] did decode the symbolic scripts. As I have said many times before, the heart of the Terma tradition is the Mind-mandate Transmission, the transferring or transmitting of the primordial wisdom from Guru Rinpoche to the disciple.

There are many Termas that can be discovered by one Terton and there are some that can be discovered by many at the same time because of various kinds of aspirations made by Guru Rinpoche at the time of the Mind-mandate Transmission. On one occasion, a Terma discovered by an incarnation of Dud jom[235] was rediscovered by an incarnation of the Lord [King *Khri Srong lDeu bTsan*] because both Dor je Dud jom and the King had received the entrustment equally. One of the reasons that the Omniscient Guru Vajradhara[236] had the authority to discover and teach the Termas of the numerous Tertons of the three times is clearly that the Dharma King Thri srong Deu tsen was present as the chief at all the Mind-mandate Transmissions of the Concealed Dharma Treasures of Guru Rinpoche.

Tertons are similar in being disciples of Guru Rinpoche, but there are differences among them—some, for example, have received the transmission of only one teaching and others of many. Some Tertons have received the transmission of many teachings, but later on because of various circumstances such as the land, friends, teachers or time, the awakening of all the transmissions in a single lifetime is not assured. Even if the Mind-mandate Transmission has been awakened, it is uncertain whether or not they will teach and spread those teachings. Because there are differences among the Discoverers that make them either Great or Minor Tertons.

Further, even in the case of some Tertons who belong to the same succession of incarnations, in some lives they discover many teachings and in others only a few. That is why, for example, it was not necessary for Ter dag Ling pa (1646–1714) to discover all the teachings that were transmitted to Vairocana. For Ter dag Ling pa is not the only incarnation of Vairocana; and Ter dag Ling pa is just one of the Tertons, while in Vairocana's incarnation lineage there are many.

The Omniscient Master Mañjuśrīghoṣa[237] was a Terton who could recite fluently without any hindrance any kind of teachings of Guru Padmasambhava discovered by himself or others when he concentrated on them. But this is a special power of his alone that he had obtained because of the power of the particular aspirations that he made during his thirteen successive lifetimes as a Terton.

Generally, Tertons can recite the discovered texts until they are formally transcribed, and then, after the completion of the transcription their memory of the particular text disappears. If the transcribed text is lost, for example in a fire, when only the first half has been transcribed, then the Terton will be able to recollect the text from the beginning and will be able to rewrite it. But if formal transcribing of the text has been finished, then even the Discoverer cannot recite the text without relying on a written copy. It is not like having memorized a text. If it were, then one should become more familiar with the text the more one writes and discusses it. But here the Mind-mandate Transmission of the teachings made through the miraculous power of Guru Rinpoche has as its purpose to conceal the teachings in the heart of the future Terton.

It is like consecrating (*Phab Pa*) and stabilizing (*brTan Par Byas*) the wisdom deity[238] (*Ye Shes Pa*) in the essence (*Thig Le*) of the heart of a disciple. So it is different from memorization.

Therefore, because of the aspirations made in the past by Guru Rinpoche—'May these teachings clearly be discovered at the appropriate time'; and because the discovery of the treasure [or symbolic] script awakens the primordial wisdom of vajra-speech that dwells at the heart [of the Discoverer], the complete words and meaning arise then just as they were originally transmitted, as, for example, when someone possessed by a deity will start shaking. When the transcribing of the Terma is finished, the purpose of concealment of the teachings is completed and the teachings will dissolve into the inner sphere of indestructible *nada* [great emptiness] and become invisible, as, for example, when a deity is consecrated or stabilized in a person he will stop shaking; but it is not like lees of chang [barley beer] with its strength completely diluted.

12 SECONDARY SYMBOLIC SCRIPTS

The secondary symbolic scripts are not the symbolic scripts that were used as a code when the Mind-mandate Transmission was given, but are scripts that appear suddenly because of the blessings of the knowledge-holders, ḍākas and ḍākinīs, as a support for awakening and understanding the Terma teachings contained in the main symbolic scripts. There are two types: the first is a version similar to a mirror divination,[239] which will be seen only by the Terton. The second is appearances that can be seen by the Discoverer of the teachings and also by others and that will be helpful in decoding the main symbolic scripts. In both types there will be countless kinds of indications, such as forms of beings or non-beings, sounds of beings or non-beings, sounds that convey meaning or no meaning, food or drink, and other daily necessities.

5 *Discovery and Reconcealment of Termas*

13 MANNER OF DISCOVERING THE TERMAS

Preparations for the Discovery

In some cases the Terton receives the prophetic guide (*Kha Byang*) before discovering the Termas, but in other cases does not.

If there is a prophetic guide, then it will explain how one should discover the teachings, whether it is necessary to do an 'effectuation of the discovery of the teachings' and, if it is necessary, how it should be done; where the place of the concealment of the Dharma teachings is; whether there is any particular time for the discovery to be made; with what kind of support [consort] and retinue of companions he has a common aspiration; whether the discovery of the teachings should be carried out secretly or in public; what the proper kinds of offerings are, what kind of reminder of the vows of the past and what command should be given to the Terma protectors; how the Terton should be protected from the ill-effects (*rDzi Dug*) of the Terma protectors; how he should recognize the signs of the teachings and the door of the concealed Termas; at what depth the Terma casket will be found from the mouth or door of the concealment place; whether or not the teachings are the inheritance of the Discoverer himself, what kind of substitute or replacement for Ter[240] it is necessary to put in; how he should reclose the concealment door; when the casket of the Terma will be opened, and so on.

If there is no prophetic guide, the Tertons should act carefully by their clear vision free from delusion as the authentic evidence, and not interpose even the slightest pretentiousness, gross conduct, nonsense, craziness, or loose character. The course of action of the Tertons is established by the order of the Blissful Guru [Padmasambhava], so every aspect of their actions has great power and virtue. But if they transgress even a single command, there will be equally grave consequences.[241] Hence the saying: 'The precious Earth Termas have the power to fulfill wishes.'

Location of Terma

Some Terma caskets will not be able to be discovered except from the actual concealment place. But sometimes if the Discoverers live in a distant place, the treasure-protector may bring the casket to them. These variations occur according to the commands of Guru Rinpoche to the treasure-keepers at the time of entrustment.

There are teachings that were entrusted to the protectors by Guru Rinpoche; he said, 'Do not hand over this Terma until the Terton comes to the concealment place.' The purpose of this is that if both the concealment and discovery of the Terma occurred at the same place, then because of the auspicious causations, the tradition of study and practice of tantric teachings will develop in that area and it will be more effective for human and non-human beings living there. Or else, since the concealment place has become a very powerful sacred place, if in addition the teachings are discovered there, then it will help the followers of this teaching not to have many obstructions. Or, since it is the source of generating and developing wishes, it will help both the followers and their accomplishments to prosper. Or if the Discoverers have travelled to the concealment place amid hardships, it helps in fulfilling their obligations, making the ḍākas and ḍākinīs satisfied so that the teaching will become more auspicious and will have great power of blessing (*Byin rLabs*), and the activities will develop and become perfect, and so on.

There are Termas that will be brought to the Discoverer wherever he or she lives. Or if there is no particular reason for the Discoverer to go to the concealment place, and if in the past before receiving the Transmission, he or she experienced hardship for the sake of the teachings and has made excellent aspirations to be able to perform beneficial actions for beings without any delay in the appropriate time, then for him or her all the power of the causes is perfected. So there is no doubt of the discovery of the teachings in his or her present lifetime. But the power of favorable conditions is required. So for this purpose, on his behalf, Guru Rinpoche should have given the command in ancient times to the Terma-keepers saying, 'Hand over this Dharma Treasure to this fortunate person wherever he lives at that time.' But even if Guru Rinpoche hasn't given such a command in the past, if all the necessary circumstances for discovering the teaching have been completed except to bring the Discoverer to the place of concealment, then Guru Rinpoche will give the instruction instantly[242] (*Phral Nyid Du*) to the Terma protector to hand over the teaching to the Discoverer, and it shall be done. This is a partial outline, but it is impossible to explain this aspect in detail.

Private and Public Discovery of the Teachings

Some Tertons withdraw their teachings in private and some in public. Sometimes when a teaching is discovered there will appear wondrous signs such as various sounds, rays of light, and a rain of flowers, while in some cases there won't be any signs. If the Terma should be discovered in public, any or all of the following conditions are fulfilled. If the Discoverers and their followers have arranged an elaborate feast offering[243] (*Tshogs*) etc. to please the ḍākinīs, then there will not be any obstruction to the discovery of the teachings in public. If the teaching is withdrawn in public it will be more effective in pacifying disease, hunger, and war in the country; or the evil effects of transgressors and harmful spirits will be eliminated. It will help many people to develop confidence in the Terma teachings and will increase the devotion of recollecting Guru Rinpoche, as the saying has it:

> In each big valley there is a great Terton,
> In each small valley there is a minor Terton.
> They are for the remembrance of Oḍḍiyāna
> [Guru Rinpoche].

Or if the discovery of the teachings in public has a special purpose, such as its having an auspicious lineage because of the auspicious causation of an excellent beginning, then the Terma should be discovered in public. If by discovering the teaching in private any important purpose is served, such as its making easier the decoding of the symbolic script or the opening of the casket of the teaching, and if the teaching will become more auspiciously beneficial; or if the discovery in public will cause extreme danger or a reversed effect and a rough situation; or if the arrangements such as meeting with the particular consort and so on are not completed, then the teachings should be discovered in private.

Various spontaneous signs and miracles will happen if they are beneficial for beings, but they will not happen during the period of secrecy of the teachings. In any case, it is impossible for Tertons not to have inner experiences such as excitement, delight and bliss at the time of discovery of the Terma.

As external signs there will be indications that virtuous gods and nāgas[244] are happy and that the teachings will be beneficial for others. Also it seems that various miracles will happen because of the different natures of Terma keepers. But I think that there is no unvarying display common to all such instances.

Destruction of the Yellow Scrolls

It is also possible to destroy the yellow scrolls after their discovery and before transcription. But actually entrustment made by Guru Rinpoche certainly endures until the attainment of enlightenment by the Terton. Also there may be many copies of the text in the realms of ḍākinīs, so it is not impossible to obtain the teachings again. Even if there is no other copy but the discovered one, and if at some point it has been destroyed, then it will certainly be rediscovered by another means as a result of the inexhaustible power of the Mind-mandate Transmission.

There are various means for their discovery. The ḍākas and ḍākinīs who have achieved the attainment of recollection[245] (*gZungs*) may rewrite the text and put it in place of the previous one. Or as foretold, the yellow scroll may appear spontaneously in the concealment place. Otherwise this teaching may also be discovered as a mind-treasure. But this kind of mind-treasure seems not to be a general mind-treasure, because it is discovered on account of the entrustment.

Generally, Guru Rinpoche has given the strict command that the script of the Terma should be reconcealed after its discovery and transcription if there is only one original, or even if there are more copies, but only one in a country like Tibet. Thus the teaching that is concealed twice is called Sub-concealed Ter (*a'Dab gTer*) and Reconcealed Ter (*Yang gTer*).

14 RECONCEALMENT OF THE TERMAS

General Way of Reconcealment

In the case of both general and specific reconcealment of the Termas the place of concealment should be either earth or water. For earth there are many places such as mountains, rocks, trees, temples and so on. For water in many texts it is said: 'permanently staying (*gTan 'Khyil*) turquoise lake.' So there is only a lake [ocean], but I think there may be distinctions between general and specific cases. Whoever reconceals the teaching, the Tertons themselves have to go to the place in order to reconceal it. Some Discoverers go to the reconcealment place miraculously through their own power or the power of the protectors, and others go there in the ordinary manner. If it is a question of reconcealment in a rock, first they dig a little hole in the rock and put the yellow scroll in it and cover the hole slightly. The next day there will be no sign of the mouth of the hole because the protectors take the teaching to the proper concealment place [or to the place of the protector himself].

Special Way of Reconcealment

a. *Handing Over the Yellow Scroll to the Terma Protector in Person*

It is easy to understand the giving back of the teaching into the hands of the protectors by the Discoverer, like a person entrusting property to someone's care. But if the Discoverers want to have the original yellow scroll for themselves so that they can give it to a fortunate person as an accomplishment-substance, then, as it is said: 'They [ḍākinīs or the Terma protectors] are the wisdom deities, but they appeared as the messengers of activity [of the doctrine and the masters]': the Terton can request the ḍākinīs or protectors to make a copy of the yellow scroll. The copying will be finished in the blink of an eye. Then if the Discoverers give the copy to the protector and ask for the original yellow scroll, they will get it back. This kind of arrangement can only be made by great Tertons who have friendship with the ḍākinīs and vow-holders as person to person and have the power of bidding them to perform their activities, but not by other ordinary Discoverers.

b. *Teleportational Reconcealment*[246] *(Thod rGal) through the Medium of any of the Four Elements*

For example, if the Terton is in Lhasa and he reconceals the teaching in Tsho ngon (*mTsho sNgon:* Kokonor, the Blue Lake) in the north, by meditative concentration of his mind (*dGongs Pa gTad*) on the concealment of the Treasure, first he digs a symbolic small hole in the earth in Lhasa and puts the text in it. In the very next moment the teaching will reach Tsho ngon lake. This is the system of reconcealing in water through the medium of the earth. In the same manner, the teachings are reconcealed in rocks at a far distance through rocks, and in temples through rocks, and in water, snow mountains, and rocks through water, and so on. By putting Terma script in fire in Druk (*a'Brug:* Bhutan) of the Mon countries it immediately reaches the reconcealment place in Kham (*Khams;* Eastern Tibet). By throwing the Terma script to the wind, it floats into the sky accompanied by sounds and will disappear and reach the reconcealment place immediately. It is a great wonder. Also there were incidents in which a Terton put the Terma script in a casket and kept it in a certain place and made a fire near the casket. Then he placed his meditative concentration on the reconcealment of the Terma script for a while. Smoke from the burning of the script appeared from the casket; and when the casket was opened, no trace was found of the script.

It is not necessary to put the script into the fire when one reconceals it by means of fire. This reconcealing performance will not be accomplished if it is seen by any person except his or her consort and the doctrine-holder (*Ch'os bDag*) who are prophesied. There are instances in which the script disappeared when the Discoverer died and left it behind. This signifies that the Terma script has been taken back by the Terma protectors. That is also a reconcealing of the Terma. I am recounting some aspects of the system of reconcealment of the Terma scripts.

c. *Reconcealment Place*

The place of reconcealment does not necessarily have to be the same place as the one in which it was originally concealed; but one cannot change the Terma Protector of the teaching.

I

2

1 *A ku tshab (sKu Tshabs, representative) of Guru Padmasambhava discovered by Nyang Nyima Odzer (1124–1192) and passed down through the generations of his family. Symbolic scripts are visible on this image. Ku tshabs are the most important and rare Terma images of Guru Padmasambhava, blessed as his own representatives by the Guru himself. Generally, there are hundreds of Terma images of him, but according to many Nyingma scriptures there are only twenty-five ku tshab images.* **2** *A ku tshab of Guru Padmasambhava, discovered by Sang gye Ling pa (1340–1396).* **3** *A ku tshab known as Guru Srin thod ma (the Image of the Master with (base of) skulll of Rākṣasa). According to Min ling Thri ch'en Rinpoche (1931–) this image was discovered either by Ratna Ling pa (1403–1478) or Padma Ling pa (1450–1521).* **4** *A ku tshab of Guru Padmasambhava. It is not known who discovered this image. It was given by Jig med Ling pa (1729–1798) to one of his chief patrons, E Lha gya thri.* **5** *Some of the Termas discovered by Ch'og gyur Ling pa (1829–1870) are arranged in the design of a flowering tree and framed in a silver and gold box with a glass window. The image at the center is a ku tshab known as Ngo drub Pal bar (blossoming*

3

Avolokiteśvara entitled De sheg Kun du (The Assemblage of All the Bliss-gone Ones) (see MEV page 84a/6). The following lines relate how Guru Padmasambhava made and consecrated this image, given in the text CTI, page 3a/5:

Having been absorbed in contemplation,
[Guru Padmasambhava] commanded the Dākinīs through the force of view and the gesture of control.
Thereupon they offered him gems of the gods and nāga realms,
Jambu-gold and sand from Manasarowar lake.
From the eight charnel grounds and the twenty-four sacred places,
Fragrant wood, essence of medicine,

attainments) and was discovered from Tsi ke Nor bu Pun sum (see SVDG page 181a/1). To the image's right is a casket from which the yellow scrolls of the texts on Ma mo Ngon dzog were discovered. To its left are some discovered relics such as hair and pieces of clothing of Guru Padmasambhava and many of his chief disciples. At the lower front of the image is the yellow scroll of a text entitled Thug drub Yid zhin Nor bu (see SVDG page 181a/6), which has six syllables written by the hand of Guru Padmasambhava. **6** *A ku tshab known as Ku tshab Thong trol ma (the representative that liberates by seeing) was discovered by Ter dag Ling pa (1646–1714) from Sha ug Tag go in 1680 with the yellow scrolls of the texts on*

4

Nectar water and ambrosia of accomplishments.
With these materials and chemical water
[The Guru] made the clay and (then the image) with his own hand,
The size of his thumb (mTshon Gang).
Inside, he put the relics (Ring bSrel) of the seven Tathagatas,
Of Prahevajra, Mañjuśrī, Śrisinha,
Vimalamitra etc., the adepts,
Hair, pieces of clothing, bodily remains and substances of accomplishment.
And the Guru's nasal red, hair and essence;

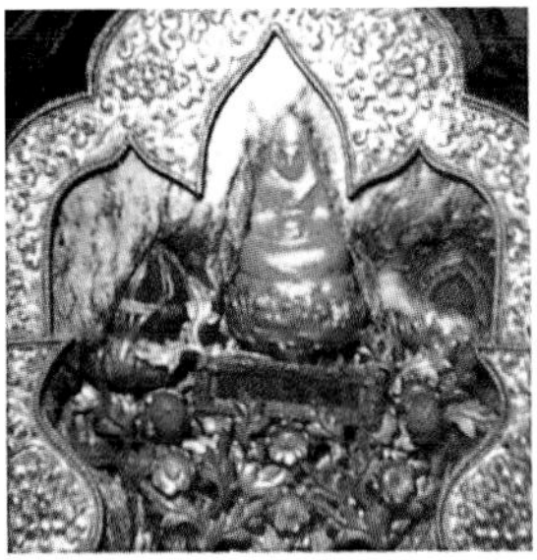

5

6

7

And ambrosia, medicine and seed and heart syllables, and so on,
As the enclosures (gZungs).
He painted it with natural vermillion
And protective color and performed the consecrations. At that time,
Numerous knowledge-holders, ḍākas and ḍākinīs
Gathered like the clouds in the sky and blessed it.
The actual body of the Guru melted into a body of light and
Dissolved for a while into the heart of the image.
Again he emerged separately and blessed it.
Originally this image was red in color but later it was painted with gold; in Tibet most of the precious images

8

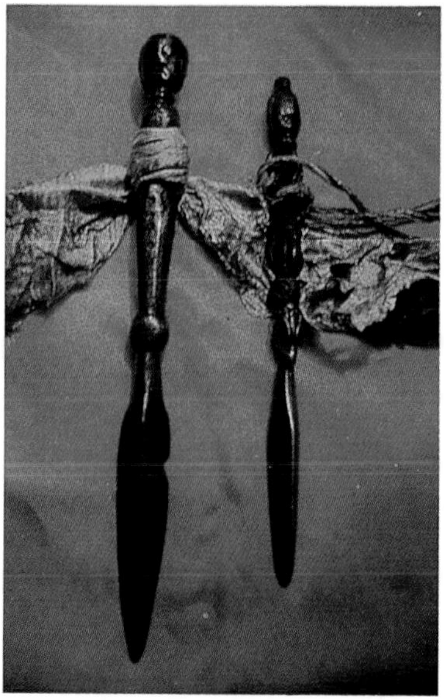

10
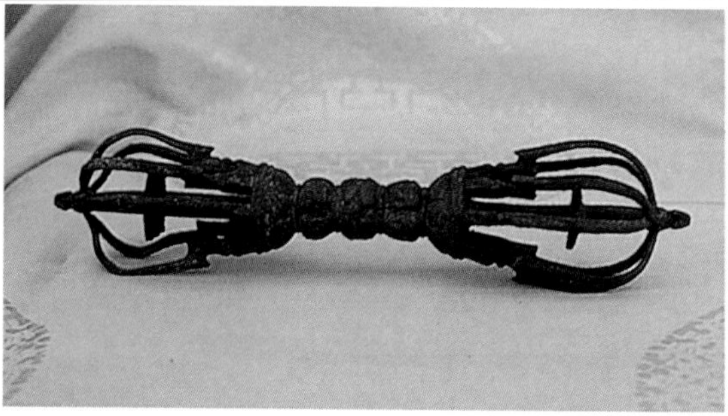

11

have been painted with gold as an act of service and respect.

7 A bronze (Li Ma) image of Guru Padmasambhava known as Padma Od bar (the radiant lotus) was discovered by Ter dag Ling pa (1646–1714) with the yellow scrolls of the texts on Yamantaka entitled Shin je shed Treg jom from Yar lung Shel trag (see MEV page 65b/5).

8 Two phur pa (sacred daggers). The longer one was discovered by Nyang Nyi ma Od zer (1124–1192); the discoverer of the shorter phur pa is unknown.

9 Two phur pa. The longer one was discovered by Tsa sum Ling pa (17th century); the discoverer of the shorter phur pa is unknown.

10 Nam chag Dor je (a sceptre made of thunderbolt metal) which was discovered *by Gyal se De ch'en Ling pa (19th century) in a cave in Padma Kod.* **11** *Ah tham Pum pa (vase sealed with* AH *letter). A vase with hand prints of Guru Padmasambhava discovered by Gyal se De ch'en Ling pa (19th century), from Sam ye Ch'im phu.* **12** *A piece of a Shog ser (yellow scroll) in Sanskrit and Wartu script. It was discovered by Tag*

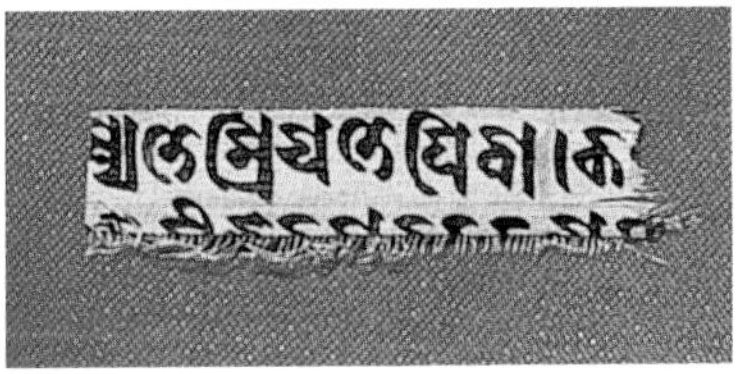

12

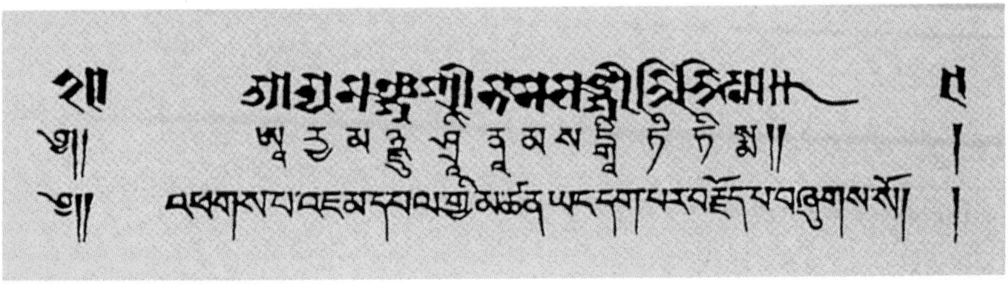

13

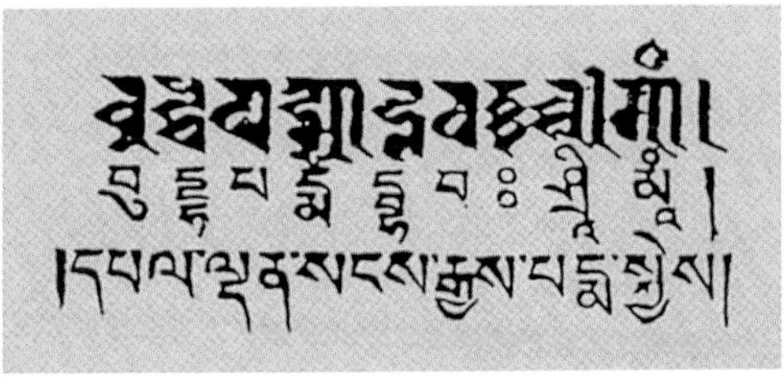

14

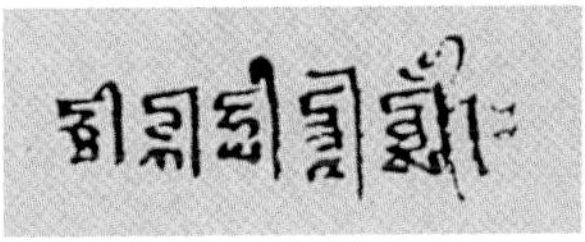

15

16

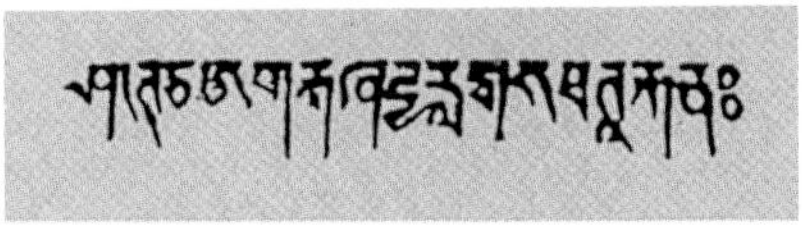

17

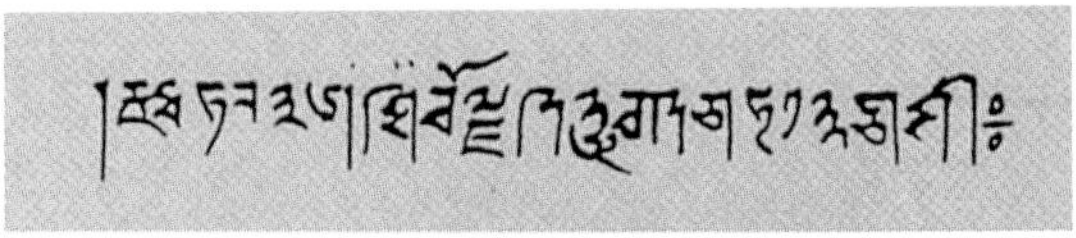

18

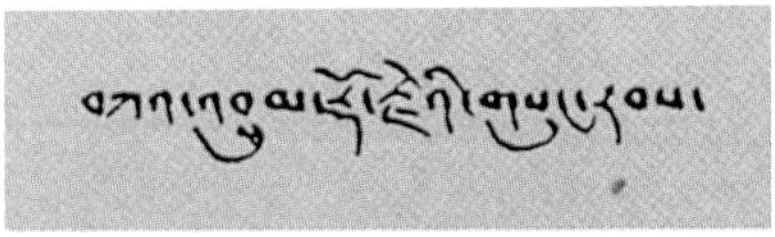

19

20

21

sham Nu den Dor Je (17th-18th century). ***13*** *The first line is in Sanskrit and in the Wartu script. The second line is a transliteration of the first line in the Tibetan Dzab (rDzab or dBu Chan) script.* ***14*** *The first line is in Sanskrit and in the Lañca script. The second line is a transliteration of the first line in the Tibetan Dzab script.* ***15*** *A copy of a*

22

symbolic script of a one-page prayer discovered as a Mind Ter by Tulku Kun zang Nyi ma (d.1858?). This symbolic script is calligraphed by the Terton himself. **16** A piece of one of the thirteen yellow scrolls which contained the series of texts on Avalokiteśvara entitled De sheg Kun du. It was discovered by Ter dag Ling pa (1646–1714), along with the image of the illustration number 6, from Sha ug Tag go in 1680. This yellow scroll is in Tibetan and in Shur (gShur or dBu Med) script and is in the form (a'God Tshul) of "complete text" (mThar Ch'ags). It is a disintegrated scroll containing page 2b, line 4–page 3a, line 5 of text SEE. One of the main receivers of this teaching from Ter dag Ling pa was the Fifth Dalai Lama (1617–1682). **17** A xylographed copy of the symbolic scripts of a five-folio text entitled Ned chang Thig kyi Drom bu from the Long ch'en Nying thig collection discovered by Jig med Ling pa (1729-1798). This was discovered as a

23

4

symbolic script of a Mind Ter. For a Mind Ter the symbolic script appears in the mind of the discoverer and awakens the concealed teachings from the enlightened nature of the discoverer's mind.
18 Ḍākinī symbolic script. It is the title of a text on Yamantaka, discovered by Ter dag Ling pa in 1667. NMP provides the translation of this phrase in Tibetan as "a'Phags Pa a'Jam dPal Nyid Khro Bo'i sKur bZhengs Pa gShin rJe'i gShed Kyi sGrub Thabs Kyi rTsa Ba'i gZhungs Lags So." (It is the root sādhana of Yamāntaka, the manifestation of noble Mañjuśrī himself in wrathful form.)
19 A line in the Tibetan Shur script.
20 Mt Drong ri (a'Brong Ri) is a sacred mountain in Golok, Tibet, dedicated to Mahākāla. From various places on this mountain many Ters were discovered for centuries by different Tertons. **21** Ter go (gTer sGo, a Ter discovering door). This square mark on the rock is the spot from where A pang Terton (d.1945) discovered a Ter from Trag Ser nya at the

Illustration number 1 was photographed by Ani Nga wang Cho dron. Number 2 is from the collection of Tulku U gyen Top gyal and the photograph was obtained through Ge long Kon ch'og Ten dzin. Numbers 3, 6, 7 and 16 are from the collection of Min trol ling monastery in Tibet and are now preserved in the collection of Kyab je Min ling Thri ch'en Rinpoche and obtained through Khen po Gyal se Tul ku. Number 4 is from the personal locket (mGul Gab) of Thrul zhig Rinpoche. Numbers 4 and 5 were obtained through Kyab je Dil go Khyen tse Rinpoche. Number 12 is from the collection of Kyab je Dil go Khyen tse Rinpoche and obtained through Ge long Kon ch'og Ten dzin. The longer phur pa of number 8 is from the collection of Kyab je Dodrup Chen Rinpoche. Number 9 is from the collections of Khenpo Pal den She rab and Khenpo Tshe wang Don gyal. Numbers 9 and 10 were photographed by Golok Od bar. Photographs of thangkas by John Cochran.

25

foot of Mt Drong ri. After discoveries of Ters from rocks the doors are usually sealed miraculously and only the marks of the door will remain visible. **22** *Ter ne (gTer gNas, a Ter discovering place). From this cliff called Trag Ser nya at the foot of Mt Drong ri, many Ters were discovered including the famous text Ngo drub Jung ba (ter) on Mahākāla which was discovered by Ch'u pho Tog den (12th century).* **23** *Kun khyen Long ch'en Rab jam.* **24** *Rig dzin Jig med Ling pa.* **25** *Jig med Thrin le Od zer, the First Dodrup Chen.* **26** *Jig med Ten pa'i Nyi ma, the Third Dodrup Chen.*

26

6 *Purpose and Greatness of Concealment*

15 THE PURPOSE AND GREATNESS OF CONCEALMENT OF TERMA SCRIPTS

In a prophetic Terma text discovered by Ratna Ling pa [Guru Rinpoche] said:

> The utmost profound and ultimate essence:
> Since Tibetans generally desire new things
> And because of strong compassion for the
>   people of the dark age
> I have filled the center and outskirts of Tibet with
>   such Dharma Treasures.
> And I made the aspiration that they may meet
>   with the fortunate sons.

In a prophetic introduction (*Kha Byang*) of Dor sem [Vajrasattva] discovered from O kar trag[247] [page lb] it is said:

> The master Padmasambhava
> In the land of the red-faced ones [Tibet]
> Lit the lamp of the esoteric and exoteric Dharma,
> Dispelled the darkness of defiled emotions.
> Since the people of the future will be loose-
>   disciplined,

They will practice the teachings with selfish view and in a narrow-minded manner. At that time
The effect of the general teachings and practices will have disappeared.
Even if they do practice it will be fruitless and tiring. Therefore
The Omniscient One [Guru Rinpoche] with his wisdom for helping living beings
All the profound teachings
Sealed with his command and concealed as the Termas.
When the various signs [for discovering] and the disciples have appeared
Those concealed teachings will appear gradually and will benefit people. For this purpose
He made the aspirations and entrustments.

In ancient times Tibet wasn't broken up into different petty states. The previous generations of Tibetans relied on the Bodhisattva Dharma King Thri srong Deu tsen and his preceptors [Guru Rinpoche and others], and they were obedient to their orders. So it was like a single nail controlling hundreds of parts of a structure. At such a time, the assembly of knowledge-holders—the Dharma Lord Guru Rinpoche, the King and the subjects—with their kindness on behalf of the future people of Tibet, agreed with one mind and concealed the teachings as Termas. This is a principal reason why the Terma teachings are more powerful in protecting the people of Tibet.

Lord Avalokiteśvara is the assigned deity for Tibetans. So, his manifesting as the knowledge-holder master [Guru Rinpoche] and making aspirations to serve the doctrine by means of the Terma tradition have great significance.

The scripts are the contemplative vajra-speech, the visible blessing and accomplishment of Padmasambhava, the possessor of the ten powers,[248] for the general and particular lands of Tibet. The Dharma teachings are not transmitted through the hands of improper people, none of whom have seen or heard those Terma teachings. Those teachings remained only in the hands of ḍākas and yoginīs, who are accomplished tantriks.

The Terma teachings are revealed because of the power of aspirations made by the assembly of Guru Rinpoche, the King, and the subjects for the benefit of the people of the dark age and because of the power of the blessings of ḍākas and ḍākinīs. That is the very reason why just by the recovery of the Termas various results occur. The power of evil human and non-human beings declines and the radiance of virtuous beings increases, and the degenerations of the dark age—disease, hunger, war and so on—are pacified. Discovery of the teachings protects the temples and monasteries of Lhasa, Sam ye, and Tha dul and Yang dul from the dangers of war, earthquake, fire, enemies and so on. They help to extend the duration of life of the canonical transmission of Guru Rinpoche and to dispel the obstructions to the lives and the activities of the masters of the doctrine.

Furthermore, in the ancient time, the Terton has received the Mind-mandate Transmission for entering the maṇḍala of indestructible essence[249] of the self-accomplished Padmasambhava into his or her mind in the form of the words and meanings of the teachings. Thereafter, during many successive lives, Mind-mandate Transmission of the teaching that has been made by the yogic method of the triple vajra[250] of the wishing gem, Guru Rinpoche, increases. Not only has the secrecy of the teachings never been broken to the improper people, but they have also never even been moved from the casket of vast expanse, the inconceivable luminosity (the true nature of the mind of the Terton), because of the power of infallible aspirations made by Guru Rinpoche and his disciples, saying:

> May the Ter teachings benefit the trainable beings of tantra, who remain in the end-age, as they did in the early (ages),

and because they [the Ters] need to be awakened by the power of the primordial wisdom of Dzogpa Chenpo, which transcends mental concepts. These Dharma Treasure scriptures are the teachings possessing the warm breath of Guru Rinpoche. So there are no adulterations and errors in them and they are praised for being powerful, having fewer obstructions to their practice, being of accomplishment easy to attain, and being of swift fruition.

Effects of Different Periods[251] of the Termas

Vajradhara Guru [Khyen tse'i Wang po] said:

> During the lifetimes of the Terton and the principal doctrine-holder, and so on, the result of the practice of such Terma teachings is apparent—this time is called 'the fruition period' (*a'Bras Bu'i Dus*) of the particular teaching. When there are many who just practice the teachings in a perfect manner, it is called 'the practice period' (*sGrub Pa'i Dus*). When there is only the proper way of transmitting the empowerments, recitation, and instructions of the teaching, it is called 'the scripture period' (*Lung Gi Dus*). Then even the declining of the transmission tradition [and the remaining of only a sign of the teaching] is 'the merely symbolic period.'

In the biography of the early Dharma Treasure[252] Discoverer and of the Later Dharma Treasure[253] Discoverer and in the discovered teachings of *Chang ter* and *Kha dro nying thig*, similar explanations are clearly given.

But even a particular fruition period is subject to the effects of other common periods and conditions. So, it is not accurate to define their effects in a generalized way.

Even in the teachings of Guru Rinpoche, there are two systems of the transmission, each being of four periods. The first is the four phases of the period of establishment of the tantric doctrine for the first time in Tibet by Guru

Rinpoche. The second system is the four periods according to the discovery of different concealed Dharma teachings at different times.

When earlier Termas were discovered, the time was also close to the fruition period of the first system, the establishment of the tantric tradition in Tibet. So for the followers it was easier to achieve tantric results in general; and especially since the time was the fruition period of the particular teaching, it was very effective.

The Termas that are being discovered today are very far away in time from [the fruition period of] the first system, so they have only the effect of their own fruition period. Thus they won't be as effective as were the teachings of the earlier Termas at the time of their discovery.

The Need and Benefit of New Discovered Termas

The tantric teachings of the canonical teachings and of the earlier Termas that were transmitted came to us through the long lineage of teachers. The power of those teachings may have declined by their falling into the hands of improper people and transgressors. The teachings may have been adulterated by individually imposed and unauthorized writings; and also in the long transmissions there tend to be obstructions. In that long period of transmission there may have been some among the lineage-holders who did not practice much and did not attain any accomplishment [so the power of the transmission becomes decayed]. There are many cases in which the followers of such teachings are not even certain about their own transmission lineage. Under such circumstances it is difficult to achieve any accomplishment. Therefore if one practices a newly transmitted Terma, it will be easier to accomplish results.

Thus, if we think about the ceaseless activities involved in the appearing of tantric teachings, we can understand that there is no one who is more gracious to the tantric disciples of this utmost end-age than Guru Rinpoche, the King and his subjects.

In this light, one can understand the reason for the appearance of Tertons in great numbers, in different phases like the seasons of the crops, and ceaselessly until the end-age.

Therefore Rig dzin Jig med Ling pa said in his *Explanation of the Empowerment of Trol thig*[254] [page 24a]:

> In the concealing of the Termas there are four great purposes: to prevent the doctrine from disappearing, the teaching from being adulterated, and the power of blessing from disappearing and to shorten the lineage of transmission.

To Pacify the Obstructions

Furthermore, Guru Rinpoche knew that from time to time numerous fears of various kinds, such as factional fighting, disease, political disorders, and the destruction of Dharma by powerful kings and ministers would occur. And for the purpose of pacifying them he blessed accomplished Tertons to appear suddenly at different times, who would discover various teachings of practices on appropriate deities, mantras and actions at the proper moment, just as different medicine is given for different sicknesses. To save many defenceless beings is one of the most important aims of the Terma teachings. That is why some of my Lamas say that it is important for there to be many sādhanas on actions (*Las Tshogs*) to be practiced in the Termas.

Concluding Summary

It is easy to recognize that there are two major elements in decoding the symbolic scripts: teaching and propagation.

Other Benefits

If the Tertons discover the teachings, then there are the

benefits mentioned before. But even if they could not discover the teachings because favorable circumstances are absent or because contrary circumstances occur, if they have made strong efforts to obtain the teachings, and if they made prayers and offerings, and performed Feast-offerings (*Tshogs 'Khor*) and Fulfilling Offerings[255] and Confession[256] and Purification (*sKong bShags*) practices, these actions will fulfill the wishes of Guru Rinpoche, and will satisfy the ḍākinīs and treasure protectors. They will repair the obligations for discovering the teaching. For this reason, as in the previous case [discovering the teachings] there will be the result of auspiciousness in the world and the subduing of evil forces. Therefore, one should not assume that if the Tertons could not discover the teachings, making efforts for its discovery was useless.

Material Objects of Religious Concern

Regarding the discovered images [representatives] (*sKu Tshab*) of Guru Rinpoche, it is said in the *Thang yig:*

> For the people who did not meet me
> The images will be the lamp for [dispelling] their darkness.

There are images built by Guru Rinpoche himself by means of his miraculous power. Even many by others have been blessed by Guru Rinpoche as inseparable from himself by merging his wisdom power into the images. So if one sees the image it will be the same as seeing Guru Rinpoche himself; if one makes offerings, pays homage and makes aspirations before the image, that will be as effective as performing these actions in front of Guru Rinpoche. The reason for the gradual discovery of the images in different periods of time (*brGyud Ma*) is the demonstration that Guru Rinpoche watches over Tibet with his kindness, forever, without ceasing; in addition it inspires his future followers to practice Dharma.

That is not the only reason. If some of the images remain in [important seats such as] the palaces of kings or meditation places, that will become the source by which the essence of the doctrine shall remain instead of disappearing. If they remain at geographically important places, it will repair the decay of the energy or spirit of the area and will prevent wars and cut off the path[257] that is frequented by harmful spirits. The images that are discovered with the Terma teachings will help to ensure that the symbolic scripts are decoded without any difficulties, and they will increase the beneficial effects of the teaching: that is, if the Discoverer has performed the preparatory practice of Terma [the effectuation of the Ter: *gTer sGrub*] using the image as an object for the practice. So the images will help to perfect various actions according to the various wishes expressed by Guru Rinpoche when he concealed them.

The same significance applies to all the other Terma objects,[258] such as instruments, ornaments of religious importance and so on.

Terma Nectars[259]

According to some interpretations, the nectar rendering liberation by tasting is praised as the best among the Terma substances since the people of this dark age have little diligence and less merit, so that they are unable to achieve any accomplishments. The nectars that were discovered as Termas have been prepared by vajra speech, Padmasambhava etc., the knowledge-holders who have achieved the supreme attainments [through their meditative power], until they have witnessed the signs that these are accomplished substances as mentioned in the great tantras. Therefore, if one takes the nectar by itself the channels (*rTsa*), essence or semen (*Khams*), energy [or air] (*rLung*) and mind (*Sems*) will receive blessings spontaneously and the excellent accomplishment will be achieved, like being intoxicated by alcohol, being made unconscious by aconite (*Bong Nga*) and being deluded with visions by datura or thorn apple (*Thang Khrom; dhattūra*); since the nectar has the extraordinary power of not depending on inner [mental] power, owing to the greatness of the skillful means of Tantra.

7 *False Termas*

Reverse Effect of Practice of Some Termas

The reason contrary and inauspicious results occur when some Termas are practiced is that there are false discovered teachings. In particular there are false texts that look like Terma script, and which are by false Tertons, the rebirths of wrongly aspiring evil ministers[260] of the ancient time who have the support of certain demonic spirits as the protectors of those Termas. Such teachings belong to demonic forces. By reciting and practicing those false teachings the follower will move only in the wrong direction.

If it is a pure teaching from a Terma of Guru Rinpoche, the embodiment of the Buddhas of the three times, then by practicing it, even if an undesirable incident of some kind should occur at the beginning, gradually nothing will be able to prevent one from obtaining the great goal because the means of enlightened activities are inconceivably vast. All the Dharma teachings concealed by Guru Rinpoche are for the accomplishment of the future followers, and it is impossible for them to have an inauspicious result. So, it is certain that the effects of those Termas themselves are not otherwise than auspicious and blissful. Nevertheless Termas have varying results. Many are auspicious, some are not. It depends on auspicious and favorable and inauspicious and unfavorable circumstances at the outset, determined by whether or not the Tertons, according to the orders of Guru Rinpoche, were able to fulfill the performance of such actions as making proper offerings to the treasure protectors, putting substitutes in the concealment place of the teachings, practicing effectuation of the Ter and maintaining the secrecy of the teachings when they have discovered them, and so on. It also depends on whether the Tertons could meet their consorts under proper circumstances, whether they were able to follow the instructions left behind by Guru Rinpoche for them, whether the doctrine-holder could practice the teachings as explained in the discovered text, and so on. In brief, the auspiciousness or inauspiciousness of the teachings result from whether or not the sacred obligations [vows: *Dam Tshig*] are properly observed. Thus one can understand not only the reasons why Termas are auspicious or not, but also that the power of the blessings and the greatness of the enlightened actions of the Termas depend upon the degree of success of preparatory performances such as effectuation of the Terma, and so on.

16 THE REASON WHY NEGATIVE ASPIRATIONS WERE MADE BY EVIL MINISTERS, ETC.

Negative aspirations were made by evil ministers in order to obstruct the enlightened activities of Guru Rinpoche. If disciples of the profound Termas of Guru Rinpoche who have the desire to achieve supreme attainment are fooled into mistaking these false teachings for pure teachings, and if they practice them, it will cause the decline of their fortunes, their life, and so on. If any short-sighted people who have no desire to attain a perpetual goal [enlightenment] should practice these false teachings, then for the time being it might seem to be helpful for increasing life, majesty and the power of speech, but [eventually] those teachings will become a cause of saṃsāra and hell for them.

17 FALSE TERMAS ON ACCOUNT OF EXTERNAL ADVENTITIOUS CIRCUMSTANCES

There are many people in this dark age whose minds are not stable, who want to do hundreds of things; who behave hastily like monkeys and start to carry out whatever ideas cross their minds without examining them. They are possessed by The ring[261] and other spirits who enjoy playing with various kinds of deceptive miracles. These spirits exhibit many deceptive illusions in various forms such as psychic vision teachings and dream teachings, and they mislead such people. They have the same negative effects as in the case of false discovered texts, mentioned earlier [as a result of negative aspirations by evil ministers].

There are also ordinary teachings such as psychic vision teachings (*Nyams sNang* or *Nyams Ch'os*) which are similar in character to the Terma liturgical texts and have not been empowered by demonic forces. If one practices them they will not have much effect, either good or bad. It is extremely important to examine very carefully since it is difficult to distinguish the pure from false teachings, and one should follow a teaching that is authentic. For if one can encounter a perfect new teaching of Guru Rinpoche it will be of great benefit, but if one is misled by a false Terma it will be a grave deception.

8 *Tertons and Doctrine-holders*

18 TERTONS ARE NOT SUBJECT TO BEING JUDGED BY THEIR BEHAVIOR

One cannot judge Tertons as inauthentic because of their imperfect and mercurial character, even to the slightest extent. Guru Rinpoche himself has said:

> The hidden enlightened beings appear in
> uncertain form;
> The fool-deceivers are great hypocritical mimics
> of the dharmic practitioner.
> O people! do not take gold and dross as equal.

Among the false Tertons there are many who are harmonious with people, who seem to have disciplined conduct, and are fortunate and charismatic. At the same time, among the authentic Tertons there are many who are loose in speech and behavior and who, without the least hesitation, get involved in many activities that people will condemn. In that way the Tertons take many grave obstructions of the doctrine on themselves in the form of infamy and ill repute and they use them for the practice of taking every experience in the great equal taste.

Likewise, there are Tertons who are unable to discover their Treasures and who have inauspicious retinues. There have been many celebrated Tertons, as illustrated by the lives of Padma Le drel Tsal[262] and Sum tshog, who got diseases or died in an inauspicious manner: all these things happened for the same reason [taking obstructions upon oneself for the sake of the tradition]. Such occurrences are also for the purpose of demonstrating that the karmic effects are unavoidable, and that there are grave consequences involved in transgressing the slightest order of Guru Rinpoche during the present lives of beings.

19 HOW TO EXAMINE A TERTON

There are two ways of examining Tertons according to the earlier Knowledge-holders (*Rig a'Dzin*). The first is to receive clarification of the authenticity of the Terton from a divinity such as one of the Three Roots. For example, Won ton Kyer gang pa[263] (*dBon sTon sKyer sGang Pa*) developed faith in the Termas discovered by Sang gye Wang chen (*Sangs rGyas dBang Ch'en*) of Nye mo (*sNye Mo*) only after receiving clarification of doubts in a pure vision from Guru Rinpoche himself.

The second way is to examine by means of proofs from scripture and reasoning. For example when Sang gye Ling pa (1340–1396) went to give long-life nectar to Ne dong ma,[264] he was trusted only after examination in debates and questioning by many scholars.

Nowadays, however, it is rare for someone to have the capacity to examine a Terton by the first means. In the second case it is difficult for no error to be made in an examination just by people who regard themselves as scholars.

As explained earlier, the ultimate place of the secret treasure or the concealment, where the power of vajra speech wisdom [Termas] is established inexhaustibly by the power of the Mind-mandate Transmission made by Guru Rinpoche, is mindness (*Sems Nyid*), the changeless dharma sphere of the Terton. Then afterwards, because of the effects of the yellow scrolls, the power of that vajra speech wisdom becomes apparent. The cause of the discovery is not at all just the Terton's looking at the yellow scroll again and again. But the aspect of awareness (*Rig Ch'a*) or the wisdom (*Shes Rab Kyi Ch'a*) of the luminescent nature (*gNyug Ma'i Od gSal*) of the Terton comes forth nakedly, and then he or she watches the symbolic scripts (*brDa Yig*) by the entering (*bChug Nas*) of the wisdom into them.

The awakening of the power of vajra speech wisdom through the conditional factor of the yellow scrolls signifies that the Termas of the dharma sphere arise as the aspect of the power of the awareness (*Rig rTsal*) or alternatively that the power of the awareness itself arises in the form of the clear and complete words and meanings of the Terma teachings. Therefore, without having a sublime realization as the basis for controlling the dharma sphere by awareness, as mentioned in the uncommon teachings of Dzog chen, to inherit the profound Termas of Guru Rinpoche is impossible. It would be like saying that you have never been to India but that you have been to Magadha [central India].

If Tertons do have such a perfect realization, then there is no chance that they will have false Terma as a result of the deceptions of gods and demons. For the primordially pure awareness can never be drawn in the wrong direction.

The reason why Tertons search for a teacher from whom to receive teachings and study instructional texts is just in order to follow the usual tradition. In reality they will have the spontaneous conviction that Guru Rinpoche is their teacher, and because of that very fact they are the natural yogis who have received the blessings spontaneously and have attained self-arisen realization of the luminescent essence. That is how they awaken their past karmic or experiential connections in the process of the Terma Transmission.

How can one know whether or not a Terton possesses such realization?

When the Terton is examined by a person who has

perfect insight into essential aspects (*Lam gNad*) of Dzog chen through the teachings of the genuine canonical transmission of Guru Rinpoche himself or of Vimalamitra, whether or not he finds that the Terton's style of expression is similar to those of the main Dzog chen texts, if the essential meanings have been properly disclosed with confidence, then that is an indication that the Terton is endowed with wisdom equal to that of the indisputable Tertons. He or she can be respected as an authentic one. These criteria are similar in a way to the statement in the *Prajñāpāramitā*[265] that whether or not a Bodhisattva is a Non-returner[266] can be judged by the signs of his discourses on Non-returner teachings.

In the lives of earlier scholars and sages it is said that if a person knows the nature of the yellow scrolls, he can judge the discoverer by examining the authenticity of the yellow scroll; but through this means one cannot judge the Mind Terma teachings.

20 EFFECTUATION OF THE TERMA

It seems that except for some practices done on activities (*Las sGrub*) for themselves and others, most of the practices done by the Tertons on their own discovered Dharma Treasure teachings may become Effectuation of the Ter (*gTer sGrub*). However, the practices performed by the Terton mainly concern the discovery of the teachings before they are transmitted to others and are then spread. In order to assist the discovery of the Ter, which must be withdrawn from the concealment place swiftly without difficulties, first the Discoverer practices on other Terma texts related to the same subject that have already been discovered and transcribed (*gTan La Phebs Zin Pa*) by himself or other Tertons. Further, after discovery of the teaching he does some practice in order to help the opening of the Ter casket (*gTer sGrom*) and the decoding of the symbolic scripts (*brDa Khrol*). Then, in addition, before transcribing the text from the symbolic scripts, he practices the Effectuation of Terma on the newly discovered teaching with the yellow scroll as the request for permission to transcribe the teachings into the 'son copy.' After transcribing, he does the Effectuation practice of the particular discovered teaching on the 'son copy' for the purpose of generating more of the blessing power of the discovered teaching, so that it will be brought to its perfect condition for being taught and disseminated.

21 SECRECY OF THE TERMAS

Why is the Terma kept secret for a long period of time after its discovery? One reason is to check carefully whether there is any need of more clarity and perfection in these decoded teachings. It is clear that this system of checking applies to the Miraculous Discovered Dharma Treasure (*'Phrul Yig Chan*).

Then also it is necessary to wait in case there is further instructional prophecy concerning the importance of a particular time for disclosing the teaching and spreading it, or what sort of appropriate circumstances are necessary in order to arrange an auspicious opportunity. Should such instructional prophecies be received after the Terton has already started transmitting and spreading the discovered teaching, it will have become too late, like a dam after a flood.

Another reason for delay is to generate the power of accomplishment contained in the Terma by its being practiced by the Discoverer himself before it is revealed to others. This is in order to prepare auspicious circumstances of interdependent causation for the future followers who will practice the teachings, so that they will achieve signs of accomplishment without any difficulties. It is said that the teachings of a teacher who himself has not practiced them will have little benefit for his disciples.

The apparent conferring of empowerments and blessings by the gurus, tutelary deities and ḍākinīs upon the Tertons while they are doing the effectuation of the Terma is a sign of their having received the power, like the sharpening of a knife's edge through the Effectuation of the Terma, but, as I mentioned before, it is not actual Terma transmission.

22 THE DOCTRINE-HOLDER

The fortunate person prophesied in the Terma prophecy as the principal figure in upholding the tradition of the Terton by studying, teaching and practicing is the Doctrine-holder (*Ch'os bDag*). There are two kinds of Doctrine-holders, the principal Doctrine-holder and the minor Doctrine-holder. Both are equal in receiving the Mind-mandate Transmission from Guru Rinpoche, but the manner is different.

The principal Doctrine-holder would have received the Mind-mandate Transmission and prophecy from Guru Rinpoche in person, along with the Terton, in the ancient time [ninth century]. The minor Doctrine-holder would not have received the Mind-mandate Transmission in person from Guru Rinpoche, and it is not necessary for him [his incarnation] to have been in that part of the land [of Tibet] at that time. But by his knowledge of the infinitely varied fortunes of future generations, Guru Rinpoche has given the prophecy and made aspirations saying: 'In a later period at a place called such and such, a person called so and so, of such and such a kind will appear, and I am empowering him to become a Doctrine-holder of this teaching.' And that becomes the Mind-mandate Transmission. The essence of the Mind-mandate Transmission is concentration of mind (*dGongs Pa gTad*), because without the concentration of his mind, Guru Rinpoche cannot make such an aspiration or prophecy. Not only that, the entire activities of Guru Padmasambhava's power of transforming all existent phenomena as he wishes comes from the power of his concentrative reflection.

It seems that it is not certain that the minds of the two kinds of Doctrine-holders will have similar abilities of clear awakening of past habituations when they see the Terma teachings—this is because the effects of the karmic system are inconceivable and there are various circumstantial influences (*rKyen*), such as defilements of the womb or birth and evil friends. There have been many incidents reflecting such eventualities.

9 *Mind and Earth Termas*

23 DIFFERENCES BETWEEN MIND AND EARTH TERMAS

Earth and Mind Termas are in general the same. Both, at the beginning, have been concealed in the center or depth of the heart, the indestructible casket, through the Mind-mandate Transmission. In the middle, both remain without any changes. Finally, when the time comes, the teachings emerge from the door of the concealment of the recollection (*Dran Pa*) of the dharmatā, the natural state (*Ch'os Nyid gNyug Ma*) opened by the sharp chisel of the wisdom of the luminous state (*Od gSal Gyi mKhyen Ch'a*).

But Mind Termas have been accepted as Termas because they remained in the treasure of the inner expanse of the mind. So it is called the Profound Mind Dharma Treasure (*Zab Pa dGongs gTer*). The Earth Termas are, as it says in a quotation:

> I [Guru Padmasambhava] have filled the land [of
> Tibet] with Dharma Treasures all over.
> If you wish accomplishments, take them from
> the concealed places.

They are Termas concealed in different external places, so they are called the Vast Earth Terma (*rGya ch'e Ba Sa'i gTer*).

The difference between Earth and non-Earth Termas lies in whether they actually rely on yellow scrolls or not, for the Mind Terma must contain its two aspects (*Zur gNyis*). If they [the Discoverers] do not have very stable luminous contemplation, then there is not the proper aspect of Mind (*dGongs Pa*) in which the teachings must be concealed. If the symbolic script is not dissolved in the mind and sealed [and concealed] in advance, then there is no aspect of the concealed Terma and there is nothing to be discovered. So if the first aspect is present but not the second, then the discovered teachings belong to the category of Pure Vision. If there is neither aspect, then they belong to the category of the Ordinary Experiential Vision or Psychic Vision (*Nyams Ch'os*). Those teachings should not be mixed with or mistaken for the Mind Dharma Treasure.

For some people, as a result of doing recitation and meditation, symbolic scripts happen to arise before them. But they are not stable or reliable since they have not arisen because of any Mind-mandate Transmission, and there is no inner meaning in those symbolic scripts that could be decoded.

In the system of receiving the Mind-mandate Transmission of the Mind Terma there are two categories. The first is the Mind-mandate Transmission of the Terma by concealing it in the Mind of the future Terton in the form of 'letters.' The second one is in the form of 'sounds.' There are three kinds of letters or script: the symbolic script of Just Visible (*sNang Tsam*), Just an Indication (rTen Tsam), and the Complete Text (*mThar Ch'ags*). The different varieties of scripts are the same as in the case of Earth Ter mentioned earlier. In the sound Mind-mandate Transmission, there are many different kinds of sounds, such as the sound of just a syllable, a noun or a word.

In Mind Terma the Mind-mandate Transmission itself is the concealment, so they take place simultaneously.

The discovery of the Ter from the depth of the mind will be in the form of either letters or sounds depending on the form in which the teachings were Mind-mandated, and there will not be any interchanges. That is why it is not certain that symbolic scripts will be present in the discovery of Mind Terma.

Likewise even the calligraphy of the discovered symbolic script will be exactly in the same form as it was entrusted. If it has been entrusted in the Chag kyu Ring po (*lChags Kyu Ring Po* curlicue script) form of calligraphy, it will be discovered only in Chag kyu Ring po form of script, and the same applies to the other cases. It is the same system for the symbols of sound also. It is said that the Lord of Victors, the Lotus-Born [Guru Padmasambhava] and his mind-sons, the King and his subjects, concealed and discovered the Termas of the most excellent teachings in the Land of Snow [Tibet]; they also acted in the same manner in many different lands such as Oḍḍiyāna, etc. the Land of Ḍākinīs, and in the Underground Land [the Land of Nāgas].

I have been told[267] that among the three syllables (*Grong Khyer*) of the symbolic script given at the beginning of the first Ter sar Do chang[268] text, the first two are in the 'Just an Indication' form of symbolic scripts for the *Do chang*.

10 *Terma System in the New Tantric Tradition*

24 TERMA SYSTEM IN THE NEW TANTRIC[269] TRADITION OF TIBET

Generally, among the followers of the New Tantric tradition there have been many Lamas such as Nyal pa Nyi ma Shey rab[270] (*gNyal Pa Nyi Ma Shes Rab*) and Nyen lo Dar ma trag[271] (*gNyan Lo Dar Ma Grags*) and so on, who have discovered Ters concealed by Guru Rinpoche. Also there were sages such as Lord Tsang pa Gya re[272] (1161–1211), Gyud chen Sang gye Gya tsho[273] and so on, who discovered Ters from other sources.[274] Also many teachers, such as Re chung Dor je Trag pa[275] (1084–?), Dro gon Chö gyal Phag pa[276] (1235–1280), Karma pa Rang chung Dor je[277] (1284–1334), Bu ton Rin chen drub[278] (1290–1364), Gyal wang Ge dun Gya tsho[279] (1476–1542), Lo drö rin chen Seng ge[280] (*Blo Gros Rin Ch'en Seng Ge*), and so on, studied and practiced the Termas of Guru Padmasambhava. But in the different schools that follow the New Tantric tradition there never appeared many Tertons, as happened in the Nyingma tradition.

11 *Purpose of this Text, and Colophon*

25 PURPOSE OF WRITING THIS TEXT

Some scholars are contemptuous of the Terma tradition, saying, 'It is the teaching from earth and stones'; and some others say, 'It is too much to say that those Termas are esoterically powerful because of their being kept in the earth for a long period of time'; others assert that 'Since the source of Ter is earth and stones, there is no lineage of transmission,' and so on without examining the subtle qualities of the Terma tradition, which are more extraordinary than those of other traditions. Even among the people who concentrate on the practice of Terma for their whole lives there are many who merely think that 'The Dharma Treasure teachings will have powers of blessing because they were concealed by Guru Rinpoche and later on they were discovered by a good Lama'; and some think, 'The Dharma Treasure teachings are powerful because they have powerful gods, demons of the snow-mountains, rocky mountains, and lakes as their protectors'; while others think, 'Whatever the Dharma Treasure teachings might be, they are the practice of my ancestors and my spiritual tradition from the past,' and they accept them as a proverb says: 'Accepting one's father's cup as clean.' Some people do not even distinguish between Terma texts and the texts composed by a Terton, and just say, 'I like this Lama and I practice his teachings,' and they even take the compositions of the Terton as equal to the Terma texts discovered by him. Some respect the Terma texts as a liturgy just for prosperity and say, 'This text was auspicious for whoever practiced it.' Many think, 'Tertons are persons who enjoy women and alcohol in a disorderly fashion, wear mixed costumes and write many unworthy compositions without carefulness.' And they say,' There is no easier thing to do than to become a Terton. I also can do it if I want to.' Some merely determine the authenticity of a Terton by whether or not he has discovered any casket or bundle of scripts or objects from the earth. So, although it seems that there is devotion in many people, and that they respect the Terma texts as important, yet if we examine their reasons and the nature of their faith, it fades, like examining a river in a mirage.

For this reason, I have written this unprecedented composition with the wish that if there could be any chance that there are a few people who are genuinely and studiously minded, may this writing help them to open a little of the smiling eyes of faith in this tradition of the Mind-mandate Transmission of the One From Oḍḍiyāna, who knows the three times.

26 COLOPHON

I, Jig med Ten pa'i Nyi ma, have written this text entitled *Wonder Ocean, A Brief and Clear Explanation of the Process of Transmission of the Discovered Dharma Treasures*, since I had the wish to write it for a long time; and then because of repeated goading in the form of requests to write it by my attendant Jig med Chö kyi Lo dro, a devotee of the oral canonical transmission of the teachings of Guru Rinpoche. I heard a brief explanation of the tradition of transmission of the Seven Streams[281] from the Lord Spiritual Father Lama Dor je Zi jid[282] (1820–1892), the illusory wisdom body inseparable from the Lord of the Victors, Padmasambhava; and later on I received a reading with explanation of *Ter gyi Do chang Chen mo* from the knowledge-holder Terton Le rab Ling pa (1856–1926); and he also gave me clarifications of my questions. Making them as the basis, I added some appropriate contributions of my own.

By the merit of writing this text, may the immaculate tradition of the Lama of Oḍḍiyāna, the essence of the doctrine of the Victor, spread in all directions and throughout all time.

May gods, demi-gods, Accomplished Ones, Knowledge-holders, and the inconceivable ocean of ḍākinīs uphold the profound Mind Treasure as in the ancient time, and may these teachings appear continuously for fortunate beings.

Appendices

1 *Bon Rituals in Ter Teachings*

Tibetan Buddhism, including the Nyingma school, and Bon, the native pre-Buddhist spiritual tradition, have many teachings in common. Bon also adopted many teachings from Buddhism. Generally Tibetan Buddhists consider that there have been two main forms of interaction between the two traditions: 1) some teachings or methods of training, including certain Bon ritual systems, have been incorporated into Buddhist methods of training, not only in the case of the Ter teachings of the Nyingma school, but by all Buddhist schools of Tibet. 2) In the scriptures of the Chab kar (Ch'ab dKar, White River) school of Bon there are a number of Buddhist texts which have been recast in Bon terminology.

1. In Tibetan tantric (esoteric) Buddhism there are methods of training, particularly ritual ceremonies such as worship of gods or spirits, which originated from or were influenced by Bon. But it is not a matter of giving up Buddhist principles and training or of polluting the purity of Buddhism. The special skill of esoteric Buddhism is transmutation by right view and pure perception, using all appropriate means of training. For example, eating food is not itself a Buddhist practice, but if one uses it as a means of training, it becomes a Buddhist training in transforming one's daily life as a Buddhist practice.

The worship of gods and spirits is one of the most noted instances of the influence of Bon on Tibetan Buddhism. As a cultural manifestation it appears to be the worship of unenlightened spirits or demonic beings with earthly offering materials, yet it is actually incorporated into esoteric Buddhist training as a meditative means. Such rituals usually take the following form: take refuge in the Buddha, Dharma and Sangha, develop the aspiration of enlightenment for the sake of all living beings, then through the contemplative state develop and perfect oneself as an enlightened one such as Avalokiteśvara. Bless the offering materials as wisdom-ambrosia, multiply them into various wish-fulfilling objects and give them to the spirits to please them and to pacify their mental negativities. The rituals conclude with teachings to the spirits and dedication of the merits for the sake of the enlightenment of living beings. Sometimes one perceives the spirits as enlightened deities, makes offerings and dedicates the merits. Sometimes one contemplates oneself as an enlightened one and blesses the spirits. So in essence it is an entirely Buddhist training.

In Buddhism we believe that there are numerous systems of living beings besides the ones that we see. What prevents us from seeing them is our lack of common karma and the limited powers of our physical eyes. So belief in the existence of gods and spirits is not contrary to the conventional belief of Buddhism. Developing compassion, generosity, devotion, giving charity and making offerings are Buddhist practice in the accumulation of merits. If we have respect, love and devotion to a being, perceiving him as a Buddha, we accumulate good karma as having devotion to a Buddha. The main factor in earning good karma is not necessarily reliance on external objects but on ourselves and on the effects of our own actions. So if we can perceive even an ordinary person as an enlightened being, we are being trained in the spiritual path. The special training of esoteric Buddhism is, through contemplative wisdom, to generate and perfect the universe as the Buddhas and their pure lands. In Tibetan Buddhist rituals there is never a question of perceiving worldly spirits as worldly beings and taking them as the ultimate refuge, or of making impure offerings such as the sacrifice of lives. If such rituals occurred, they were not at all part of Buddhist practice.

2. In the Chab kar school of Bon there are many teachings which are similar to or even identical to Buddhist teachings. With the exception of the Bon technical terms in which they are written, all the systems of ten stages, five paths

and nine vehicles of training in these teachings are quite similar to Buddhism in general and Nyingma in particular. Many Buddhist scholars believe that many Buddhist scriptures were translated into Bon technical terms, and that many esoteric teachings of Buddhism were concealed and discovered as Ter teachings of Bon; and that some Buddhist teachers, reincarnated as Bon masters, taught Buddhist teachings under the label of Bon for the benefit of Bon followers. There were many Buddhist Tertons who discovered teachings of Buddhism as Bon teachings. Among them were: Drub thob Ngo drub, Ku sa Men pa, Pon po Lha bum, Khyung po Pal ge, Ra shag Cho bar, Won se Khyung thog, Yag shar Ngon mo, Ten Nyee Ling pa Padma Tshe wang Gyal po, Khung po Trag pa Wang chug, Sum pa Chang chub Tshul thrim, Dre She rab La ma, Nyag ton Lha bar, Rig dzin Ngo drub Gyal tshen, and Long sal Nying po.

Some scholars of the Sar ma schools (which began in Tibet in the eleventh century) thought that many original tantras of the Nyingma school (which were brought from India to Tibet between the seventh and the eleventh century) are not Buddhist texts which came from India because the Sanskrit originals of these tantras were not available during the period of Sar ma translation. One of those scriptures was the *gSang Ba sNying Po* (*Guhyagarbha*) tantra of which the Sanskrit original was discovered later. The discovery showed the error of the attempt in later centuries to prove that because the original Sanskrit manuscripts had not been found, these tantras were not Indian in origin and therefore not Buddhist. During the later centuries, while the Sanskrit originals of some of the Nyingma tantras had not been found, but the same texts existed among the Bon scriptures, some scholars concluded that these were Bon and not Buddhist teachings. Here it is very important to understand that when Buddhism reached Tibet, for various reasons many great Buddhist and Bon scholars translated and taught Buddhist scriptures in Bon terms and preserved them as Bon scriptures. For example, all the volumes of *Sher Phyin a'Bum Pa* (*The Prajñāpāramitā in One Hundred Thousand Verses*) are preserved in the Bon canon as Khams Ch'en, and no Buddhist scholar has any doubt that it is the *Prajñāpāramitā sūtra* of Buddhism. So it was neither wise nor just to say that many of the Nyingma tantras were not Buddhism because their Sanskrit originals could not be found in later centuries and they were found in the Bon canon. The important means of verifying whether or not a text is Buddhist is to ascertain the essence of the meaning rather than relying on words, presumptions and stories. In order to prove the authenticity of Mahāyāna Buddhist scriptures as pure teachings, and for the purpose of following the teachings, four aspects should be emphasized and four others discounted:

1. Depend on the meaning and not on the words.
2. Depend on the teaching and not on the person.
3. Depend on the definitive meaning and not the interpretable meaning.
4. Depend on wisdom and not on consciousnesses.

The existence of Bon rituals in Ter scriptures and of Tertons who are teachers of both Bon and Buddhism only demonstrate the openness and great skillful means of Buddhists in teaching and transmuting all the appropriate aspects both of the secular life and spiritual training of other religions as ways of Buddhist training. If we use them properly enlightenment will be achieved, but if we misunderstand or misuse them, then even so-called pure Buddhist teachings will be of little help.

2 *Description of Empowerment of Rig dzin Dü pa*

Rig dzin Dü pa (*Rig a'Dzin a'Dus Pa*) (*The Assemblage of Knowledge-holders*) is the first of the three principal sādhanas of the Long chen Nying thig cycle discovered by Kun khyen Jig med Ling pa (1729–1798). It illustrates the general structure and contents of the empowerment transmissions of the tantras. This paradigm of the *Rig dzin Dü pa* empowerment synthesizes the contents of two texts by the first Dodrup Chen Rinpoche, *Khyen tse'i Zhal ngom* and *Lha wang Padma Ra ka'i Threng wa,* which themselves are based on the root-empowerment text of *Rig dzin Dü pa, Gyal thab Ch'i lug,* by Jig med Ling pa.

A. PRELIMINARY SECTION

1. Purification of defilements by the water from the Vase. (The disciples rinse their mouths and take their seats.)
2. Dispelling of obstacles to empowerment by the Master.
3. Visualization and blessing for protection against obstacles.
4. Distribution of blindfolds, symbolizing blindness caused by ignorance.
5. Distribution of flowers for offering to the maṇḍala when introduced.
6. Long historical description of the transmission lineage of the Dzog chen Sem de in general and Rig dzin Dü pa in particular.

7 Offering maṇḍala by disciples to the Master as request for giving empowerment.

8 Request by the disciples to give the empowerment. (Repeat three times after the Master.)

9 Accepting the request and explaining the importance of the precepts (vows).

10 Taking refuge:

a. Explanation of importance of taking refuge and how to take it.

b. Taking refuge. (Repeat three times after Master.)

c. The precepts and the benefits of taking refuge.

11 Developing Bodhicitta:

a. Explanation of importance of developing Bodhicitta.

b. Development of Bodhicitta (repeat three times after the Master).

c. The precepts and the benefits of developing Bodhicitta.

12 Accumulation of merits by the seven aspects of devotional practice:

a. Explanation of the seven aspects.

b. Repetition three times after the Master.

c. Benefits.

13 Taking the three precepts (repeat after the Master).

14 For development of absolute and relative Bodhicitta, visualize the Bodhicitta in the form of a vajra upon a sun and moon seat in one's heart as the symbol, and repeat the mantra after the Master.

15 Receiving the water which binds you to your vow from the Master, and taking the vow of observing the precepts. (Repeat the mantra after the Master.)

16 Requesting the Master to open the door of the maṇḍala, the dwelling of the Assemblage of Deities.

17 The disciples think of themselves as entering through the four doors of the maṇḍala. They touch their folded hands to the three places and repeat the mantras after the Master in order to pay homage.

18 The disciples enter the internal, signless wisdom maṇḍala by following the instruction to visualize themselves as Guru Padmasambhava. They invite and merge the wisdom deities into the visualized deities.

19 In order to determine which Buddha family they belong to, the disciples cast their flowers into the maṇḍala. (Repeat after the Master.)

20 Take off the blindfolds as indication of receiving the blessing of dispelling ignorance. (Repeat after the Master.)

B. THE ACTUAL SECTION

21 The Master reveals the maṇḍala.

22 Let the disciple recollect that one's mind and the events of the mind are in their real nature the maṇḍala of the deities.

23 The Master invokes the Buddhas and with offerings and homage requests them to confer the empowerments.

The Common Empowerments of the Five Buddha Families

24a *Vase Empowerment* to purify the defilement of anger, transform it into the Wisdom of the Ultimate Sphere (Dharmadhātu) and to receive the blessing of the Buddha Akṣobhya. (Drink the sacred water.)

25b *Crown Empowerment* to purify the defilement of pride, transform it into the Equalizing Wisdom, and to receive the blessing of the Buddha Ratnasambhava. (Put the crown on head.)

26c *Vajra Empowerment* to purify the defilement of desire, transform it into the Discriminating Wisdom and to receive the blessing of the Buddha Amitābha. (Touch the vajra to right hand.)

27d *Bell Empowerment* to purify the defilement of jealousy, transform it into the All-Accomplishing Wisdom and to receive the blessing of the buddha Amoghasiddhi. (Touch the bell to left hand.)

28e *Name Empowerment* to purify ignorance and transform it into the Mirror Wisdom and to receive the blessing of the Buddha Vairocana. (Master rings the bell with vajra over the head of the disciple.)

29 *Vajrācārya* (Dor je Lopon) *Empowerment*, sowing the

seed of Primordial Buddhahood. (With vajra and bell make the gesture of embracing).

The Fourfold Uncommon Empowerments and Recitation, Torma and Text Empowerment

30a *Victorious Vase Empowerment.* The vase as a form of the complete maṇḍala of Rig dzin Dü pa giving the blessing of the body of the Buddhas. (The Master puts the vase on the disciples' heads and gives them water to drink.)

31 *Empowerment of Deities*: The Master blesses tsaklis (miniature pictures) as the actual deities. The disciple should perceive with confidence that they are the actual deities and receive blessings from them. The tsaklis which the Master shows introduce the following figures:

a. Guru Rinpoche (*Padmasambhava*)
b. Ga rab Dor je (*Prahevajra*)
c. Kun tu Zang po (*Samantabhadra*) with consort
d. The Eight Knowledge-holders (*Vidyādhara*) one after another
e. The Twenty-five Chief Disciples of Guru Rinpoche one after another
f. The Four Door Protectors of the maṇḍala

32 *Torma Empowerment*: Blessing of the torma as the complete maṇḍala of Rig dzin Dü pa by the Master. The disciples should visualize with confidence that the torma is the complete maṇḍala of the Rig dzin Dü pa.

33b *Secret Empowerment*: by tasting the essence. Giving the blessing of the speech of the Buddhas.

34 *Recitation Empowerment*: The disciples are given a rosary for reciting mantras.

35c *Wisdom Empowerment*: Conferring the capacity to practice the wisdom of the fourfold blessing and the blessing of the Minds of the Buddhas. (The disciples are shown the tsakli of the consort and should touch it with the ring-fingers of their left hands.)

36d *Symbolic or Verbal Empowerment*: The Master displays a crystal with a mirror symbolizing the spontaneously arisen wisdom free from all concepts. It conveys the capacity for verbal understanding of the absolute nature and confers the blessing of vajra wisdom.

37 *Text Empowerment*: Empowering the disciples to perform practices and to preach the doctrine. (The text is placed on the disciples' heads.)

C. CONCLUDING SECTION

38 *Empowerment of Auspiciousness:*
   a. The seven precious attributes of lordship.
   b. The eight auspicious symbols.
   c. The eight auspicious substances.

39 Explanation of the precepts of empowerment.

40 Offering of the maṇḍala to the Master in gratitude for performing the empowerment.

41 Prayer of dedication of merits.

3 *Categories of Texts in* The Collection of the Ancient Tantras

This is brief schema of the categories of texts in *The Collection of Ancient Tantras* (*rNying Ma rGyud a'Bum*), the original esoteric scriptures of the Nyingma school transmitted through unabridged lineages.

Kun khyen Jig med Ling pa (1729–1798) wrote the first catalogue of the Collection of Ancient Tantras on the basis of the collections made by Ratna Ling pa (1403–1478), Ter dag Ling pa (1646–1714) and Lo chen Dharmaśrī (1654–1717/8). Later the Collection of Ancient Tantras was carved in wooden blocks and published at De ge Gon chen monastery (built in 1616) in twenty-five volumes, and Ge tse (*dGe rTse*) Mahāpaṇḍita of Ka thog monastery (built in 1159) wrote the history of the Ancient Tantric tradition and the catalogue for the new publication. In the 1970s His Holiness Dil go Khyen tse Rinpoche (1910–) published *The Collection of Ancient Tantras* in thirty-three volumes in Delhi, India.

Each volume is numbered alphabetically in Tibetan, according to the De ge edition.

	Volumes
1 The Instructions, Atiyoga	Ka–Ch'a
A. The Category of the Secret Instructions (*Man Ngag sDe*)	Ka–Cha
a. Most Secret Sublime Tantras	Ka–Nga
i Yang ti (*Yang Ti*)	Ka–Kha
ii Chi ti (*sPyi Ti*)	Kha–Ga
iii Ati (*A Ti*)	Ga–Nga
b. Secret Tantras	Nga
c. Outer and Inner Tantras	Nga–Cha
B. The Inner Tantras, the Great Expanse	Cha

(*Klong sDe*)	
C. The Outer Tantras, the Category of the Mind, (*Sems sDe*)	Cha–Ch'a
a. Text of the Cycle of Kun ched Gyal po	Cha–Ch'a
b. The Eighteen Tantras on the Cycle of Mind	Ch'a
c. The Other Texts of the Cycle of Mind	Ch'a
2 The Precepts, Anuyoga	Ja–Nya
A. The Four Root Sūtras	Ja–Nya
B. The Six Tantras	Nya
C. The Twelve Rare Tantras	Nya
3 The Development, Mahāyoga	Ta–Ra
A. The Eighteen Tantras (*rGyud sDe*)	Ta
a. Root Tantra: Guhyagarbhamāyājāla-tantra	Ta–Da
b. The Seventeen Explanatory Tantras	Da
i The Five Root Tantras of Body, Speech, Mind, Virtues and Actions	Da–Na
ii The Five Tantras of Explanation of the Method of Practice	Pa
iii The Five Tantras on the Aspect of Conduct	Pa
iv The Two Additional Tantras	Pa–Pha
B. The Eight Sādhanas of the Eight Great Maṇḍalas	Pha
a. Terma Texts	Pha–Ba
i La ma Gong du by Sang gye Ling pa	Pha
ii Yi dam De sheg Du pa by Nyang Nyi ma Od zer	Pha–Ba
b. Canonical Tantras	Ba–Ra
i The Tantras of the Body, Mañjuśrī	Ba–Tsa
ii The Tantras of Speech, Padma	Tsa–Tsha
iii The Tantras of the Mind, Yang dag	Tsha–Dza
iv The Tantras of Virtues, Amṛta	Dza–Wa
v The Tantras of Actions, Vajrakīla	Wa–Za
vi The Tantras of Inciting and Dispatching, Ma mo	Za–A'
vii The Tantras of Offering and Praise to the Worldly Deities	Ya–Ra
viii Tantras of Terrifying Mantras of Exorcism	Ra

4 *Categories of Texts in* The Collection of Canonical Literature

This is a brief schema of the categories of texts in The Collection of Canonical Literature (Ka ma, *bKa' Ma*) of the Nyingma school. The canonical scriptures, mostly tantric teachings, were first brought together by Ter dag Ling pa (1646–1714) and his brother Lo chen Dharmaśrī (1654–1717/8), and later by Gyal se Zhen phen Tha ye (1800– ?) of Dzog chen monastery (built in 1685). Gyal se Zhen phen Tha ye also printed them for the first time, in an edition of 9 volumes. He established the annual seven day sādhana or ritual ceremony on each of the thirteen major maṇḍalas of the Canonical Literature at Dzog chen monastery, which was adopted by certain other monasteries.

Each volume is numbered alphabetically in Tibetan, according the to the edition published by Mr. Sonam Kazi in Delhi, India.

	Volumes
1 Texts of the Sūtric (exoteric) vehicle	Ka
A. The Prātimokṣa (monastic discipline) texts	Ka
B. The Bodhisattva teachings	Ka
2 Texts on the Tantric (esoteric) vehicle	Ka–Ta
A. Three Outer Tantras	Ka–Kha
a. Kriyāyoga: texts on the Medicine Buddha, Od zer Dri med and Tsug tor Dri med	Ka–Kha

b.	Caryāyoga: Nam nang Ngon chang (*rNam sNang mNgon Byang*)	Kha
c.	Yogatantra: Ngen song Jong wa (*Ngan Song sByong Ba*)	Kha
B.	Three Inner Tantras	Kha–Ta
a.	Mahāyoga	Kha–Cha
i	The Five Root Tantras: The Tantras of Body, Speech, Mind, Virtues and Action	Kha
ii	The Five Tantras of Manifestations (*Rol Ba*)	Kha–Ga
iii	The Five Branch Tantras of Action (missing)	
iv	The Two Additional Tantras (missing)	
v	The General Tantras, the Tantras of Peaceful and Wrathful Deities and their Supplementary Texts	Nga–Cha
b.	Anuyoga	Cha–Ch'a
i	Root Tantras: Kun du Rig pa'i do (*Kun a'Dus Rig Pa'i mDo*)	
ii	Explanatory Tantras: Chi do Gong pa Du pa (*sPyi mDo dGongs Pa a'Dus Pa*) etc.	
c.	Atiyoga	Nya–Ta
i	Sem de (*Sems sDe* – Mind Category): Ka gyed Dzong threng (*bKa' brGyad rDzongs a'Preng*)	Nya–Ta
ii	Long de (*Klong sDe* – the Texts on the Great Expanse): Dor je Zam pa (*rDo rJe Zam Pa*)	Ta
iii	Men ngag de (*Man Ngag sDe* – Category of Instructions): The Seventeen Tantras	Ta

5 *Categories of Texts in* The Precious Treasury of Termas

This is a brief schema of the categories of texts in The Precious Treasury of Termas, (*Rin Ch'en gTeṛ Gyi mDzod*), a collection of some major termas (*gTer Ch'os*) of each major Terton (*gTer sTon*) of the Nyingma school. This collection was arranged by Kong tul Yon ten Gya tsho (1813–1899) and published in xylographic blocks in Pal pung (dPal sPungs) monastery (built in 1727) and Tshur phu (mTshur Phu) monastery (built in 1189) in 60 volumes. In 1974 H.H. Dil go Khyen tse Rinpoche (1910–) published this collection in Delhi, India. The following outline of contents is based on the catalogue – *The Key to a Hundred Doors of Accomplishment* – by Kong tul Yon ten Gya tsho.

1 Histories and Biographies
2 Mahāyoga
- A. Cycle of Tantras (*rGyud sDe*): Vajrasattva and Peaceful and Wrathful Deities
- B. Cycle of Sādhanas (*sGrub sDe*):
  - a. Root Sādhanas:
    - i Sādhanas on the deities of the Three Roots collectively
    - ii Sādhanas on the individual deities of the Three Roots
      - (1) Sādhanas on the Guru, the source of blessing power

(A) Outer Sādhanas in the form of prayers
(B) Inner Sādhanas on the Guru in Peaceful form
(a) In the form of the Dharmakāya
(b) In the form of the Sambhogakāya
(c) in the form of the Nirmāṇakāya
(C) Secret Sādhanas on the Guru in Wrathful Form
(2) Sādhanas on the Peaceful and Wrathful Tutelary Deities, the source of accomplishments:
(A) Sādhanas on the Tutelary Deities collectively
(B) Sādhanas on the individual Tutelary Deities
(a) Sādhanas on the Maṇḍala of the Body, Mañjuśrī:
(i) Peaceful Mañjuśrī
(ii) Wrathful Mañjuśrī
(b) Sādhanas on the Maṇḍala of Speech, the Padma:
(i) Peaceful form: Amitāyus and Avalokiteśvara
(ii) Wrathful form: the Red Hyagrīva of the Padma family and the Black Hyagrīva of the Karma family
(c) Sādhanas on the Maṇḍala of the Mind, Yang dag:
(i) Peaceful form: Vajrasattva
(ii) Wrathful form: Vajraheruka
(iii) Associated Deity: Vajrapāṇi
(d) Sādhanas on the Maṇḍala of Virtues: Amṛta
(i) The Actual Sādhanas
(ii) The Related Texts
(e) Sādhanas on the Maṇḍala of Action: Vajrakīla
(f) Sādhanas on Inciting and Dispatching: Ma mo
(g) Sādhanas on Offering to and Praising Worldly Deities
(h) Sādhanas on Terrifying Mantras and Exorcism
(3) Sādhanas on the ḍākinīs, the source of activities:
The Sādhanas and teachings on Vajravarāhī,

Thro ma Nag mo (Khros Ma Nag Mo), Ye shey Tsho gyal and Tārā
(4) The Texts on Dharmapālas
b. The Branch texts related to Different Activities
i The Branch texts useful for recitation and practice (*bsNyen sGrub*)
(1) Empowerments
(2) General teachings important for practice
(3) Tor ma (*gTor Ma*) offerings
(4) Feast Offering (*Tshogs*)
(5) Consecration of Sacred Objects
(6) Rituals for Death and Dying
(7) Fire (*Homa*) Offering Ceremony
ii Texts on Various Specific Actions
3 Anuyoga
(There are only a few texts in this category.)
4 Atiyoga
A. The Cycle on the Mind (*Sems sDe*)
B. The Cycle on the Great Expanse (*Klong sDe*)
C. The Cycle on Instructions (*Man Ngag sDe*)
a. The Category of Ati:
i The Tradition of Vimalamitra
ii The Tradition of Padmasambhava
iii The Tradition of Vairocana
iv The Tradition of the United Teachings of the Three Teachers
b. The Category of Chi ti (*sPyi Ti*)
c. The Category of Yang ti
5 The Concluding Texts: the Instructions and Aspirational Prayers

6 *Names of Earth, Mind and Pure Vision Tertons*

1. EARTH TERTONS GIVEN IN *THE PRECIOUS GARLAND OF LAPIS LAZULI*

1 Sang gye Lama (*Sangs rGyas Bla Ma*) (11th century)
2 Gya Lo tsa wa, Dor je Zang po (*rGya Lo Tsa Ba, rDo rJe bZang Po*) (11th century)
3 Na nam Thub pa Gyal po (*sNa Nam Thub Pa rGyal Po*) (11th century)
4 Dum gya Zhang throm (*Dum rGya Zhang Khrom*) (11th century)
5 Nyi ma Seng ge (*Nyi Ma Seng Ge*) (11th century)
6 Wu ru Ton pa, Shakya Od (*dBu Ru sTon Pa Shakya A'od*) (1284–1339)
7 Pon po Trag tshal (*Bon Po Brag Tshal*) (11th century)
8 Nye mo Zhu ye (*sNye Mo Zhu Yas*) (12th century)
9 Drub thob Ngo drub (*Grub Thob dNgos Grub*) (12th century)
10 Tsug lag Pal ge (*gTsug Lag dPal dGe*) (11th century)
11 Ku sa Men pa, Padma kyab (*Ku Sa sMan Pa Padma sKyab*) (12th century)
12 Pon po Lha bum (*Bon Po Lha a'Bum*) (11th century)
13 Khyung po Pal ge (*Khyung Po dPal dGe*) (11th century)
14 Sha mi Dor je Gyal po (*Sha Mi rDo rJe rGyal Po*) (11th century)
15 Dang ma Lhun gyal (*lDang Ma Lhun rGyal*) (11th century)
16 Tra wa Ngon shey, Wang chug bar (*Gra Ba mNgon Shes, dBang Phyug a'Bar*) (1012–1090?)
17 Ra shag, Cho bar (*Ra Shag, Ch'os a'Bar*) (11th century)

18 Nyang ral Nyi ma Od zer (*Nyang Ral, Nyi Ma A'od Zer*) (1124–1192)
19 Won (Pon) se Khyung thog tsal (*dBon (dPon) gSas* (or *Sras) Khyung Thog rTsal*) (11th century)
20 Ra mo Shel men (*Ra Mo Shel sMan*) (12th century)
21 Guru Cho kyi Wang chug (*Guru Ch'os Kyi dBang Phyug*) (1212–1270)
22 Guru Cho tshe (*Guru Jo Tshe*) (13th century)
23 Gya ton, Padma Wang chug (*rGya sTon, Padma dBang Phyug*) (13th century)
24 Do pan Gya tsho (*Do Ban rGya mTsho*) (14th century)
25 Rakshi Ton pa (*Rakshi sTon Pa*) (13th century)
26 E yi Ton pa Nyi od sel (*E Yi sTon Pa Nyi A'od gSal*) (12th century)
27 Tra gom Cho kyi Dor je (*Gra sGom Ch'os Kyi rDo rJe*) (14th century)
28 Yag char Ngon mo (*gYag Phyar sNgon Mo*) (12th century)
29 Trum dang Khar nag (*Grum Dang mKhar Nag*) (13th century)
30 Lha tsun Ngon mo (*Lha bTsun sNgon Mo*) (11th century)
31 Kham pa Nyi ma Trag pa (*Khams Pa Nyi Ma Grags Pa*) (13th century)
32 Rin chen Tshul dor or Padma Le drel tsel (*Rin Ch'en Tshul rDor* or *Padma Las a'Brel rTsal*) (13th century)
33 Tshe ten Gyal tshen (*Tshe brTan rGyal mTshan*) (13th century)
34 Rin chen Ling pa (*Rin Ch'en Gling Pa*) (14th century)
35 O gyen Ling pa (*O rGyan Gling Pa*) (1329–1360/7)
36 Dri med Od zer or Long chen Rab jam (*Dri Med A'od Zer* or *Klong Ch'en Rab a'Byams*) (1308–1363)
37 Dag po, Rog je Ling pa or Cho je Ling pa (*Dvags Po, Rog rJe Gling Pa* or *Ch'os rJe Gling Pa*) (17th century)
38 Ter dag Ling pa or Gyur med Dor je (*gTer bDag Gling Pa* or *a'Gyur Med rDo rJe*) (1646–1714)
39 Kun kyong Ling pa (*Kun sKyong Gling Pa*) (15th century)
40 Do ngag Ling pa Chog den Gon po (*mDo sNgags Gling Pa mCh'og lDan mGon Po*) (15th century)
41 Ten Nyee Ling pa Padma Tshe wang Gyal po (*bsTan gNyis Gling Pa Padma Tshe dBang rGyal Po*) (15th century)
42 Dor je Ling pa (*rDo rJe Gling Pa*) (1346–1405)

43 Sang gye Ling pa or Rin chen Ling pa (*Sangs rGyas Gling Pa* or *Rin Ch'en Gling Pa*) (1340–1396)
44 Padma Ling pa (*Padma Gling Pa*) (1450–1521)
45 Ja tson Nying po or Le thro Ling pa (*a'Ja' Tshon sNying Po* or *Las a'Phro Gling Pa*) (1585–1656)
46 Sam ten Ling pa (*bSam gTan Gling Pa*) (14th century)
47 Zhig po Ling pa Gar kyi Wang chug (*Zhig Po Gling Pa Gar Gyi dBang Phyug*) (1524–1583)
48 De chen Ling pa (*bDe Ch'en Gling Pa*) (16th century)
49 Gya pan Dor je od (*rGya Ban rDo rJe A'od*) (11th century)
50 Guru Hung bar (*Guru Hung a'Bar*) (11th century)
51 Lha tsun Chang chub od (*Lha bTsun Byang Ch'ub A'od*) (11th century)
52 Jo wo je Atīśa Dīpaṁkaraśrījñāna (11th century)
53 Zhang tsun Darma Rin chen (*Zhang bTsun Dar ma Rin Ch'en*) (11th century)
54 Rong zom, Cho kyi Zang po (*Rong Zom, Ch'os Kyi bZang Po*) (11th century)
55 Dor bum Cho kyi Trag pa (*rDor a'Bum Ch'os Kyi Grags Pa*) (11th century)
56 Sang gye bar (*Sangs rGyas a'Bar*) (11th century)
57 Se ton Ring mo (*Se sTon Ring Mo*) (11th century)
58 Gya phur bu (*rGya Phur Bu*) (11th century)
59 Ge shey Dor je Kun trag (*dGe bShes rDo rJe Kun Grags*) (11th century)
60 Lha je Nub chung (*Lha rJe gNubs Ch'ung*) (11th century)
61 Gya ton, Tson dru Seng ge dar (*rGya sTon, rTson a'Grus Seng Ge Dar*) (11th century)
62 Che tsun Seng ge Wang chug (*lChe bTsun Seng Ge dBang Phyug*) (11th century)
63 Che gom Nag po (*lChe bsGom Nag Po*) (11th century)
64 Zhang ton, Tra shee Dor je (*Zhang sTon, bKra Shis rDo rJe*) (1097–1167)
65 Sar pan Chog med (*Sar Ban Phyogs Med*) (11th century)
66 Nyen Lo tsa wa, Dar ma trag (*gNyan Lo Tsa Ba Dar Ma Grags*) (11th century)
67 Śākya od or Śākya Zang po (*Śākya A'od or Śākya bZang Po*) (12th century)
68 Lama Zang ri Re pa (*Bla Ma Zangs Ri Ras Pa*) (12th century)

69 Nyal pa Jo se or Nyal ton Nag po (*gNyal Pa Jo Sras* or *gNyal sTon Nag Po*) (12th century)
70 Nye mo Gya Gong ri pa, Sang gye Wang chen (*sNye Mo rGya Gong Ri Pa, Sangs rGyas dBang Ch'en*) (11th century)
71 Chu pho Tog den (*Ch'u Pho rTogs lDan*) (12th century)
72 Pa khal Mug po (*Ba mKhal sMug Po*) (12th century)
73 Nga dag Mol mi khyil (*mNga' bDag Mol Mi a'Khyil*) (12th century)
74 Tru gu Yang wang (*Gru Gu Yang dBang*) (12th century)
75 Sum pa Chang chub Lo dro (*Sum Pa Byang Ch'ub Blo Gros*) (12th century)
76 Tag lung pa Sang gye Won po (*sTag Lung Pa Sangs rGyas dBon Po*) (12th century)
77 Nyal pa Nyi ma Shey rab (*gNyal Pa Nyi Ma Shes Rab* (12th century)
78 Thro phu Lo tsa wa Cham pa'i pal (*Khro Phu Lo Tsa Ba Byams Pa'i dPal*) (12th century)
79 Ye pan Ya pon (*gYas Ban Ya Bon*) (12th century)
80 Pal po Ah hung bar (*Bal po Ah Hung a'Bar*) (12th century)
81 A jo Pal po (*Ah Jo dPal Po*) (12th century)
82 Kyang po Trag pa Wang chug (*rKyang Po Grags Pa dBang Phyug*) (12th century)
83 Sum pa Chang chub Tshul thrim (*Sum Pa Byang Ch'ub Tshul Khrims*) (12th century)
84 Dre Shey rab La ma (*a'Bre Shes Rab Bla Ma*) (12th century)
85 Nyag ton Lha bar (*gNyags sTon Lha a'Bar*) (12th century)
86 Drub thob Dar char wa (*Grub Thob a'Dar Phyar Ba*) (12th century)
87 Du ku Rin chen Seng ge (*Du Gu Rin Ch'en Seng Ge*) (12th century)
88 Tsang pa Lab Ring mo or Tsang ring Shey Rab (*gTsang Pa Lab Ring Mo* or *gTsang Ring Shes Rab*) (12th century)
89 Tul ku La tod Mar po or Dam pa Mar po (*sPrul sKu La sTod dMar Po* or *Dam Pa dMar Po*) (12th century)
90 Jo mo Men mo (*Jo Mo sMan Mo*) (1248–1283)
91 Me long Dor je (*Me Long rDo rJe*) (1243–1303)
92 Kal den Chee Pa (*sKal lDan Byis Pa*) (13th century)
93 Trang-ti Gyal nye khar pu (*Brang Ti rGyal Nye mKhar Bu*) (13th century)

94 Gom chen Drug pa (*sGom Ch'en a'Brug Pa*) (13th century)
95 Nyenton Dzam bha la (*gNyan sTon Jambhala*) (13th century)
96 Don drub Seng ge (*Don Grub Seng Ge*) (13th century)
97 Padma Trag Pa (*Padma Grags Pa*) (13th century)
98 Dung tsho Re pa (*Dung mTsho Ras Pa*) (First) (13th century)
99 Kha dro ma Kun ga bum (*mKha' a'Gro Ma Kun dGa' a'Bum*) (13th century)
100 Dung tsho Re pa (*Dung mTsho Ras Pa*) (Second) (13th century)
101 Ba dzar Ma ti (*Vajramati*) (?)
102 Gyal se Leg pa (*rGyal Sras Legs Pa*) (1290–1366?)
103 O gyen Zang po (*O rGyan bZang Po*) (14th century)
104 Shey rab Me bar (*Shes Rab Me a'Bar*) (14th century)
105 Nyi da Sang gye (*Nyi Zla Sangs rGyas*) (14th century)
106 Le thro Ling pa (*Las a'Phro Gling Pa*) (14th century)
107 Tul ku Zang po Trag pa (*sPrul sKu bZang Po Grags Pa*) (14th century)
108 Dri med Lhun po (*Dri Med Lhun Po*) (14th century)
109 Dri med Kun ga (*Dri Med Kun dGa'*) (14th century)
110 Rig dzin Ngo drub Gyal tshen or God dem (*Rig a'Dzin dNgos Grub rGyal mTshan* or *rGod lDem*) (1337–1408)
111 Lang po wa, Pal Gyal tshen or Chang chub Ling pa (*Lang Po Ba, dPal rGyal mTshan* or *Byang Ch'ub Gling Pa*) (14th century)
112 Kar ma Ling pa (*Karma Gling pa*) (14th century)
113 Jam yang La ma (*a'Jam dByangs Bla Ma*) (14th century)
114 Thang tong Gyal po (*Thang sTong rGyal Po*) (1385–1509)
115 Gon po Rin chen (*mGon Po Rin Ch'en*) (15th century)
116 Ratna Ling pa (*Ratna Gling Pa*) (1403–1478)
117 Kal den Dor je (*sKal lDan rDo rJe*) (?)
118 Chog den Dor je (*mCh'og lDan rDo rJe*) (15th century)
119 Chag Chang chub Ling pa (*Ch'ag Byang Ch'ub Gling Pa*) (15th century)
120 Yol mo Tul ku Śākya Zang po (*Yol Mo sPrul sKu Śākya bZang Po*) (15th century)
121 Dro dul Le thro Ling pa (*a'Gro a'Dul Las a'Phro Gling Pa*) (15th century)
122 Jam pal Dor je (*a'Jam dPal rDo rJe*) (?)

123 Pen chen Padma Wang gyal (*Pan Ch'en Padma dBang rGyal*) (1487–1542)
124 Mi gyur Le thro Ling pa Kun ga Pal zang (*Mi a'Gyur Las a'Phro Gling Pa Kun dGa' Pal bZang*) (16th century)
125 Dri gung Rin Chen Phun tshog or Nam chag Me bar (*a'Bri Gung Rin Ch'en Phun Tshogs* or *gNam lChag Me a'Bar*) (1509–?)
126 Threng po Dro dul Ling pa Shey rab Od zer (*Phreng Po a'Gro a'Dul Gling Pa Shes Rab A'od Zer*) (1517–1584)
127 Nga ree Rig dzin Leg den Dor je (*mNga' Ris Rig a'Dzin Legs lDan rDo rJe*) (16th century)
128 Matiratna (16th century)
129 Tshe ring Dor je (*Tshe Ring rDo rJe*) (16th century)
130 Ne sar Khyen tse'i Wang chug Do ngag Ling pa (*gNas gSar mKhyen brTse'i dBang Phyug mDo sNgags Gling pa*) (1524–1587?)
131 Cho gyal Wang po'i de or Chang dag Trashee Tob gyal (*Ch'os rGyal dBang Po'i sDe* or *Byang bDag bKra Shis sTobs rGyal*) (1550–1602?)
132 Dor trag Rig dzin Ngag gi Wang po (*rDor Brag Rig a'Dzin Ngag Gi dBang Po*) (1580–1639)
133 Gar wang Le thro Ling pa (*Gar dBang Las a'Phro Gling Pa*) (16th century)
134 Yong dzin Ngag wang Trag pa (*Yong a'Dzin Ngag dBang Grags Pa*) (16th century)
135 Ngag chang Tra shee Tshe ten (*sNgags a'Ch'ang bKra Shis Tshe brTan*) (17th century)
136 Ra zhi Padma Rig dzin (*Ra Zhi Padma Rig a'Dzin*) (17th century)
137 Dud dul Ling pa (*bDud a'Dul Gling Pa*) (17th century)
138 Rig dzin Dud dul Dor je (*Rig a'Dzin bDud a'Dul rDo rJe*) (1615–1672)
139 Rig dzin Long sal Nying po (*Rig a'Dzin Klong gSal sNying Po*) (1625–1692)
140 Mog drub Nam kha Cho wang (*rMog Grub Nam mKha' Ch'os dBang*) (17th century)
141 Yol mo Tul ku Ten dzin Nor bu (*Yol Mo sPrul sKu bsTan a'Dzin Nor Bu*) (17th century)
142 Zang po Dor je (*bZang Po rDo rJe*) (17th century)
143 Dor je Gyal po (*rDo rJe rGyal Po*) (17th century)

144 Gar wang Da wa Gyal tshen (*Gar dBang Zla Ba rGyal mTshan*) (17th century)
145 Yong ge Mi gyur Dor je (*Yongs dGe Mi a'Gyur rDo rJe*) (17th century)
146 Cha tang Ku chog or Ngag gi Dor je (*Bya bTang sKu mCh'og* or *Ngag Gi rDo rJe*) (17th century)
147 Won(Pon) se Khyung thog (*dBon(dPon) gSas Khyung Thog*) (17th century)
148 Rig dzin Tag sham Dor je or Sam ten Ling pa (*Rig a'Dzin sTag Shams rDo rJe* or *bSam gTan Gling Pa*) (17th century)
149 Ra ton, Tob den Dor je or Padma Tshe wang tsal (*Ra sTon, sTobs lDan rDo rJe* or *Padma Tshe dBang rTsal*) (17th century)
150 Ngag wang Kun ga Ten dzin (*Ngag dBang Kun dGa' bsTan a'Dzin*) (17th century)
151 Rig dzin Rol pa'i Dor je (*Rig a'Dzin Rol Pa'i rDo rJe*) (17th century)
152 Rong ton, Padma De chen Ling pa (*Rong sTon Padma bDe Ch'en Gling Pa*) (17th century)
153 Padma Cho gyal (*Padma Ch'os rGyal*) (17th century)
154 Padma Wang chug (*Padma dBang Phyug*) (17th century)
155 Khyung trag Dor je or O gyen Phun tshog (*Khyung Brag rDo rJe* or *O rGyan Phun Tshogs*) (17th century)
156 Pe yul, Rig dzin Tshe wang Nor bu (*dPal Yul, Rig a'Dzin Tshe dBang Nor bu*) (17th century)
157 Tsa sum Ter dag Ling pa (*rTsa gSum gTer bDag Gling Pa*) (17th century)
158 Rig dzin Thug chog Dor je (*Rig a'Dzin Thugs mCh'og rDo rJe*) (17th century)
159 Dri med Ling pa (*Dri Med Gling Pa*) (18th century)
160 Kun zang De chen Dor je or Mon Lam Dor je (*Kun bZang bDe Ch'en rDo rJe* or *sMon Lam rDo rJe*) (18th century)
161 Rog je Ling pa Dro dul tsal (*Rog rJe Gling Pa a'Gro a'Dul rTsal*) (17th century)
162 Drug thang De chen Gyal po (*a'Brug Thang bDe Ch'en rGyal Po*) (18th century)
163 Cho ling, Gar wang Chi med Dor je (*Ch'os Gling, Gar dBang a'Ch'i Med rDo rJe*) (1763–?)
164 Dor je Thog med or Ten dzin Da od Dor je (*rDo rJe Thogs Med* or *bsTan a'Dzin Zla A'od rDo rJe*) (18th century)

165 Da wa'i Od zer (*Zla Ba'i A'od Zer*) (18th century)
166 Chog gyur De chen Zhig po Gling Pa (*mCh'og Gyur bDe Ch'en Zhig Po Gling Pa*) (1829–1870)
167 Rig dzin Cho gyal Dor je (*Rig a'Dzin Ch'os rGyal rDo rJe*) (19th century)
168 Padma Do ngag Ling pa or Khyen tse'i Wang po (*Padma mDo sNgags Gling Pa or mKhyen brTse'i dBang Po*) (1820–1892)

Earth Tertons of uncertain dates

169 Da ben Zi jid bar (*Zla a'Ban gZi brJid a'Bar*)
170 Rog pen, Shey rab od (*Rog Ban Shes Rab A'od*)
171 Drom, Cho kyi Nying po (*a'Brom, Ch'os Kyi sNying Po*)
172 Od zer Ton pa (*A'od Zer sTon Pa*)
173 Me nyag Trag jung (*Me Nyag Grags a'Byung*)
174 Da wa Dor je (*Zla Ba rDo rJe*)
175 Tsang gi Nyag ton, Shey rab Trag pa (*gTsang Gi Nyag sTon, Shes Rab Grags Pa*)
176 Tsang ton, Cho bar (*gTsang sTon, Ch'os a'Bar*)
177 Kham pa, Me zor (*Khams Pa, Me Zor*)
178 Ngag chang Wang chen Zang po (*sNgags a'Ch'ang dBang Ch'en bZang Po*)
179 Sar po Chau gon (*Sar Po Byau mGon*)
180 Kye wu Zang ling Wang chug (*sKye Bu Zangs Gling dBang Phyug*)
181 Yang Pon Ri throd Pa seng (*Yang Bon Ri Khrod Pa Seng*)
182 Chang men Don drub Dar gye (*lChang sMan Don Grub Dar rGyas*)
183 Go Padma (*a'Gos Padma*)
184 Rang chung Ye shey (*Rang Byung Ye Shes*)
185 Se pen Nyi ma'i Nying po (*Se Ban Nyi Ma'i sNying Po*)
186 Lho trag pa, Kun ga Zang po (*Lho Brag Pa, Kun dGa' bZang Po*)
187 Drug gom Zhig po (*a'Brug sGom Zhig Po*)
188 Lha sum Chang chub Pal mo (*Lha gSum Byang Ch'ub dPal Mo*)
189 Mahā Badzar (*Mahāvajra*)

2. MIND AND PURE VISION TERTONS

1 Chang chub Sem pa, Da wa Gyal tshen (*Byang Ch'ub Sems dPa', Zla Ba rGyal mTshan*) (11th century)
2 Re chung, Dor je trag (*Ras Ch'ung, rDo rJe Grags*) (1084–1161)
3 Kha che Pendita, Śākyaśrī (*Kha Ch'e Paṇḍita, Śākyaśrī*) (1127–?)
4 Yu thog Yon ten Gon po (*gYu Thog Yon Tan mGon Po*) (second) (12th century)
5 Kyer gang, Cho kyi Seng ge (*sKyer sGang, Ch'os Kyi Seng Ge*) (11th century)
6 Karma pa, Rang chung Dor je (*Karmapa, Rang Byung rDo rJe*) (1284–1339)
7 Long chen Rab jam (*Klong Ch'en Rab a'Byams*) (1308–1363)
8 Lho trag Le kyi Dor je (*Lho Brag, Las Kyi rDo rJe*) (14th century)
9 Phen yul wa, Pal den Dor je (*a'Phan Yul Ba, dPal lDan rDo rJe*) (15th century)
10 Nag kyi Rin chen (*Nags Kyi Rin Ch'en, Vanaratna*) (1384–?)
11 Cho je, Kun ga Pal jor (*Ch'os rJe, Kun dGa' dPal a'Byor*) (15th century)
12 Nam kha Sod nam (*Nam mKha' bSod Nams*) (?)
13 Karma pa, Thong wa Don den (*Karmapa, mThong Ba Don lDan*) (1416–1453)
14 Re chen, Pal jor Zang po (*Ras Ch'en, dPal aByor bZang Po*) (15th century)
15 Tog den, Sang gye Gon po (*rTogs lDan, Sangs rGyas mGon Po*) (?)
16 Kun khyen, Padma Kar po (*Kun mKhyen, Padma dKar Po*) (1527–1592)
17 Gyal se, Ten pa'i Jung ne (*rGyal Sras, bsTan Pa'i a'Byung gNas*) (16th century)
18 Nang sal Rig dzin Tra shee Gya tsho (*sNang gSal Rig a'Dzin bKra Shis rGya mTsho*) (16th century)
19 Dri gung pa Zhab drung, Kon chog Rin chen (*a'Bri Gung Pa Zhabs Drung, dKon mCh'og Rin Ch'en*) (16th century)
20 Dri gung, Cho kyi Trag pa (*a'Bri Gung, Ch'os Kyi Grags Pa*) (17th century)

21 Lha tsun Nam kha Jig med (*Lha bTsun Nam mKha' aJigs Med*) (1597–1650?)
22 Sang dag Thrin le Lhun drub (*gSang bDag a'Phrin Las Lhun Grub*) (1611–1662)
23 Fifth Dalai Lama, Dor je Thog med tsal (*Fifth Ta La'i Bla Ma, rDo rJe Thogs Med rTsal*) (1617–1682)
24 Ne sar, Khyen tse'i Wang chug (*gNas gSar, mKhyen brTse'i dBang Phyug*) (1524–1587?)
25 Dri gung, Rin chen Phun tshog (*a'Bri Gung, Rin Ch'en Phun Tshogs*) (1509–1557)
26 Drub chen Nyi da Long sal (*Grub-Ch'en Nyi Zla Klong gSal*) (19th century)
27 Nam cho Mi gyur Dor je (*gNam Ch'os Mi a'Gyur rDo rJe*) (1645–1667)
28 Kar ma Chag med (*Karma Ch'ags Med*) (17th century)
29 Kun zang Cho kyi Dor je (*Kun bZang Ch'os Kyi rDo rJe*) (17th century)
30 Rig dzin Thug kyi Dor je (*Rig-a'Dzin Thugs Kyi rDo rJe*) (18th century)
31 Si tu, Padma Nyin ched Wang po (*Si Tu Padma Nyin Byed dBang Po*) (1774–1853)
32 Pa wo Tsug lag, Cho kyi Gyal po (*dPa' Bo gTsug Lag, Ch'os Kyi rGyal Po*) (19th century)
33 Fourth Chag med, Kar ma Ten dzin Thrin le (*4th Ch'ags Med, Karma bsTan a'Dzin Phrin Las*) (19th century)
34 Nga phod Ge gen, Padma Gyey pa (*Nga Phod dGe rGan, Padma dGyes Pa*) (18th century)
35 Tshe wang Mi gyur Dor je (*Tshe dBang Mi a'Gyur rDo rJe*) (18th century)
36 Kun khyen, Jig med Ling pa (*Kun mKhyen a'Jigs Med Gling Pa*) (1729–1798)
37 Pal ri Tul ku, Padma Cho jor Gya tsho (*dPal Ri sPrul sKu Padma Ch'os a'Byor rGya mTsho*) (18th century)
38 Do drub chen, Jig-med Thrin le Od zer (*rDo Grub Ch'en, a'Jigs Med a'Phrin Las A'od Zer*) (1745–1821)
39 Khe drub Ngag wang Dor je (*mKhas Grub Ngag dBang rDo rJe*) of E ne ring. (18th century)
40 Ka thog pa, Kun zang Nge don Wang po (*Ka Thog Pa, Kun bZang Nges Don dBang Po*) (18th century)
41 4th Dzog chen, Mi gyur Nam kha'i Dor je (*4th rDzogs Ch'en Mi a'Gyur Nam mKha'i rDo rJe*) (1793–?)

3 A FEW NAMES OF TERTONS NOT GIVEN IN *THE PRECIOUS GARLAND OF LAPIS LAZULI*

There are many important Tertons whose names or biographies are not given in *The Precious Garland of Lapis Lazuli*. Some of them are:

1 Rig dzin Nyi ma Trag pa (*Rig a'Dzin Nyi Ma Grags Pa*) (1647–1710)
2 Che yo, Rig dzin Chen Mo (*Ch'e Yos, Rig a'Dzin Ch'en Mo*) (18th century).
3 Sog po Cho gyal, Ngag gi Wang po (*Sog Po Ch'os rGyal Ngag Gi dBang Po*) (18th century)
4 Gam po pa, O gyen Dro dul Ling pa (*sGam Po Pa, O rGyan a'Gro a'Dul Gling Pa*) (18th century)
5 Rig dzin Dor je Thog med (*Rig a'Dzin rDo rJe Thogs Med*) (18th century)
6 Long chen Rol pa tsal (*Klong Ch'en Rol Pa rTsal*) (19th century)
7 Do Khyen tse, Ye shey Dor je (*mDo mKhyen brTse, Ye Shes rDo rJe*) (1800–1866).
8 Cho ying Top den Dor je (*Ch'os dByings sTobs lDan rDo rJe*) (19th century)
9 Ter ton, De chen Dor je of Re kong (*gTer sTon, bDe Ch'en rDo rJe of Re bsKong*) (19th century)
10 Nyag la, Pe ma Dud dul (*Nyag Bla, Padma bDud a'Dul*) (19th century)
11 Gyal se, De chen Ling pa (*rGyal Sras, bDe Chen Gling Pa*) (19th century)
12 Shug gang, Rig dzin Pe ma Du pa tsal (*Shugs sGang, Rig 'Dzin Padma'Dus Pa rTsal*) (1810–1872)
13 Kong tul, Yon ten Gya tsho (*Kong sPrul Yon Tan rGya mTsho*) (1813–1899)
14 Ge ter, Dud jom Ling pa (*rGes gTer, bDud a'Joms Gling Pa*) (1835–1903)
15 Khor dong, Nu den Dor je (*a'Khor gDong, Nus lDan rDo rJe*) (19th century)
16 A dzom Drug pa, Dro dul Dor je (*A a'Dzom a'Brug Pa, a'Gro a'Dul rDo rJe*) (1842–1925/6)
17 Ju Mi pham, Jam yang Nam gyal Gya tsho (*a'Ju Mi Pham, a'Jam dByangs rNam rGyal rGya mTsho*) (1846–1912)

18 Cho gyal Ling pa of Rong tha (*Ch'os rGyal Gling Pa of Rong Tha*)
19 Gar ra Long yang (*mGar Ba Klong Yangs*) (d.1912?)
20 Nyag la, Le rab Ling pa (*Nyag Bla, Las Rab Gling Pa*) (1856–1926)
21 Do mang, De chen Dor je Ling Pa (*mDo Mang, bDe Ch'en rDo rJe Gling Pa*) (1879–?)
22 Tulku Tri med (*sPrul sKu Dri Med*) (1881–1924)
23 Se ra Kha dro, De wa'i Dor je (*Se Ra mKha' a'Gro, bDe Ba'i rDo rJe*) (1899–1952?)
24 Je trung, Cham pa Jung ne (*rJe Drung, Byams Pa a'Byung gNas*)
25 Pal me Khyen tse, Kun zang De chen Dor je (*dPal Me mKhyen brTse, Kun bZang bDe Ch'en rDo rJe*) (1897–1946)
26 Khyung po, O gyen Kun trol Ling pa (*Khyung Po, O rGyan Kun Grol Gling Pa*)
27 Gar wa Gyal se, Pe ma Nam gyel (*mGar Ba rGyal Sras, Padma rNam rGyal*) (d.1951)
28 A pang Ter ton, O gyen Thrin le Ling pa (*A Pang gTer sTon, O rGyan Phrin Las Gling Pa*) (d.1945)
29 A kya Ter ton, Kha chod Ling pa (*A Kya gTer sTon, mKha' sPyod Gling Pa*) (1893–1939)
30 Nyag La, Chang chub Dor je (*Nyag Bla Byang Ch'ub rDo rJe*)
31 Khyen tse, Cho kyi Lo dro (*mKhyen brTse, Ch'os Kyi Blo Gros*) (1893–1959)
32 Tul ku Dor je Dra dul (*sPrul sKu rDo rJe dGra a'Dul*) (1894?–1958?)
33 Nga wang Ten dzin (*Ngag dBang bsTan a'Dzin*)
34 Gya rong Nam tul, Dro dul Gar gyi Dor je (*rGya Rong Nam sPrul, a'Gro a'Dul Gar Gyi rDo rJe*) (d.1956)
35 Lo Ter ton of Rab kha da (*Glo gTer sTon of Rab Kha mDa'*)
36 U ra Ter ton of A kyong Gong ma (*A'u Ra gTer sTon of A sKyong Gong Ma*)
37 Ling ter of Thra ling gar (*Gling gTer of Khra Gling sGar*)
38 Ga Ter ton of Nga wa (*rGa gTer sTon of rNga Ba*)
39 Chig Ter ton of Mar Bi tsha (*mCh'ig gTer sTon of sMar sBi Tsha*)

40 Dud jom, Jig tral Ye shey Dor je (*bDud a'Joms, a'Jigs Bral Ye Shes rDo rJe*) (1904–1987)
41 Tulku Kun zang Nyi ma (*sPrul sKu Kun bZang Nyi Ma*) (d.1958?)
42 Tulku Sod nam De tsen (*sPrul sKu bSod Nams lDeu bTsan*) (d.1958?)
43 Dil go Khyen tse, Tra shee Pal jor (*Dil mGo mKhyen brTse, bKra Shis dPal a'Byor*) (1910–)
44 Ka jur pa, Long chen Ye shey Dor je (*bKa' a'Gyur Pa, Klong Ch'en Ye Shes rDo rJe*) (d.1975)
45 Se ra Yang Tul (*Se Ra Yang sPrul*) (1926–1988)
46 Ga ra Gyal se, Pad lo (*mGar Ba rGyal Sras, Pad Lo*) (1927–?)
47 Do drup chen, Rig dzin Ten pa'i Gyal tshen (*rDo Grub Ch'en, Rig a'Dzin bsTan Pa'i rGyal mTshan*) (1927–1961)
48 Ta re Lha mo Nam Khay Pu mo (*Ta Re Lha Mo Nam mKha'i Bu Mo*) (1937–)

Key to Abbreviations
Bibliography
Notes
Glossary
Index

Key to Abbreviations

ADL Autobiography of the Terton Dud jom Ling pa.

AM The Noble Absorption – The Accumulation of All Merits.

BBT A Brief Biography of the Terton (Ja tshon Nying po) from the Kon ch'og Chi du Cycle.

BRL Biography of Guru Ratna Ling pa.

BT The Blessing Treasure, a Liturgy of Empowerment of Sādhanas of the Peaceful and Wrathful Eight Divinities (of the Cycle of) 'The Total Perfection of Esoteric Attainments.'

CCDS Compilation of Chronological Data from All Sources.

CLT The Celebration of the Illumination of the Teachings, a Brief Explanation of the Doctrine of the Early Translation of the Tantric Tradition.

CO The Chariot of Omniscience, a Commentary on the Resultant Vehicle of the Precious Treasure of Virtues.

CPW The Condensed Perfection of Wisdom.

CQSV The Mirror of Wisdom and Compassion with Hundreds of Radiances, a Commentary on the Quintessential Sublime Vision.

CT The Chariot of Two Truths, a Commentary on the Causal Vehicle of the Precious Treasure of Virtues.

CTI From the Cycle of the Assemblage of the Bliss Gone Ones, the Profound Path (on Avalokiteśvara) – the Catalogue of (the Contents of) the Two Images, Which are Liberating-by-Seeing.

EBT Entering the Bodhisattva's Training.
EMP Entering the Middle Path.
ER The Autobiography of Padma Ling pa – The Exquisite Ray.
ETV The Perfection of Wisdom in Eight Thousand Verses.
FIW The Root Empowerment Text of Tsa sum Rig dzin Srog drup – The Fruit of Immortal Wisdom.
GGD The Mind Sādhana of the Great Glorious Deities from the Long chen Nying thig Cycle.
GLE The Great Liturgy of Empowerment of the Sādhanas of the Eight Divinities (of the Cycle of) the Total Perfection of Esoteric Attainments.
GPUV The Elegant Teachings of the Golden Pin for Untying the Vajra-knots, a Commentary on the Precious Treasure of Virtues.
GSND Account of Long chen Nying thig – The Great Secret Narration of the Ḍākinīs.
HGC The Great History of the Terma of Guru Chö Wang.
HHVE The History of the Hidden Vajra Essence, the Key to the Visions of the Knowledge-Holders from the Cycle of Rig dzin Srog drup.
HKN History (of Kha dro Nying thig).
HRL The Great History of the Termas of Ratna Ling pa – The Clear Lamp.
HSL The Great History of the Termas of Sang gye Ling pa.
IC The Immortal Celebration, the Empowerment Liturgy of the Text for Extracting the Essence for Prolonging Longevity (Discovered by the Fifth Dalai Lama).
KHDA Catalogue of the Precious Treasury of the Termas and the Lineage of the Transmission of Empowerment, Instructions and Supplementary Teachings – The Key to a Hundred Doors of Accomplishment.
KPT The Key to the Precious Treasure, an Outline of the Glorious Esoteric Essence.
LGB The Lamp Illuminating the Great Blissful Path, a Note-Commentary on the Root-Sādhana of the Queen of Great Bliss, the Mother Knowledge-Holder.
MC The Mind Casket of the Crucial Prophetic Guide of Long chen Nying thig.
MCCM The Miraculous Clear Crystal Mirror, a New Clear and

Complete Chronicle of the Royal Lineages of the Great Land of Snow, Tibet.

MEV The Inner Biography of the Venerable Lama, the Great Terton, the King of the Dharma (i.e., Ter dag Ling pa) – The Music of Enormous Virtue.

NMP Notes on Main Points, a Note-Commentary to Clear the Meaning of the Root Text on Manjushri Yamantaka Entitled the Destroyer of Wrath.

OWC The Ornament of the Vision of Wisdom and Compassion, a Liturgy of Empowerment of the Essence of Liberation.

OID Autobiography of Tantrik Ja lu Dor je (or mDo mKhyen brTse Ye Shes rDor rJe) – The Oral Instructions of Ḍākinīs.

OS The Oral Instructions of the Master of the Secret Doctrine, a Commentary on the Glorious Esoteric Essence, the Ultimate Meaning.

PCD The Noble Perfect Condensation of the Doctrine.

PG History of the Kha dro Nying thig – The Precious Garland.

PGL A Brief History of the Profound Termas and Tertons – The Precious Garland of Lapis Lazuli.

PGV The Prophetic Guide from the Mind Sādhana of Vajrasattva Cycle.

POM The Prosperous Ocean of Marvels, a Biography of the Lord of Knowledge-Holders, Padmasambhava.

PPB The Noble Absorption: the Presence of the Present Buddha.

PV The Shower of Joy, a Precious Treasure of Virtues.

PWM Account of the Great Secret Experiences and Visions (of Jig med Ling pa) – The Play of the Water-moon.

RLST A Rough List of Scholars and Translators of the Land of Snow, Tibet.

RMP The Verses of the Root of the Middle Path Entitled 'Wisdom.'

RO Verses of the Refutation of the Objections.

RSKN The Noble Teachings at the Request of Sāgara, a King of the Nāgas.

SEE The Stages of Elaborated Empowerment, from the Cycle of Assemblage of the Bliss-Gone Ones, the

	Profound Path (on Avalokiteśvara).
SSR	The Verses of Sixty Stanzas on Reasoning.
ST	A Summary of the Theories in the Precious Wishing Treasure.
SVDG	The Authentic and Clear History of the Entire Buddha-Doctrine of the Land of Snow – The Sound of the Victory Drum of the Gods.
TOW	The Noble Teachings at the Request of Ocean Wisdom.
TPG	The Precious Garland.
WD	The Longer Version of Prayers to the Tertons – The Waves of Devotion.
WGL	A Brief Account of the Throne Successors of Both New and Old Tantric Schools of the Land of Snow, Tibet – The Wonder Garden of Lotuses.
WGU	A Brief Biography of the Lord, Omniscent Lama Khyen tse'i Wang po Kun ga Ten pa'i Gyal tsen – The Wonder Garden of Udamwara.
WL	White Lotus, the Commentary on the Precious Wishing Treasure (volumes I and II).
WO	A Brief and Clear Explanation of the Transmission of Termas – The Wonder Ocean.

Bibliography of Works Cited

1: HISTORY

ADL Autobiography of the Terton Dud jom Ling pa (1835–1903). gTer Ch'en Ch'os Kyi rGyal Po Khrag a'Thung bDud a'Joms Gling Pa'i rNam Par Thar Pa Zhal gSung Ma. Dud jom Ling pa. Published by Dupjung Lama 1978.

BBT A Brief Biography of the Terton (Ja tshon Nying po) (1586–1656) From the Kon ch'og Chi du Cycle. Yang Zab dKon mCh'og sPyi a'Dus Las, gTer sTon Gyi Lo rGyus rNam Thar Nying bsDus. Gampo pa Mi pham Ch'ö kyi Wang ch'ug.

BRL Biography of Guru Ratna Ling pa. Guru Ratna Gling Pa'i rNam Par Thar Pa'i mDzad Pa. Dro dul Ling trag. Published by Taglung Tsetrul Pema Wangyal 1979.

CCDS Compilation of Chronological Data From All Sources. bsTan rTsis Kun Las bTus Pa. Tshe ten Zhab trung (1910–). Published by mTsho sNgon Mi Rigs dPe bsKrun Khang, China.

CTI From the Cycle of the Assemblage of the Bliss Gone Ones, the Profound Path (on Avalokiteśvara)—the Catalogue of (the Contents of) the Two Images, Which are Liberating-By-Seeing. Zab Lam bDe gShegs Kun a'Dus Las, mThong Grol sKu rTen gNyis Kyi dKar Ch'ag bZhugs. Ter dag Ling pa. Published by Khorchen Tulku 1976.

DND A Dictionary of Numerical Divisions. rNam Grang rGya mTsho'i g Ter by Pe ma Rig dzin. Published by Lama Dodrup Sangyay 1977.

ER — The Autobiography of Padma Ling pa – The Exquisite Ray. Padma Gling Pa'i rNam Thar A'od Zer Kun mDzes Zhal gSung Ma completed by Gyal wa Don dup. Padma Ling pa. Published by Kunsang Tobgay 1975.

FIW — The Root Empowerment Text of Tsa sum Rig dzin Srog drup – The Fruit of Immortal Wisdom. rTsa gSum Rig a'Dzin Srog sGrub Kyi rTsa Ba'i dBang bsKur Ma Bu Zungs a'Brel blTas Ch'og Tu bKod Pa a'Ch'i Med Ye Shes Myu Gu. Lo drö Tha ye. Published by Jamyang Khyentse.

GSND — Account of Long chen Nying thig – The Great Secret Narration of the Ḍākinīs. Klong Ch'en sNying Gi Thig Le'i rTogs Pa brJod Pa Ḍākki'i gSang gTam Ch'en Mo. Jig med Ling pa (1729–1798). Published by Jamyang (Dilgo) Khyen tse.

HGC — The Great History of the Terma of Guru Chö Wang. Guru Ch'os dBang Gi gTer a'Byung Ch'en Mo. Guru Chö Wang (1212–1270). Published by Ngodrup and Sherab Drimay 1980. HGC

HHVE — The History of the Hidden Vajra Essence, the Key to the Visions of the Knowledge-Holders From the Cycle of Rig dzin Srog drup. Rig a'Dzin Srog sGrub Las, Lo Gyus Gab sBas rDo rJe'i Srog sNying Rig a'Dzin dGongs Pa'i lDeu Mig. Lha tsun Nam kha Jig med (1597–1650?). Published by Palace Temple, Sikkim.

HKN — History (of Kha dro Nying thig). (mKha' a'Gro sNying Thig Gi) Lo rGyus rGyal Ba gYung Gis mDzad Pa. Gyal wa yung. Published by Taglung Tsetrul Pema Wangyal 1976.

HPT — History of the Precious Ter Discovery. *gTer a'Byung Rin Po Ch'e'i Lo rGyus* (Vol. Om, mKha' 'Gro sNying Thig). Dri med Od zer. Published by Sherab Gyaltsen Lama.

HRL — The Great History of the Termas of Ratna Ling pa – The Clear Lamp. Guru Ratna Gling Pa'i gTer a'Byung Ch'en Mo gSal Ba'i sGron Me. Ratna Ling pa (1403–1478). Published by Taglung Tsetrul Pema Wangyal 1979.

HSL — The Great History of the Termas of Sang gye Ling pa. sPrul sKu Sangs rGyas Gling Pa'i gTer a'Byung

Ch'en Mo. Sang gye Ling pa (1340–1396).

IC The Immortal Celebration, the Empowerment Liturgy of the Text for Extracting the Essence for Prolonging Longevity (Discovered by the Fifth Dalai Lama). Tshe sGrub a'Chi Med Dangs Ma bChud a'Dren Gyi dBang Ch'og Ch'i Med dGa's Ton. Khyen tse'i Wang Po. Published by Gonpo Tseten 1977.

KHDA Catalogue of the Precious Treasury of the Termas and the Lineage of the Transmission of Empowerment, Instructions and Supplementary Teachings – The Key to a Hundred Doors of Accomplishment. Rin Po Ch'e gTer Gyi mDzod Ch'en Por Ji lTar bZhugs Pa'i dKar Ch'ag Dang sMin Grol rGyab rTen Dang bChas Pa'i brGyud Yig dNgos Grub sGo brGya a'Byed Pa'i lDeu Mig. Kong tul Yon ten Gya tsho. Published by Jamyang Khyentse.

MC The Mind Casket of the Crucial Prophetic Guide of Long chen Nying thig. Klong Ch'en sNying Gi Thig Le Las, gNad Byang Thugs Kyi sGrom Bu. Jig med Ling pa. Published by Jamyang Khyentse.

MCCM The Miraculous Clear Crystal Mirror, A New Clear and Complete Chronicle of Royal Lineages of the Great Land of Snow, Tibet. Gangs Chan Bod Ch'en Po'i rGyal Rabs a'Dus gSal Du bKod Pa sNgon Med Dvangs Shel a'Phrul Gyi Me Long. Jig tral Ye shey Dor je (1904–1987). Published by Duplung Lama 1978.

MEV The Inner Biography of the Venerable Lama, the Great Terton, the King of the Dharma (i.e., Ter dag Ling pa) – The Music of Enormous Virtue. rJe bTsun Bla Ma Dam Pa gTer Ch'en Ch'os Kyi rGyal Po'i Nang Gi rTogs Pa brJod Pa Yon Tan mTha' Yas rNam Par bKod Pa'i Rol Mo. Dharmaśrī. Published by Khorchen Tulku 1976.

OID Autobiography of Tantrik Ja lu Dor je [or mDo mKhyen brTse Ye Shes rDo rJe (1800–?)] – The Oral Instructions of Ḍākinīs. Rig a'Dzin a'Jigs Med Gling Pa'i Yang Srid sNgags a'Ch'ang a'Ja' Lus rDo rJe'i rNam Thar mKha' a'Gro'i Zhal Lung. Ja lu Dorje. Published by Dodrup Chen Rinpoche.

PG History of Kha dro Nying thig – The Precious Garland. mKha' a'Gro sNying Thig Gi Lo rGyus Rin Po Che'i Phreng Ba. Cha tral wa Zod pa. Published by Taglung Tsetrul Pema Wangyal 1976.

PGL A Brief History of the Profound Termas and Tertons – The Precious Garland of Lapis Lazuli. Zab Mo'i gTer Dang gTer sTon Grub Thob Ji lTar Byon Pa'i Lo Gyus mDor bsDus bKod Pa Rin Po Ch'e Baidurya'i Phreng Ba. Yon ten Gya tsho (1813–1899). Published by Ngodrup and Sherab Drimed 1977.

PGV The Prophetic Guide From the Mind Sādhana of Vajrasattva Cycle. rDor Sems Thug Kyi sGrub Pa Las, Zab gTer Kha Byang bZhugs So. Gyur med Dor je (1646–1714). Published by Khorchen Tulku 1976.

POM The Prosperous Ocean of Marvels, a Biography of the Lord of Knowledge-Holders, Padmasambhava. Rig a'Dzin Grub Pa'i dBang Phyug Ch'en Po Padma a'Byung gNas Kyi rNam Par Thar Ba Ngo mTshar Phun Sum Tshogs Pa'i rGya mTsho. Cham pa Ngag wang Sod nam Wang po Trag pa Gyal tshen (or Chang dag Tra shi Top gyal, 1550–1602?). Published by Sherap Gyaltsen Lama 1976.

PWM Account of the Great Secret Experiences and Visions (of Jig med Ling pa) – The Play of the Water-moon. gSang Ba Ch'en Po Nyams sNang Gi rTogs brJod Ch'u Zla'i Gar mKhan. Jig med Ling pa. Published by Jamyang Khyentse.

RLST A Rough List of Scholars and Translators of the Land of Snow, Tibet. Gangs Chan Gyi Yul Du Byon Pa'i Lo Pan rNams Kyi mTshan Tho Rag Rims Tshigs bChad Du sDebs Pa. Khyen tse'i Wang po. Published by Gonpo Tseten 1977.

SVDG The Authentic and Clear History of the Entire Buddha-Doctrine of the Land of Snow – The Sound of the Victory Drum of the Gods. Gangs lJongs rGyal Ba'i bsTan Pa Rin Po Ch'e Ji lTar Byung Ba'i Tshul Dag Ching gSal Bar brJod Pa Lha dBang gYul Las rGyal Ba'i rNga Bo Ch'e'i sGra dByangs. Jig tral Ye shey Dor je (1904–1987). Published by Dudjom Rinpoche 1967.

WD The Longer Version of Prayers to the Tertons – The Waves of Devotion. gTer sTon Rim Par Byon Pa rNams Kyi gSol a'Debs rGyas Par bKod Pa Mos Gus rGya mTsho'i rLabs a'Phreng. Yon ten Gya tsho. Published by Jamyang Khyentse.

WGL A Brief Account of the Throne Successors of Both New and Old Tantric Schools of the Land of Snow, Tibet – The Wonder Garden of Lotuses. Gangs Chan Bod Kyi Yul Du Byon Pa'i gSang sNgags gSar rNying Gi gDan Rabs mDor bsDus – Ngo mTshar Padmo'i dGa' Tshal. Khyen tse'i Wang po (1820–1892). Published by Gonpo Tseten 1977.

WGU A Brief Biography of the Lord, Omniscient Lama Khyen tse'i Wang po Kun ga Ten pa'i Gyal tsen – The Wonder Garden of Udamwara. rJe bTsun Bla Ma Thams Chad mKhyen Ching gZigs Pa a'Jam dByangs mKhyen brTse'i dBang Po Kun dGa' bsTan Pa'i rGyal mTshan dPal bZang Po'i rNam Thar mDor bsDus Pa Ngo mTshar U Dum Wa Ra'i dGa' Tshal. Lo dro Tha ye. Published by Jamyang (Dilgo) Khyentse.

WO A Brief and Clear Explanation of the Transmission of Termas – The Wonder Ocean. Las a'Phro gTer brGyud Kyi rNam bShad Nyung gSal Ngo mTshar rGya mTsho. Jig med Ten pa'i Nyi ma. Published by Dodrup Chen Rinpoche 1974.

2. SCRIPTURES AND COMMENTARIES

AM The Noble Absorption – The Accumulation of All Merits. a'Phags Pa bSod Nams Thams Chad sDud Pa'i Ting Nge a'Dzin. Āryasarva-puṇyasamucca-yasamādhi. Vol. Na, Do de, Kajur, Dege Edition.

BT The Blessing Treasure, a Liturgy of Empowerment of the Sādhanas of the Peaceful and Wrathful Eight Divinities (of the Cycle of) 'the Total Perfection of Esoteric Attainments'. Zhi Khro bKa' brGyad gSang Ba Yongs rDzogs Kyi dBang Gi Ch'o Ga Byin rLabs gTer mDzod by Sang gyey Ye shey (?). Published by Ngodrup and Sherab Drimay, Bhutan, 1979.

CIT The Celebration of the Illumination of the Teachings, a Brief Explanation of the Doctrine of the

Early Translation of the Tantric Tradition. gSang sNgags sNga a'Gyur rNying Ma Pa'i bsTan Pa'i rNam bZhag mDo Tsam brJod Pa Legs bShad sNang Ba'i dGa' sTon by Jig tral Ye shey Dor je (1904–1987). Published by Zang dog Pal ri monastery, Kalimpong.

CO The Chariot of Omniscience, a Commentary on the Resultant Vehicle of the Precious Treasure of Virtues. Yon Tan Rin Po Ch'e'i mDzod Las, a'Bras Bu'i Theg Pa'i rGya Ch'er a'Grel Ba rNam mKhyen Shing rTa by Jig med Ling pa. Published by Sonam T. Kazi.

CPW The Condensed Perfection of Wisdom. a'Phags Pa Shes Rab Kyi Pha Rol Tu Phyin Pa sDud Pa Tshigs Su bChad Pa. Aryaprajñāpāramitā-sañcayagāthā. Vol. Ka, Sher Phyin, Kajur, Dege edition.

CQSV The Mirror of Wisdom and Compassion with Hundreds of Radiances, a Commentary on the Quintessential Sublime Vision. dGongs a'Dus rNam bShad mKhyen brTse'i Me Long A'od Zer brGya Pa by Jig med Ling pa. Published by Sonam T. Kazi.

CT The Chariot of Two Truths, a Commentary on the Causal Vehicle of the Precious Treasure of Virtues. Yon Tan Rin Po Ch'e'i mDzod Las, rGyu'i Theg Pa'i rGya Ch'er a'Grel Ba bDen gNyis Shing rTa by Jig med Ling pa. Published by Sonam T. Kazi.

EBT Entering the Bodhisattva's Training. Byang Ch'ub Sems dPa'i sPyod Pa La a'Jug Pa. Bodhicaryāvatāra by Śāntideva. Vol. La, Madhyamaka, Tenjur, Dege Edition.

EMP Entering the Middle Path. dBu Ma La a'Jug Pa. Madhyamakāvatāra by Candrakīrti. Vol. A', Madhyamaka, Tenjur, Dege Edition.

ETV The Perfection of Wisdom in Eight Thousand Verses. a'Phags Pa Shes Rab Kyi Pha Rol Tu Phyin Pa brGya sTong Pa. Āryaprajñāpāramitā-aṣṭasāhasrikā. Vol. Ka, Sher Phyin, Kajur, Dege Edition.

GEE The Glorious Esoteric Essence, the Illusory Net. dPal gSang Ba sNying Po sGyu a'Phrul Drva Ba. Guhyagarbhamāyājālatantra. Vol. Kha, Nying Gyud, Kajur, Dege Edition.

GGD The Mind Sādhana of the Great Glorious Deities From the Long chen Nying thig Cycle. Klong Ch'en sNying Gi Thig Le Las, Thugs sGrub dPal Ch'en a'Dus Pa discovered by Jig med Ling pa (1729–1798). Published by Dodrup Chen Rinpoche.

GLE The Great Liturgy of Empowerment of the Sādhanas of the Eight Divinities (of the Cycle of) 'the Total Perfection of Esoteric Attainments.' bKa' brGyad gSang Ba Yongs rDzogs Kyi dBang Ch'og Ch'en Mo discovered by Guru Chö Wang Published by Ngodrup and Sherab Drimay, Bhutan 1979.

GPUV The Elegant Teachings of the Golden Pin for Untying the Vajra-knots, a Commentary on the Precious Treasure of Virtues. Yon Tan Rin Po Ch'e'i mDzod Kyi dKa' gNad rDo rJe'i rGya mDud a'Grol Byed Legs bShad gSer Gyi Thur Ma by (Sog po) Ten dar Lha ram pa (1759–?). Published by Jamyang (Dilgo) Khyentse.

KPT The Key to the Precious Treasure, an Outline of the Glorious Esoteric Essence. dPal gSang Ba sNying Po'i sPyi Don Rin Ch'en mDzod Kyi lDeu Mig by Jig med Ten pa'i Nyi ma (1865–1926). Published by Dodrup Chen Rinpoche.

LGB The Lamp Illuminating the Great Blissful Path, a Note-Commentary on the Root-Sādhana of the Queen of Great Bliss, the Mother Knowledge-Holder. Rig a'Dzin Yum Ka bDe Ch'en rGyal Mo'i sGrub gZhung Gi Zin Bris bDe Ch'en Lam bZang gSal Ba'i sGon Me by Jig med Ten pa'i Nyi ma. Published by Dodrup Chen Rinpoche 1974.

NMP Notes on Main Points, a Note-Commentary to Clear the Meaning of the Root Text on Mañjuśrī Yamantaka Entitled the Destroyer of Wrath. a'Jam dPal gShin rJe'i gShed Dregs Pa a'Joms Byed Kyi rTsa Ba 'i gZhungs Don gSal Byed Kyi mCh'an a'Grel rTsa Tho Zin Bris by Dharmaśrī (1654–1717/ 8).

OWC The Ornament of the Vision of Wisdom and Compassion, a Liturgy of Empowerment of the Essence of Liberation. Grol Thig dBang Ch'og mKhyen brTse'i dGongs rGyan by Jig med Ling pa. Published by Sonam T. Kazi.

OS — The Oral Instructions of the Master of the Secret Doctrine, a Commentary on the Glorious Esoteric Essence, the Ultimate Meaning. gSang Ba'i sNying Po De Kho Na Nyid Nges Pa'i rGyud Kyi a'Grel Ba gSang bDag Zhal Lung by Dharmaśrī. Published by Min trol ling monastery.

PCD — The Noble Perfect Condensation of the Doctrine. a'Phags Pa Ch'os Thams Chad Yang Dag Par sDud Pa. Ārya-dharmasaṁgīti. Vol. Zha, Do de, Kajur, Dege Edition.

PPB — The Noble Absorption: The Presence of the Present Buddha. a'Phags Pa Da lTar Gyi Sangs rGyas mNgon Sum Du bZhugs Pa'i Ting Nge a'Dzin. Ārya-pratyutpanne-buddhasamukhā-vasthita-samādhi. Vol. Na, Do de, Dege Edition.

PV — The Shower of Joy, a Precious Treasure of Virtues. Yon Tan Rin Po Ch'e'i mDzod dGa' Ba'i Ch'ar by Jig med Ling pa. Published by Sonam T. Kazi 1971.

RMP — The Verses of the Root of the Middle Path Entitled 'Wisdom.' dBu Ma rTsa Ba'i Tshigs Leur Byas Pa Shes Rab Zhes Bya Ba. Prajñā-nāma-mūlamadhyamaka-karikā by Nāgārjuna. Vol. Tsa, Madhyamaka, Tenjur, Dege Edition.

RO — Verses of the Refutation of the Objections. rTsod Pa bZlog Pa'i Tshigs Leur Byas Pa. Vigrahavyāvartanī-kārikā by Nāgārjuna. Vol. Tsa, Madhyamaka, Tenjur, Dege Edition.

RSKN — The Noble Teachings at the Request of Sāgara, a King of the Nāgas. a'Phags Pa Klu'i rGyal Po rGya mTshos Zhus Pa. Āryasāgaranāgarājaparipṛccha-sūtra. Vol. Pha, Do de, Kajur, Dege Edition.

SEE — The Stages of Elaborated Empowerment, from the Cycle of the Assemblage of the Bliss-Gone Ones, the Profound Path (on Avalokiteśvara). Zab Lam bDe gShegs Kun a'Dus Las, sPros bChas dBang Gi Rim Pa discovered by Ter dag Ling pa (1646–1714).

SSR — The Verses of Sixty Stanzas on Reasonings. Rigs Pa Drug Chu Pa'i Tshigs Leur Byas Pa. Yuktiṣaṣṭikakārikā by Nāgārjuna. Vol. Tsa, Madhyamaka, Tenjur, Dege Edition.

ST — A Summary of the Theories in the Precious Wishing Treasure. Yid dZhin mDzod Kyi Grub mTha' bsDus Pa by Mi pham Nam gyal (1846–1912). Published by Dodrup Chen Rinpoche.

TOW — The Noble Teachings at the Request of Ocean Wisdom. a'Phags Pa Blo Gros rGya mTshos Zhus Pa. Ārya-sāgarmatiparipṛcchā. Vol. Pha, Do de, Kajur, Dege Edition.

TPG — The Precious Garland. Rin Po Ch'e'i Phreng Ba. Ratnavali by Nāgārjuna. Vol. Ge, sPring Yig, Tenjur, Dege Edition.

WL — White Lotus, the Commentary on the Precious Wishing Treasure (Volume I and II). Yid bZhin Rin Po Ch'e'i mDzod Kyi a'Grel Pa Pad Ma dKar Po by Long chen Rab jam (1308–1363). Published by Dodrup Chen Rinpoche.

Notes

PART ONE

1 See Appendix 2
2 WL Vol. II, page 71– 9
3 RO page 28a
4 RMP page 1b
5 RMP page 14b
6 Quoted in WL Vol. II, page 756
7 EBT
8 EMP Page 15a
9 RO page 28a
10 RMP page 6a
11 RO page 29a
12 RMP page 15a
13 SSR page 22b
14 ETV page 142b
15 PG page 115a
16 EBT
17 EBT
18 CPW page 2b
19 EMP page 16b
20 EBT
21 EBT
22 WL Vol. II, page 79b
23 Hevajra-tantra quoted in WL Vol. II, page 80a
24 PV page 48b
25 OS page 35a

26 Quoted in CLT page 22b
27 Quoted in SVDG page 19a
28 According to SVDG (page 396b/6) the king was born in the Fire Ox Year (617ad). According to MCCM he was born in the Fire Ox Year (617ad) (page 18b/5) and died in the Earth Dog Year (698 ad) (page 69a/3).

The views of several historians are presented in CCDS as follows: *Chronicle of Royal Lineages of Tibet* by Sa chen Trag pa Gyal tshen, *History of Buddhism* by Bu ton Rin chen grub, *Chronicle of Royal Lineages of Tibet* by Pan chen Sod trag, *Khey pa'i Ga ton (mKhas Pa'i dGa' sTon), The Dharma History* by Tsug lag Threng wa, *The Red Annals* by Tshal pa Kun ga Dor je, *Pag sam Jon zang (dPag bSam lJon bZang), The Dharma History* by Sum pa Khen po Ye shey Pal jor and CCDS agree that the king was born in the Fire Ox Year (617 ad) and died in the Earth Dog Year (698 ad) at the age of 82. Also *Thub ten Sal war Ched pa'i Nyin ched (Thub bs Tan gSal Bar Byed Pa'i Nyin Byed), The Dharma History* by Long chen Rab jam, *Chronicle of Royal Lineages of Tibet* by Sa kya Lama Sod nam Gyal tshen and the writings of Jam yang Zhed pa agree that he was born in the Fire Ox Year (617 ad). However, *The Blue Annals* by Go lo Zhon nu Pal, Dzog den Zhon nu'i Ga ton (*rDzogs lDan gZhon Nu'i dGa' sTon*), *Chonicle of Royal Lineages of Tibet* by the Fifth Dalai Lama, *The White Lapis Lazuli* by De sid Sang gye Gya tsho and the writings of Jig med Ling pa and Pal tul Jig med Cho kyi Wang po, Ju Mi pham Nam gyal and *My Land and My People* by the Fourteenth Dalai Lama agree that he was born in the Earth Ox Year (629 ad).

29 According to SVDG the king was born in the Iron Horse Year (790 ad) (page 396b/3) and died in the Earth Dragon Year (848ad) (page 81b/3) at the age of 59. According to *Ka thang Zang ling ma* (*bKa' Thang Zangs Gling Ma*) (page 72b/2) discovered by Nyang Nyi ma Od zer, PGL (page 12b/5), and MCCM (page 163a/3) he was born in the Iron Horse Year (790 ad) but died in the Earth Tiger Year (858 ad) at the age of 69.

The views of several historians are presented in CCDS as follows: *Chronicle of Royal Lineages of Tibet* by Sa chen Trag pa Gyal tshen, *The Red Annals* by Tshal pa Kun ga Dor je, *Sal wa'i Me long, Cronicle of Royal Lineages of Tibet* by Sod nam Gyal tshen, *The Dharma History* by

Sum pa Khen po and CCDS agree that the king was born in the Iron Horse Year (790 ad) and died in the Wood Ox Year (845 ad). *My Land and My People* by the Fourteenth Dalai Lama also agrees that the king was born in the Iron Horse Year (790 ad). However, among others, *The History of Buddhism* by Bu ton and *Chronicle of Royal Lineages of Tibet* by Pan chen Sod trag agree that he was born in the Earth Horse Year (778 ad) and died in the Fire Tiger Year (846 ad).

PART TWO

30 See Appendix 3 and 4
31 See Appendix 3
32 See Appendix 3
33 HKN page 204b
34 Concerning the duration of Guru Padmasambhava's stay in Tibet the differing views of historians range from 6 months to over 55 years.

According to SVDG (page 81b/1 and 396b/3), PGL (page 12b/5), MCCM (page 163a/3) and *The Biography of Guru Padmasambhava* (page 37b/6) by Sog dog pa Lo tro Gyal tshen he came to Tibet in the Iron Tiger Year (810 ad) and after staying for fifty-five years and six months he left Tibet in the Wood Monkey Year (864 ad).

CCDS assembles the views of some historians, some of which are listed here. According to *The White Lapis Lazuli* by De sid Sang gye Gya tsho he came to Tibet in the Earth Ox Year (749 ad) and left in the Wood Monkey Year (804 ad). According to the writings of Min ling Lo chen Dharmasri, Pal tul Jig med Cho kyi Wang po and Ju mi pham Nam gyal he came to Tibet in the Water Tiger Year (822 ad) and left in the Fire Monkey Year (876 ad).

PART THREE

35 Quoted in SVDG page 19a
36 GGD page 116b

37 TOW page 139a
38 AM page 96b
39 PGL page 56
40 PGL page 50
41 See Appendix 5
42 OWC page 24a
43 CQSV page 24b
44 HKN page 208b
45 HKN page 209b
46 HKN page 210a
47 WO page 46
48 CQSV page 25a
49 CQSV page 40a
50 WO page 4b
51 PGL page 125b
52 WO page 106
53 WGL page 20a
54 See Appendix 6
55 See Appendix 6, part 3
56 HRL Page 38a
57 PGL page 82b
58 MEV page 62a
59 ADL page 48b
60 HRL page 107b
61 ER page 245
62 HSL page 18b
63 ADL page 49b
64 MEV page 65a
65 ADL page 51a
66 PGL page 86a
67 HRL page 64b
68 HRL page 61b
69 HGC page 36a
70 HGC page 49a
71 WGU page 88a
72 WGU page 89b
73 WGU page 91b
74 WO page 8a
75 OID page 90b
76 PGL page 225a

77 WO page 16b
78 ADL page 51a
79 WGU page 93a
80 GSND
81 MC
82 IC page 4a
83 HHVE page 3b
84 WO page 33b
85 WGU page 113a
86 WO page 30–31a

PART FOUR

87 OID page 93b
88 GPUV page 270a
89 WD page 15a
90 S. Padmasambhava, T. *Padma a'Byung gNas*. The Lotus Born. One of the greatest tantric siddhas (those who have attained the result of esoteric Buddhist practice). His visit to Tibet during the reign of King Thri srong Deu tsen (750–858) accomplished three major aims: (1) Through his enlightened miraculous power he subdued both human and non-human negative forces obstructing the introduction of Buddhism. (2) He was chiefly responsible for establishing Buddhism in Tibet, notably esoteric, tantric Buddhism, by translating texts, teaching and transmitting empowerments. (3) He was almost solely responsible for concealing esoteric teachings as Ter (*gTer*) for the benefit of future followers. He achieved deathless attainment, and after fifty-five years and six months in Tibet, he departed for his pure land, Copper Colored Mountain, without leaving his body behind. He is popularly known as Guru Rinpoche, the Precious Teacher, or Lobpon Rinpoche (*Slob dPon Rin Po Ch'e*), the Precious Master.
91 S. Tantra, T. Sang ngag (*gSang sNgags*), the esoteric teachings. In Buddhism there are thousands of tantric teachings related to hundreds of different levels of maṇḍalas (cycles) of deities. Through tantric practice

Buddhahood, enlightenment, can be achieved in this very life or within the next few lives, while through common Mahāyāna practice it requires countless eons. The Hinayāna scriptures teach that Buddhahood is just possible for an ordinary person. The goal of their practice is Arhathood, the cessation of emotions and suffering. The Nyingma tradition divides the tantras into six categories: Three Outer Tantras and Three Inner Tantras. The Three Outer Tantras are: Kriyāyoga emphasizing physical practices; Caryāyoga emphasizing both physical practices and view, and Yogatantra emphasizing the view. The Three Inner Tantras are: Mahāyoga emphasizing the Development Stage (S. *Utpannakrama*, T. *bsKyed Rim*); Anuyoga, emphasizing the Perfection Stage (S. *Sampannakrama*, T. *rDzogs Rim*); and Atiyoga, in which the practice is contemplation on the inseparability of the Development and Perfection Stages, the Great Perfection (S. *Mahasandhi*, T. *rDzogs Pa Ch'en Po*). This is the highest esoteric teaching and practice of the Nyingma. It is a method of practice to introduce one to or to realize the natural state of mind, which is Buddhahood. In respect to transmission, there are two categories of tantras in the Nyingma: Ka ma (S. *Vacana*, T. *bKa' Ma*), the original teachings which came through the long lineage, transmitted from teacher to disciple; and Terma (*gTer Ma*), transmitted through the short lineage from the concealer to the discoverer.

92 Nyingma (*rNying Ma* or *gSang sNgags rNying Ma*), the followers of the Ancient Tantric Tradition, the oldest Buddhist school in Tibet.

93 Canonical Teachings, Ka ma (*bKa' Ma*), include both exoteric (S. *Sūtra*, T. *mDo*) and esoteric (S. *Tantra*, T. *gSang sNgags*) teachings. Unlike the Termas, they are transmitted lineally from teacher to disciple. It is called Long Transmission of Canonical Teachings.

94 Ter ma (*gTer Ma*). The transmission system of Discovered Esoteric Dharma Treasure teachings. *Ter* means treasure and *Ter chö* means Dharma Treasure teachings.

95 Pure Vision, Dag nang (*Dag sNang*), are teachings which a spiritual master receives in pure vision from a Buddha, sage, guru or deity.

96 S. Samantabhadra, T. Kun tu Zang po (*Kun Tu bZang Po*), the Primordial Buddha. In the Nyingma tantric tradition Samantabhadra refers to the dharmakāya, the ultimate body of the three bodies of the Buddha, a Mahāyāna doctrine. The three bodies are: dharmakāya, saṃbhogakāya and nirmāṇakāya. Dharmakāya is free from visual form, dialectic expression or conceptual conventions. In art, the Nyingma tradition represents Samantabhadra as a naked blue Buddha symbolizing freedom from obstructions and changes, like the sky or space. (The Bodhisattva Samantabhadra is a different figure.)

97 S. Vajrasattva, T. Dor je Sem pa (*rDo rJe Sems dPa'*), a Buddha in Saṃbhogakāya form. Saṃbhogakāya or the Enjoyment Body is pure and subtle form which can be perceived only by accomplished persons. It is endowed with the qualities of five certainties and 112 major and minor signs and marks. It is attired in the thirteenfold saṃbhogakāya costumes and ornaments. Although in general Vajrasattva is the head of the Vajra family of Buddhas and the presiding Buddha of the eastern Pure Land, in Nyingma tantric practice he figures as the main Buddha and his maṇḍala as the pervading one of all the deities. He is also worshipped particularly for purification of emotional defilements and evil deeds.

98 Mind Transmission, Gong gyud (*dGongs brGyud*), is the first of three ways of transmitting esoteric teachings according to the Nyingma scriptures. It is the way of transmitting teachings or power between Buddhas themselves. It is also known as Gyal wa Gong gyud (*rGyal Ba dGongs brGyud*), the Mind Transmission of the Buddhas. The teacher transmits the teachings to a disciple without using words or indication, the disciple being inseparable from the teacher as is a reflection of the moon in still and clear water.

99 Indication Transmission, Da gyud (*brDa brGyud*), is the way of transmitting the teachings and powers by a knowledge-holder or Buddha to a knowledge-holder or highly accomplished person. The disciples receive and understand the whole teachings and power just by an indication or gesture, verbal or physical, by the master. It is known as Rig dzin Da gyud (*Rig a'Dzin brDa*

brGyud), the Indication Transmission of Knowledge-holders.

100 Hearing or Aural Transmission, Nyen gyud (*sNyan brGyud*), is the way of transmitting teachings to ordinary people by realized and ordinary masters. It is known as Nal jor Na gyud (*rNal a'Byor rNa brGyud*), Hearing Transmission Between Yogis (esoteric practitioners) or Kang zag Nyen gyud (*Gang Zag sNyan brGyud*), Hearing Transmission Between People. In this system the complete verbal empowerment and instructions are transmitted by master to disciple from mouth to ear.

101 Ter ton (*gTer sTon*) means Treasure Discoverer; in the Nyingma tradition one who withdraws texts and sacred objects of Dharma from their places of concealment.

102 Doctrine-holder, Chö dag (*Ch'os bDag*), the chief receiver and holder of a Terma; the most important figure in the lineage after the Terton himself.

103 Eight Great Maṇḍalas, Drub pa Ka gyed (*sGrub Pa bKa' br Gyad*), a sādhana of eight maṇḍalas, cycles, of eight deities; one of the most important esoteric sādhana scriptures in the Nyingma tradition. It belongs to the Mahāyoga category in the classification of the nine yānas or six tantras of the Nyingma. Many Tertons have discovered sādhana texts on this maṇḍala of deities. Although it is actually a maṇḍala of eight assemblages of deities, the maṇḍalas of La ma Rig dzin (*Bla Ma Rig a'Dzin*) are added to them making a sequence of nine maṇḍalas:

1. Che chog Dud tsi Yon ten (*Ch'e mCh'og bDud rTsi Yon Tan*), the deity of quality
2. Yang dag (*Yang Dag*), the deity of mind
3. Jam pal Shin je shed (*S. Mañjuśrī Yamantaka*), the deity of body
4. Padma Ta drin (S. *Padma Hyagriva*, T. *Padma rTa mGrin*), the deity of speech
5. Dor je Phur pa (S. *Vajrakīla*, T. *rDo rJe Phur Pa*), the deity of action
6. Ma mo Bod tong (*Ma Mo rBod gTong*), the worldly deities of inciting and dispatching

7. Rig dzin Lob pon (*Rig a'Dzin Slob dPon*) or La ma Rig dzin (*Bla Ma Rig a'Dzin*), the Guru (spiritual master)
8. *Jig ten Chod tod* (*a'Jigs rTen mCh'od brTod*), the worldly deities of offering and praise
9. *Mod pa Trag ngag* (*dMod Pa Drag sNgags*), the worldly deities of exorcism

104 *Sang dzog* (*gSang rDzogs*) is a Terma text in six volumes discovered by Guru Chö Wang (1212–1270), one of the two greatest Tertons of the Nyingma school. The full title is *Ka gyed Sang wa Yong dzog* (*bKa' brGyad gSang Ba Yongs rDzogs*). It is one of the three major Termas on the Eight Great Orders of Maṇḍalas of Eight Deities (*sGrub Pa bKa' brGyad*).

The following quotation is from GLE (page 52), one of the many texts which comprise the *Sang dzog*. I used an incomplete edition published by Ngodrup and Sherab Drimay, 1979 in Bhutan. There are different readings in the quotations given in *Wonder Ocean* and similar passages in GLE. *Wonder Ocean* may have used one of the other texts which is missing from the edition I read, or it could even be that the variants occurred because of different editions or calligraphers. Also *Wonder Ocean* may have been quoting from *Rang shar*, which I was unable to find. However, the most important points in both versions are identical. They explain in one voice the way of transmitting the teachings to the Tertons by Guru Padmasambhava and how the teachings are discovered by the Tertons by the awakening of the traces or recollections (*Bag Ch'ags*) of the transmissions which they received in their past lives from Guru Padmasambhava. In GLE (page 4b/4) it is said:

> Thus all the aspects of the stream of empowerment were transmitted to me, *U gyen [Oḍḍiyāna = Padmasambhava]*. I opened the door of the empowerment of *Zhi ba Dor je Ying* (*Zhi Ba rDo rJe dByings*) at Yang le shod in Nepal and transmitted it to Vimala (mitra). I bestowed the eight different empowerments of divinities of Eight Great Maṇḍalas upon

the Eight Great Fortunate Ones at eight different sacred places in Tibet. At the summit (the main temple) of Sam ye [monastery] I conferred the great empowerment of De sheg Du pa (*bDe gShegs a'DusPa*) on the Lord [king] and his subjects, the twenty-five chief disciples. After that, I transmitted the complete empowerment of Sang wa Yong dzog (*gSang Ba Yongs rDzogs*) to the Lord [king], subject (*Nam mKha'i sNying Po*), and friend (*Ye Shes mTsho rGyal*) and to the rest, the nine heart-sons. Thus I explained how the stream of empowerment has been transmitted without being broken. [Now I shall give] the prophecy of the future course of the unbroken stream of empowerment. In future, when the time is close to the age of struggles and dregs, a rebirth [i.e. Nyang Nyi Ma A'od Zer, 1124–1192] of the Lord, yourself, will encounter my heart-secret teachings such as the cycle of *Ka gyed De sheg Du pa (bKa' brGyad bDe gShegs a'Dus Pa,* in nine or thirteen volumes) in a valley which has the shape of the opened corpse of a red horse to the south west of Sam ye, and the unbroken stream of empowerment will be maintained. Because, (*Nyang Nyi Ma A'od Zer*) having awakened the recollection (*Bag Ch'ags*) of today's completion of the stream of empowerment which is (vested) in you, Lord, he will be endowed with the transmission (*bKa' Babs*). Then, having perfected his spiritual training, he (Nyang) will go to the Blissful (*T. bDe Ba Chan, S. Sukhavati*) Pure Land. Not long after that, a Bodhisattva, subduer of beings, an incarnation of yourself, and a heart-son of mine [i.e. *Guru Ch'os dBang*], will enjoy the transmission/command (*bKa' Babs*) of the excellent *Yong dzog* [i.e. *gSang Ba Yongs rDzogs*]. In that very life of his, I will cause to awaken in him the recollections (*Bag Ch'ags*) of the great empowerment of *Yong dzog*. He will also discover the Ters of my mind-treasures and the precious teachings given exclusively to the lord, subject and friend. Make sure that no doubts about the authenticity of the stream of empowerment arise in the minds of future followers, and keep the [teachings] strictly [secret] from inappropriate people.

105 Rang shar (*Rang Shar*). One of the three major Termas on the *Eight Great Orders of Maṇḍalas of Eight Deities*. Its full title is *Ka gyed Trag po Rang chung Rang shar* (*bKa' brGyad Drag Po Rang Byung Rang Shar*, four volumes), discovered by Rig dzin God dem (1337–1408), who founded the Chang ter (*Byang gTer*) sub-school of the Nyingma.

106 Empowerment or Initiation, Wang (S. *Abhiṣekha*, T. *dBang*). In tantric Buddhism empowerment is the entrance to practice. Its purpose is the transmission of esoteric power by a master to his disciples. Usually empowerments take place in ceremonies, each tantric scripture having its own empowerment. Without it one is not permitted to practice or even to read an esoteric scripture. Tantric empowerments and teachings were conferred in great secrecy in ancient times, and often this is still the case. Empowerment is for the purpose of awakening through an external support, such as the blessing power of the master, the inner power or enlightened nature which we possess. After the empowerment the disciples observe the obligations (*samaya*) and meditate on the awakened realization achieved during the empowerment. They practice the two major aspects of tantric meditation, the Development and Perfection Stages, perfecting the realization into a fully enlightened state. Empowerment is the most important key to esoteric practice and is only for people who have prepared themselves to receive it by finishing all the necessary preliminary practices. Nowadays in Tibetan communities hundreds of people obtain empowerments without any preparation. Although they will not receive any special power or realization without preparation, if they have devotion they will receive a special blessing, which is the reason why lamas consent to perform these ceremonies. Empowerments vary according to tantras and texts. An empowerment of an Inner Tantra (*Nang*

rGyud) of the Nyingma may begin with the Common Preliminary and Uncommon Preliminary Empowerments, followed by four actual Empowerments: Vase, Secret, Wisdom and Symbolic or Verbal Empowerments, and concluding empowerments.

107 S. Oḍḍiyāna, T. O gyen (*O rGyan* or *U rGyan*) was a province of ancient India. Many masters, including Guru Padmasambhava, came from that center of tantric teachings. Modern scholars recognize the Swat valley in Pakistan as the location of Oḍḍiyāna.

108 Yang le shöd, a place in Nepāl where, in a cave, Guru Padmasambhava did the practice of the maṇḍalas of the deities Yang dag (S. Vajraheruka) and Dor je Phur pa (S. Vajrakīla, T. *rDo rJe Phur Pa*) for three years with the spiritual support of one of his consorts, Śākyadevi of Nepāl. He attained the state of Mahamudrā Vidyādhara. Today the place is known as Pharping.

109 S. Vimalamitra, T. Tri med Shey nyen (*Dri Med bShes gNyen*), one of the greatest Indian Buddhist scholars. He went to Tibet in the ninth century and taught, wrote and translated many teachings on sutric and tantric scriptures. One of his innermost teachings is on Nying thig (S. *Cittatilaka*, T. *sNying Thig*), the Innermost Essence of Dzog pa Chen po (S. *Mahāsandhi*, T. *rDzogs Pa Ch'en Po*) or Atiyoga, which became known as Vima Nying thig.

110 Eight Fortunate People. The transmission of empowerment (S. *Abhiṣekha*, T. *dBang*) of the Eight Great Orders of Maṇḍalas (*sGrub Pa bKa' brGyad*) was given by Guru Padmasambhava to his eight fortunate disciples in Tibet:

1. Che chog (*Ch'e mCh'og*) to King Thri song Deu tsen
2. Yang dag to Nub Nam kha'i Nying po
3. Yamantaka to Nub Sang gye Ye shey
4. Hyagriva to Gyal wa Chog yang
5. Vajrakīla to Ye shey Tsho gyal
6. Ma mo to Drog mi Pal gyi Ye shey
7. Jig ten Chod tod (*a'Jigs rTen mCh'od bsTod*) to Lang Pal gyi Ye shey
8. Mod pa Trag ngag (*dMod Pa Drag sNgags*) to Vairocana

According to BT (page 5a/6) Che chog or Dud tsi Che chog (*bDud rTsi Ch'e mCh'og*) was transmitted to Nyag Jñāna Kumāra (S. *Jñānakumāra*, T. *gNyag*) instead of to the King.

111 Sam ye (*bSam Yas*), the oldest monastery in Tibet, was built in the ninth century by King Thri srong Deu tsen (790--858) under the guidance of Guru Padmasambhava and Śāntarakṣita, a celebrated scholar of Mahāyāna Buddhism and abbot of Nālandā, the famous monastic university in India. Sam ye has a huge three-story temple at the center and large temples on the four sides, eight smaller temples between, and stūpas at the four corners. They are surrounded by a high wall topped by 108 small stūpas. The temples were used as halls of worship, teaching, translation and meditation. They were filled with scriptures and religious objects both Tibetan and from India, Nepāl and Central Asia.

112 De sheg dü pa (*bDe gShegs a'Dus Pa*) is one of the three Termas on the Eight Great Orders of Maṇḍalas in nine volumes. It was discovered by Nyang Nyi ma Od zer (1124–1192), one of the two greatest Tertons of the Nyingma.

113 Lord, Je (*rJe*) here indicates King Thri srong Deu tsen, the thirty-seventh king of the Chö gyal (*Ch'os rGyal*) dynasty (127 BC – 906 AD). He was the chief patron of Guru Padmasambhava and the Buddhist scholars of Tibet.

114 Subjects, Bang (*a'Bangs*) here refers to the twenty-five chief disciples of Guru Padmasambhava. There are two ways to count them: In the first, the twenty-five are the lord and the subjects, excluding either Yu dra Nying po (*gYu sGra sNying* Po) or Drog mi Pal gyi Ye shey (*a'Brog Mi dPal Gyi Ye Shes*). In the second they are the twenty-five subjects, with both Yu dra Nying po and Drog mi Pal gyi Ye shey but not the King. According to the second list, the twenty-five chief disciples are:

1. Nub chen Sang gye Ye shey (*gNub Ch'en Sang rGyas Ye Shes*), one of the greatest tantric masters of Tibet, an accomplished one through the practice of Yamantaka (T. Shin je shed, *gShin rJe gShed*).
2. Ngen lam Gyal wa Chog yang (*Ngan lam rGyal Ba*

mCh'og dByangs), one of the first seven monks of Tibet, achieved esoteric accomplishments through practice on Hyagriva (T. Ta drin, *rTa mGrin*).

3. Nam kha'i Nying po (*Nam mKha'i sNying Po*), a famous monk and translator. He became an accomplished one through esoteric practice on Vajraheruka (T. Yang dag).
4. Nyag Lo Ye shey Zhon nu (S. *Jñānakumāra*, T. *gNyag Lo Ye Shes gZhon Nu*), one of the greatest sources of tantric teachings among Tibetans and a great translator. He accomplished his attainments through the deity Vajrakīla (T. Dor je Phur pa, *rDo rJe Phur Pa*) among others.
5. Ye shey Tsho gyal (S. *Jñānasāgara*, T. *Ye Shes mTsho rGyal*), the consort of Guru Padmasambhava and the greatest female enlightened being in Tibet. She became an accomplished one through practice of the Vajrakīla maṇḍala.
6. Drog mi Pal gyi Ye shey (*a'Brog Mi dPal Gyi Ye Shes*), a translator who achieved accomplishment through practice of the maṇḍala of Ma mo.
7. Lang Pal gyi Seng ge (*Lang dPal Gyi Seng Ge*), a powerful tantrik who became an accomplished one through practice of the maṇḍala of Jig ten Chod tod (*a'Jigs rTen mCh'od brTod*).
8. S. Vairocana, T. Nam par Nang dzed (*rNam Par sNang mDzad*), the greatest translator Tibet ever produced. One of the first seven monks, he translated a number of scriptures of sūtra and primarily of tantra. He became an accomplished one through practice on Mod pa Trag ngag (*dMod Pa Drag sNgags*).
9. Yu dra Nying po (*gYu sGra sNying Po*), a translator and disciple of Guru Padmasambhava and Vairocana. He was a great master of the Sem de (*Sems sDe*) and Long de (*Klong sDe*) categories of Dzog chen.
10. Na nam Dor je Dud jom (*sNa Nam rDo rJe bDud a'Joms*) achieved accomplishment through practice of the Vajrakīla maṇḍala.
11. Ye shey yang (*Ye Shes dByangs*), one of the eight

great calligraphers during the time of Guru Padmasambhava.

12. Sog po Lha pal (*Sog Po Lha dPal*), an accomplished one through practice of Vajrakīla. He was a disciple of both Guru Padmasambhava and Nyag lo Ye shey Zhon nu.
13. Na nam Ye shey (*sNa Nam Ye Shes*), an accomplished one through practice of the Vajrakīla maṇḍala. According to scholars he is the famous translator Zhang gi Ban De Ye shey de (*Zhang Gi Ban De Ye Shes sDe*), who was one of the three great translators second only to Vairocana.
14. Khar chen Pal gyi Wang chug (*mKhar Ch'en dPal Gyi dBang Phyug*), brother of Ye shey Tsho gyal, the consort of Guru Padmasambhava. An adept of Vajrakīla, he traveled with Guru Padmasambhava to various sacred places in Tibet.
15. Dan ma Tse mang (*lDan Ma rTse Mang*), a translator who attained the power of unforgetting recollection (S. *Dharana*, T. *Mi brJed Pa'i gZungs*). He was one of the great calligraphers of the symbolic scripts of Ter.
16. Ka wa Pal tseg (*sKa Ba dPal brTsegs*), one of the three great translators next only to Vairocana; one of the first seven monks of Tibet.
17. Shud pu Pal gyi Seng ge (*Shud Pu dPal Gyi Seng Ge*), an adept of Vajrakīla, Ma mo and Yamantaka.
18. Dre Gyal wa'i Lo drö (*a'Bre rGyal Ba'i Blo Gros*), a disciple of both Guru Padmasambhava and the Indian Hūṁkāra; a translator and one who attained deathless accomplishment.
19. Khye chung Lo tsa (*Khyeu Ch'ung Lo Tsa*) became a translator in his youth. A scholar and tantric adept.
20. Tren pa Nam kha (*Dran Pa Nam mKha'*), a great master of Bon who became a disciple of Guru Padmasambhava and a translator.
21. O tren Pal gyi Wang chug (*O Bran dPal Gyi dBang Phyug*), a great scholar and practitioner of tantras.
22. Ma Rin chen chog (*rMa Rin Ch'en mCh'og*), one of the first seven monks and a great translator. He was

a master of the *Guhyagarbha Tantra.*

23. Lha lung Pal gyi Dor je (*Lha Lung dPal Gyi rDo rJe*), a disciple of Guru Padmasambhava and Vimalamitra who became a highly accomplished one.
24. Lang tro Kon Chog Jung ne (*Lang Gro dKon mCh'og a'Byung gNas*), a great tantrik and translator.
25. La sum Gyal wa Chang chub (*La gSum rGyal Ba Byang Ch'ub*), one of the first seven monks, a famous scholar and translator.

115 The Subject, Bang (*a'Bangs*) refers to Vairocana, respected as the greatest translator of Tibet, not only by the followers of the Earlier Translated Doctrine, the Nyingmapas, but also by the followers of the Later Translated Doctrine, the Sarmapas. A translator of the later period, Ngog lo Lo den Shey rab (*rNgog Lo Blo lDan Shes Rab* 1059–1109), wrote:

> Vairocana is equal to the expanse of the sky.
> Ka and Chog are like the sun and moon (referring to Ka wa Pal tseg and Chog ro Lu'i Gyal tshen),
> Rin chen Zang po (the greatest translator of the later period) is only like the dawn star,
> And we are merely fireflies.

According to BT (page 6a/2), the excellent one among the Subjects is Nam kha'i Nying po (*Nam mKha'i sNying Po*) instead of Vairocana.

116 Friend, Trog (*Grogs*) refers to Ye shey Tsho gyal, the consort of Guru Padmasambhava. She was born in the Khar chen family and became a devout yoginī, undergoing many hardships to inspire others in the Dharma. Her husband, King Thri srong Deu tsen, offered her to Guru Padmasambhava. She became his consort and chief disciple, devoting her life to serving the Guru, his followers and the teachings. She performed wonders through her enlightened power. Ye shey Tsho gyal requested the Ter teachings, arranged them, and completed their concealment for the benefit of future followers. At the end of her life, she departed for the manifested pure land of Guru Padmasambhava without

leaving mortal remains. She is respected by Nyingmapas as a Wisdom Ḍākinī or Enlightened Being who assumed human form for the sake of others, and as the greatest female teacher. She is one of the twenty-five siddhas or accomplished disciples of Guru Padmasambhava.

117 Nine Heart-sons, Thug se gu (*Thugs Sras dGu*), the greatest accomplished disciples of Guru Padmasambhava in Tibet:

1. King Thri srong Deu tsen
2. Nub chen Sang gye Ye shey
3. Ngen lam Gyal wa Chog yang
4. Nub Nam kha'i Nying po
5. Nyag Ye shey Zhon nu
6. Ye shey Tsho gyal
7. Drog mi Pal gyi Ye shey
8. Lang Pal gyi Seng ge and
9. Vairocana

But in BT (page 6a/1), Nub Sang gye Ye shey (*gNubs Sangs rGyas Ye Shes*) and Drog mi Pal gyi Ye shey (*a'Brog Mi dPal Gyi Ye Shes*) are replaced by Ka wa Pal tseg (*Ka Ba dPal br Tsegs*) and Chog ro Lu'i Gyal tshen (*Chog Ro Klu'i rGyal mTshan*).

118 S. Bodhisattva, T. Chang chub Sem pa (*Byang Ch'ub Sems dPa'*), an adherent of Mahāyāna Buddhist practice who has vowed to serve all living beings for their happiness and enlightenment. Until he completes the tenth stage and reaches the fifth path, which is Buddhahood, he will be called a Bodhisattva. The two types are ordinary people practicing Mahāyāna disciplines and beings who are manifestations of the Buddhas and Bodhisattvas, such as Avalokiteśvara and Mañjuśrī, in order to serve living beings.

119 Central deity, Tso wo (*gTso Bo*). When a tantric master confers an empowerment, the disciple first casts a flower into the maṇḍala to determine to which family of deities he belongs. This text refers to the Mind-mandate Transmission given to a person whose flower has fallen upon the central deity. In a footnote the author clarifies the

statement by saying that in order to receive the Mind-mandate Transmission of great teachings such as Gong dü Chen mo, it is necessary for the flower to fall in the center, but not in the case of other teachings.

120 This point refers to some major Termas such as Gong dü chen mo (*dGongs a'Dus Ch'en Mo*) and the three texts on the Eight Great Maṇḍalas. but it should be understood that there are differences between the major and minor Termas. Gong dü chen mo (*dGongs a'Dus Ch'en Mo*) is the name of a vast and famous Terma in thirteen volumes. Generally known as La ma Gong dü (*Bla Ma dGongs a'Dus*), it was discovered by Sang gye Ling pa (*Sang rGyas Gling Pa*, 1340–1396). He is one of the previous lives of Dodrup Chen Rinpoche, author of *Wonder Ocean.*

121 Mind-mandate Transmission, (*gTad rGya*). The main instrument for the concealing of Ter. The transmission and concealment take place in the essential nature of the mind of a disciple by his power of concentration. The Guru integrates his enlightened mind with the awareness state of the mind of his disciple, and that integration is the absolute transmission and concealment of the teaching. Concealment of symbolic script etc. are supports of transmission.

122 End-age, Dü tha (*Dus mTha'*). Age of dregs and dark age are synonyms. The present time of war, disease, famine and emotional struggles might be a golden age for science and technology, but to spiritual eyes it might be the end-age.

123 Instruction, Thrid (*Khrid*). After empowerment or initiation into the maṇḍala of a tantric deity one receives instructions on how to practice.

124 Recitation transmission, Lung. Transmission of a scripture by recitation of the entire text. One of the three essential requirements for starting esoteric practice. The other two are empowerment and instruction.

125 S. Ḍākinī, T. Kha dro (*mKha' a'Gro*). A possessor of spiritual power in female form. There are two kinds of ḍākinīs: S. Jñāna Ḍākinī, T. Ye shey Kha dro ma (*Ye Shes mKha' A'Gro Ma*), who are fully enlightened and are in

the pure form of a female body possessing the five certainties of the Saṃbhogakāya; and ordinary ḍākinīs, who have taken birth as beings possessing varying degrees of spiritual power and realization. Ḍākinīs protect the Termas, hand them over to the Tertons and protect the followers of the teachings. The majority of Terma protectors are in female form since it is a natural quality of the female to care for and preserve. This point is briefly explained in the notes of Yum ka De chen Gyal mo (LGB page 4) by the Third Dodrup Chen Rinpoche. In Tibet 'Kha dro' is an honorific term of address for consorts of tantric masters.

126 Casket, Drom bu (*sGrom Bu*). The container of the symbolic scripts written on yellow scrolls for the concealment of the Termas.

127 Yellow Scroll, Shog Ser. The paper scrolls of symbolic script which the Tertons discover.

128 Prophetic Terma text, Ter lung (*gTer Lung*). In addition to religious objects and instructions on meditation and ritual, Termas include texts foretelling future events and giving advice.

129 Dri med Kun ga (*Dri Med Kun dGa'*) was born in the Fire-Pig (1347) year in Tra chi (*Gra Phyi*), southern Tibet. He discovered many sādhanas on Guru Padmasambhava and Avalokiteśvara and Dzog chen teachings. Most of them disappeared and were rediscovered by Khyen tse'i Wang po (*mKhyen brTse'i dBang Po*, 1820–1892) as Yang ter (*Yang gTer*) or rediscovered Ter.

130 Three realms, S. Tribhūmi, T. Sa sum (*Sa gSum*). The realms of gods above the earth, human beings on the earth, and nāgas under the earth.

131 This phrase is part of a dharani recited by the master while conferring the name or prophetic empowerment (*Ming dBang*). Uttered by a master conferring a tantric empowerment, it sows in the mind of the disciple the seed of becoming a Buddha of that name by the master's blessing of transmission and the disciple's devotion and realization. Dharani: *O Vajra* [put disciple's tantric name here] *Tathagata-siddhi-samayas tvam bhur bhuva svah.*

132 Ter dag Ling pa (*gTer bDag Gling Pa*). Popularly known as Min ling Ter chen (*sMin Gling gTer Ch'en*), Gyur me Dor je (*a'Gyur Med rDo rje*, 1646–1714). One of the greatest Nyingma tantric authorities. An incarnation of Vairocana, he discovered many Ter and compiled esoteric and exoteric teachings. In 1676 he built Min trol ling (*sMin Grol Gling*) monastery, one of the two major Nyingma monasteries in central Tibet. A teacher and a disciple of the Fifth Dalai Lama.

133 Meaning, Tshon cha don (*mTshon Bya Don*). The meaning which is to be symbolized; the actual transmission, meaning or essence of attainment conveyed by symbolic means. In the Terma tradition, it is the Mind-mandate Transmission.

134 Text, Tshon ched Da'i Pe (*mTshon Byed brDa'i dPe*). Symbolic text which indicates the meaning in the transmission of esoteric powers. In the Terma tradition, it is the Entrustment of symbolic scripts to Ḍākinīs.

135 Vow-holders, Dam chen (*Dam Chan*). Powerful beings of different classes who have received teachings from Guru Padmasambhava and have taken vows to protect his teachings, his followers and the Terma tradition. Some of them are enlightened ones who have assumed various forms to serve others. They appear in male and female, wrathful and peaceful forms.

136 Perfection Stage (S. *Sampannakrama*, T. *rDzogs Rim*). All the inner tantric practices are classified into two stages or categories: Development Stage (*S. Utpannakrama*, T. *bsKyed Rim*) and Perfection Stage. The Development Stage is meditation on the clarity of perceiving phenomena as pure lands and enlightened deities. The Perfection Stage is generating wisdom, the union of great bliss and emptiness, by means of the channels, energy and essence of the vajra-body, and dissolving all phenomena into the meditative state, the primordial wisdom.

137 Mother (i.e. root) and son (i.e. commentarial) texts of Kha dro nying thig. Mother or Root Kha dro nying thig (*mKha' a'Gro sNying Thig*) is one of the two major texts on Nying thig teachings in Tibet. The other important text is Vima Nying thig, the teachings brought to Tibet by

Vimalamitra. Kha dro Nying thig teachings were brought to Tibet by Guru Padmasambhava in the ninth century and transmitted to Lha cham Padma Sal (*Lha lCham Padma gSal*), daughter of King Thri srong Deu tsen and others, and concealed as Terma. Padma Le drel tsal (*Padma Las a'Brel rTsal* 1291?–1315?), a rebirth of Lha cham Padma sal, discovered the Terma of the Nying thig teachings. It became known as Kha dro Nying thig because it had been transmitted through the Kha dro or female teacher Lha cham Padma sal and her incarnations. The son (commentarial) texts of Kha dro Nying thig, known as Kha dro Yang tig, is the commentary on Kha dro Nying thig written by Kun khyen Long chen Rab jam (*Kun mKhyen Klong Ch'en Rab a'Byams*, 1308–1363), the supreme scholar of the Nyingmapa and author of over 200 treatises. Kun khyen also wrote commentaries on Vima Nying thig, entitled La ma Yang tig (*Bla Ma Yang Tig*), and a commentary on both Kha dro and Vima Nying thig entitled Zab mo Yang tig. The texts written by Kun khyen on Nying thig teachings are classified by many scholars of Nyingma as Mind Termas.

138 Nying thig (*S. Cittatilaka*, T. *sNying Thig*). The main emphasis of Nying thig teachings is on the Men ngag de category of Dzog chen or Atiyoga. Dzog chen, the Great Perfection, has three major categories:

1. Sem de (S. *Cittavarga*, T. *Sems sDe*) on Mind.
2. Long de (S. *Abhyantaravarga*, T. *Klong sDe*) on the Great Expanse.
3. Men ngag de (S. *Upadeśavarga*, T. *Man Ngag sDe*), Instructions on the Essential Point.

Whether or not they are called Nying thig, there are teachings in almost all major Termas on the Men ngag de aspect of Dzog chen. The two major texts of Nying thig are Kha dro Nying thig and Vima Nying thig with commentaries by Kun khyen Long chen Rab jam. Long chen Nying thig (*Klong Ch'en sNying Thig*) is another well known Nying thig text. Through the blessing of Kun khyen Long chen Rab jam in pure visions Rig dzin Jig med Ling pa discovered Nying thig teachings as

Mind Terma and named them Long chen Nying thig.

139 Rig dzin Jig med Ling pa (*Rig a'Dzin a'Jigs Med Gling Pa*, 1729–1798) is one of the greatest teachers of sūtra and tantra, notably of Dzog chen. He wrote nine volumes including the Long chen Nying thig, which he discovered as a Mind Terma from the natural state of mind without relying on the external support of symbolic scripts. He was the founder of the Long chen Nying thig sub-school of the Nyingmapa. The First Dodrup Chen Rinpoche (1745–1821) was the Root Doctrine-holder of Long chen Nying thig.

140 Symbolic script (*brDa Yig*). Script written on yellow scrolls, the key to discovery of Earth Termas.

141 Miraculous script, Thrul yig (*a'Phrul Yig*). A type of symbolic script which changes rapidly or unclearly when the Terton reads it.

142 Alphabet (*Ka dPe*). Since most symbolic scripts are not Tibetan, the Tibetan alphabetical equivalent is sometimes found with them. A non-Terton is then able to read the script.

143 Rubrics (*Phyag bZhes*). Guides for the performance of recitations, rituals, disciplines, meditation and celebrations.

144 Phag pa Da tar.... Title of a scripture of the Buddha which includes these verses from PPB page 37a:

> In future, after my passing away,
> When the funeral ceremonies have been completed
> elaborately,
> The Buddhas and Bodhisattvas will preserve
> [memorize] them [sūtras],
> Transcribe them and put them in caskets.
> Afterward in stūpas, rocks, mountains
> And in the hands of gods as well as nāgas
> The sūtras will be concealed or entrusted.
> Then the Buddhas and Bodhisattvas will go to fulfill
> the lives of celestial beings; and
> In a later period,
> Leaving behind that kind [of existence], they will
> return to this land.

Having taken the form of a Buddha or Bodhisattva,
They shall fulfill the wishes [of beings].
They will go from place to place where the Dharma is needed,
And will rediscover the sūtras.

145 S. Sūtra, (T. *mDo* or *mDo sDe*). A collection of discourses of the Śākyamuni Buddha to his common disciples. One of the three categories of common teachings known as Tripiṭaka (*sDe sNod gSum*), the three baskets or collections.

146 Phag pa Sod nam. . . . Title of a scripture of the Buddha. (AM)

147 Phag pa Cho yang dag. Title of a canonical scripture. From PCD, page 84b:

> Bodhisattva Sthiramati said, "O Victorious One! Well-being of mind is the root of all Dharma. Whoever does not have that mind is far from the Dharma of the Buddha. O Victorious One! People who have well-being of mind, even if the Buddha is not present, will receive Dharma from the midst of the sky, walls or trees. For those Bodhisattvas whose minds are pure, instructions and teachings will appear just by the thoughts in their minds."

148 S. Vajrayāna, T. Dor je Theg pa (*rDo rJe Theg Pa*). The Adamantine Vehicle. A synonym for the tantric or esoteric teachings and practices of Buddhism. *Vajra* means diamond, that which is indestructible, or the most extraordinary material. *Yāna* means vehicle and means: It is the extraordinary means to reach the supreme goal of enlightenment.

149 S. Yoga, T. Nal jor (*rNal a'Byor*). Esoteric practices of the outer, inner and secret teachings of Tantra involving vigorous physical and mental discipline.

150 S. Yogin, T. Nal jor pa (*rNal a'Byor Pa*). An ascetic layman or monk who practices yoga.

151 S. Sādhana, T. Drub thab (*sGrub Thabs*). Means of accomplishment. Texts used in the tantric practices of worshipping, reciting, visualizing and meditating on the maṇḍala of a deity.

152 Liberation by seeing, Thong trol (*mThong Grol*). One of the five swiftly liberating skillful means of tantra:

1. S. Cakra, T. Khor lo (*a'Khor Lo*). A diagram which liberates by seeing. In the case of Termas, the symbolic scripts.
2. S. Mantra, T. Zung ngag (*gZungs sNgags*). Syllables which liberate by hearing.
3. S. Amṛta, T. Dud tsi (*bDud rTsi*). Ambrosia, substances which liberate by tasting.
4. S. Mudrā, T. Chag gya (*Phyag rGya*). A consort, the source of wisdom of united bliss and emptiness, who liberates by touching.
5. Pho wa (*a'Pho Ba*). Meditation on transferring the consciousness, which liberates by thinking.

153 Spirit Lake, La tsho (*Bla mTsho*). A lake which can be seen at Drag da (*sBrags mDa'*) about twenty-five miles south of Lhasa, said to have emerged spontaneously at the moment of birth of the great ḍākinī Ye shey Tsho gyal (*Ye Shes mTsho rGyal*), the consort of Guru Padmasambhava. Hence the name Tsho gyal, Queen of the Lake or Victorious Lake.

154 T. Nga yab ling, S. Cāmaradvīpa (*rNga Yab Gling*). The Western sub-continent of the Southern Continent, Jambudvīpa, in Indian cosmology. In 864 ad after fifty-five years and six months in Tibet, Guru Padmasambhava left for Cāmaradvīpa, flying through the sky by his enlightened power. He had attained deathless accomplishment and still remains in the middle of Cāmaradvīpa in a manifested pure land called Copper Colored Mountain (*Zangs mDog dPal Ri*), visible only to realized beings. This sub-continent is also known as the Land of Rākṣas (*Srin Po'i Gling*).

155 Local spirits, S. Bhūmipāla, T. Zhi dag (*gZhi bDag*). Buddhists believe that there are countless types of beings other than humans and animals. Some are more powerful, happier and more intelligent than humans, and others less. Usually, if there is no common karma, or karmic connection, beings of different types will not encounter each other. Spirits are not necessarily births of

the ancestors from a particular locality, but may have come from any kind of birth or realm. Before Buddhism came, Tibetans believed in the presence of powerful beings or spirits in various parts of the land and they worshipped them. The practice established a relationship between people and spirits. When Buddhism reached Tibet, spirits caused obstructions because the goal of Buddhist practice was not the worship of spirits. One of the major purposes of Guru Padmasambhava's visit to Tibet was to pacify the spirits. He controlled all the local spirits and bound them by oath to protect Buddhism and Buddhists. They became known as Dharmapālas, protectors of the Dharma.

156 Auspicious or favorable circumstances, omen or sign, Ten drel (*rTen a'Brel*). In Mahāyāna Buddhism, the ultimate meaning of all phenomena is emptiness, free from conceptualizations and beyond reasoning. In relative reality, apparent phenomena are generated and degenerate totally because of positive and negative circumstances, the causes and conditions. If favorable circumstances coexist, every possible result will occur as a magical display. Thus the discovery of Terma totally depends on the occurrence of favorable circumstances. Even a good omen, such as someone's saying an auspicious word, greatly affects the discovery of a Terma and its effectiveness. In Tibetan philosophical texts Ten drel (S. *Pratītyasamutpāda*) is translated as interdependent causation, but in other contexts it means sign and omen. Favorable circumstances or good omen is the proper translation in this case.

157 Omniscient Lord, S. Sarvajñā, T. Tham ched Khyen pa (*Thams Chad mKhyen Pa*). Here it refers to Khyen tse'i Wang po (*mKhyen brTse'i dBang Po*, 1820–1892), a great Terton and teacher. He was an incarnation of both King Thri srong Deu tsen and Vimalamitra, and of Jig med Ling pa. The Third Dodrup Chen, author of *Wonder Ocean*, was one of his main disciples.

158 Terma Protectors, Ter sung (*gTer Srung*). When Guru Padmasambhava concealed the symbolic scripts and religious objects he entrusted them to powerful beings

such as nāgas, yakṣas, and gods. Many of these Terma Protectors are highly realized ones and even manifestations of Buddhas, who have taken various forms in order to serve the teachings for the benefit of beings. Others are worldly beings but are devoted to the Dharma and are holders of the vow to protect the teachings and followers.

159 Four elements, Jung wa Zhi (*a'Byung Ba bZhi*). Fire, air, water and earth.

160 Triple Gem, S. Triratna, T. Kon chog Sum (*dKon mCh'og gSum*). The three gems or precious ones are: the Buddha, the precious teacher, the Dharma, the precious teaching and attainment, and the Saṅgha, the precious community of Dharma followers.

161 Obligations, S. Samaya, T. Dam tshig. The effective connection between cause and result is the only means which generates and maintains all phenomenal existents. For spiritual development a strong spiritual connection between a realized master, the source of transmission of esoteric power, and the disciple, and between the esoteric teachings and the practitioner are crucial for strengthening conventional attainments in order to reach the ultimate goal, the fully enlightened state.

162 S. Mantra, T. Rig ngag (*Rig sNgags*). A string of syllables or a phrase of esoteric meaning and power. A manifestation of supreme enlightenment in the form of sacred syllables and sounds. Some mantras have linguistic meaning, others do not. Both types have potential natural power and purity of sound and speech. Mantras differ in purpose and effect: for rituals of deities, worshipping deities, invoking the blessing power of deities, bestowal of blessings, protection from negative influences, and achievement of various wishes. They may be chanted loudly but are usually chanted or recited quietly and kept secret.

163 Actions, S. Karma and Krīyā, T. Le (*Las*). Practices which are not the main practice but are related, and which can only be practiced if one has some esoteric accomplishment. They are for dispelling bad circumstances and fulfilling the wishes of oneself or others in accordance

with Dharma. Generally they are classified into four: peaceful, expanding or developing, controlling or subjugating and wrathful.

164 Thang yig. Termas of religious history and biography. Two famous ones are Padma Ka yi Thang yig (*Padma bKa' Yi Thang Yig*) and Thang yig De nga (*Thang Yig sDe lNga*) by O gyen Ling pa (*O rGyan Gling Pa*, 1323–?).

165 Great Prophecy of Gong dü, Gong dü Lung ten Chen mo (*dGongs a'Dus Lung bsTan Ch'en Mo*). A famous text of confidential prophecy from La ma Gong dü.

166 Eastern Terma includes the Terma of Pe ma Le drel tsal (*Padma Las a'Drel rTsal*, 1291?–1315?), who discovered the Kha dro Nying thig, and the Termas of Sang gye Ling pa (1340–1396), who discovered the La ma Gong dü, among others. However, according to DND p. 98a/5, this is the Ters discovered by Dor je Ling pa (1346–1405).

167 Southern Terma includes the Terma discovered by Nyang Nyi ma Od zer (1124–1192), Guru Chö wang (1212–1270) and Padma Ling pa (1450–1521). However, according to popular belief it is the Ters of Ter dag Ling pa (1646–1714) and according to DND (page 98a/6), this is also the Ters of Ratna Ling pa (1403–1478).

168 Western Terma: According to HPT (page 47a/3) and DND (page 98a/5), this is the Ters discovered by Pe ma Ling pa (1450–1521).

169 Northern Terma includes the Termas of Rig dzin God dem (1337–1408), the Chang ter (*Byang gTer*). According to DND (page 98a/6), this is also the Ters of Kar ma Ling pa (14th century).

170 Central Terma includes the Termas of Ter dag Ling pa (1646–1714). According to DND (page 98a/5): this is the Ters of Sang gye Ling pa (1340–1396).

171 S. Anuttarayoga, T. Nal jor La med (*rNal a'Byor Bla Med*). The Unexcelled Yoga: the three Inner Tantras according to the Nyingma division of Buddhist teachings into nine yānas.

172 Easy to understand. Most Termas are on Anuttara tantras, the most profound and difficult of tantric teachings. They are also the most direct and uninterpretable expositions presented simply and practically with great skill, making the teachings easy to understand, practice,

and realize.

173 Guru Sādhana. Practice on the Spiritual Master. Practice on Guru Padmaśambhava as the union of all the enlightened ones. Guru Sādhana texts are divided according to purpose into root scriptures and branch or supplementary texts.

174 S. Atiyoga or Mahāsandhi, T. Dzog pa Chen Po (*rDzogs Pa Ch'en Po*). According to Nyingma tradition, the summit of the nine yānas and the most profound teaching of all. Atiyoga is the direct approach to the essential nature of the mind, which is the Buddha nature (*S. tathāgatagarbha*, T. *De bZhin gShegs Pa'i sNying Po*), through the recognition of the naked awareness state of one's own mind.

175 S. Avalokiteśvara, T. Thug je Chen po (*Thugs rJe Ch'en Po*) or Jigten Wang chug (*a'Jigs rTen dBang Phyug*). The Bodhisattva of compassion, the most popular deity in Tibet. Also known in Tibetan as Chen re zig (*sPyan Ras gZigs*).

176 Tsa sum Ka du (*rTsa gSum bKa' Dus*). Texts on the Three Roots (guru, tutelary deity and ḍākinī) providing a condensed practice on Buddhist doctrine.

177 Chi pung (*sPyi sPungs*). Texts in which various deities of the Three Roots are practiced on in an assembled form.

178 Ne gyur (*gNas bsGyur*). Texts at different stages of which deities are changed to their different forms.

179 Tso du (*gTso bsDus*). Texts in which the practice is on the assemblage of the main deities only.

180 Chig dril (*gChig Dril*). Texts in which the practice is on one deity for the purpose of various accomplishments.

181 Peaceful Guru. Texts in which the practices are on Guru Padmasambhava in peaceful form. In general, deities have three aspects: peaceful form, wrathful form, and semi-wrathful form.

182 Wrathful Guru. Texts of practice on Guru Padmasambhava in wrathful form. While an enlightened one in peaceful form is easily understood, the wrathful form and the form of sexual union are misunderstood by those who are ignorant of the tradition. The significance of the enlightened aspects includes the following points:

1. In Buddhism whether an expression is wrathful or

peaceful makes no difference; they are equal in being illusory phenomena far from their true state. But these expressions are assumed by the enlightened ones as a necessary skillful means to guide beings to the true state.

2. In relation to Dharma practitioners, a person who has little spiritual experience needs to avoid expressions of a negative and unvirtuous nature such as anger and to make efforts to develop virtuous expressions such as compassion. A person of middling spiritual potential can subdue unvirtuous expressions by their antidotes, for example, anger by compassion. Persons of high spiritual experience can accept as training whatever negative expressions occur. Whatever emotion they experience, they will use the power generated by it as a virtue, transforming it into an enlightened state.
3. The wrathful form is not a reflection of negative emotions of the deities but an appropriate demonstration, a means to pacify or transform the emotions of beings into enlightened power. The manifestation of an angry form is not different from the Buddha's enlightened manifestation as a human being for human beings, an animal for animals and a musician for musicians.
4. There are nine major expressions for any type of Buddha in wrathful form: three physical expressions:
haughty, heroic and fearful; three expressions of speech: laughing, reviling and fierce; three mental expressions: compassionate, vigorous (courageous) and peaceful. The purpose of any expression is to manifest a virtuous meaning, to strengthen positive energy through skillful means, and to attain the state of equalness by transforming anger, for example, into mirror-like wisdom.

183 Tutelary deities, S. Iṣṭadevatā, T. Yi dam. A deity chosen as the main object of one's meditative practice. The Buddhist tantras include hundreds of sādhanas of deities, any of which can be used for practice on a tutelary deity.

184 S. Cakrasaṁvara and Hevajra, T. Khor lo De chog (*a'Khor Lo bDe mCh'og*) and Kye Dor je (*Kyai rDo rJe*). Two of the major deities and tantras of the New Tantra (*gSar Ma*) tradition of Tibetan Vajrayāna. The New Tantras are the texts translated into Tibetan from Sanskrit and other Indian languages in and after the eleventh century AD.

185 Peaceful and wrathful deities, Zhi thro (*Zhi Khro*). Tantric texts on a cycle of one hundred deities (forty-two peaceful deities and fifty-eight wrathful deities); one of the principal Ancient Tantras of the Nyingma school. The root text is S. Guhyagarbhamāyājālatantra, T. Gyu thrul Dra wa Sang wa Nying po (*sGyu a'Phrul Dra Ba gSang Ba sNying Po*). Many commentaries and Termas are devoted to this tantra.

186 Three categories of worldly deities, Jig ten pa'i De sum (*a'Jigs rTen Pa'i sDe gSum*). Ma mo Bod tong (*Ma Mo rBod gTong*), Jig ten Chod tod (*a'Jigs rTen mCh'od bsTod*) and Mod pa Trag ngag (*dMod Pa Drag sNgags*), three maṇḍalas of the Eight Great Maṇḍalas (*bKa' brGyad*).

187 Eight Siddhis, Drub chen Gyed (*Grub Ch'en brGyad*). The Eight Great Accomplishments. They are the accomplishments of the celestial land, sword, pill, swift feet, vase, yakṣa (spirit), elixir and eye lotion.

188 Extraction of nutrients, Chud len (*bChud Len*). There are texts on extracting the essence of flowers or stones for practitioners to live on without food. The purpose is to purify one's body, generate pure energy, and refine one's mental functions for spiritual attainments.

189 Sang dü or La ma Sang dü (*Bla Ma gSang a'Dus*). Text on the practice of Guru Padmasambhava discovered by Guru Chö wang (1212–1270).

190 Chö gyal Ka bum (*Ch'os rGyal bKa' a'Bum*). The teachings of King Srong tsen Gam po (617–698) of Tibet.

191 Yang nying Dü pa (*Yang sNying a'Dus Pa*). Text discovered by Guru Chö wang.

192 Gong pa zang thal (*dGongs Pa Zangs Thal*). Famous text on Dzogchen discovered by Rig dzin God dem (1337–1408).

193 Knowledge-holders, S. Vidyādhara, T. Rig dzin or Rig pa Dzin pa (*Rig Pa a'Dzin Pa*). A sage of the esoteric tradition of Buddhism, holder of esoteric wisdom, pow-

er and teachings. There are eight famous knowledge-holders of ancient India according to Nyingma tantras. They are Hūṁkāra, Mañjuśrī, Nāgārjuna, Prabhahasti, Dhanasaṃskṛta, Vimalamitra, Rombuguhya (or Guhyacandra) and Śāntigarbha.

194 Hūṁ letters. When Guru Padmasambhava visited Sam ye, local spirits rained rocks on him. Just by his uttering HŪṀ the rocks were suspended in the form of a HŪṀ letter, and the rock formation is known as Dza mo Hung dra ma (*rDza Mo Hung 'aDra Ma*), the HŪṀ-like rocky mountain.

195 Four rocky mountains. Guru Padmasambhava left his foot-prints on four rocks, as if on mud, to become objects of homage. There are many footprints, hand-prints and body-marks imprinted on rocks in Tibet by Guru Padmasambhava. The author mentions the four major footprints on rock, specifying the one at Pa tro (*sPa Gro*) in Bhutan. Chang dag Tra shee Tob gyal (*Byang bDag bKra Shis sTobs rGyal* 1557?–?) mentions four footprints on rock in his biography of Guru Padmasambhava, (POM page 300a) but does not include the footprint at Pa tro. He locates the eastern footprint at Ser gyi dam (*gSer Gyi a'Dam*) near Tsa ri in Kong po valley and the southern one at Lho trag Khar chu (*Lho Brag mKhar Ch'u*). The western footprint was on the Gung thang pass in Mang province but was later brought to Sam ye. The northern footprint is at the base of Dar ko (*rDar Ko*) snow mountains.

196 Four Lakes. Guru Padmasambhava left huge hand-prints which can still be seen on four lakes. The four lakes are Nam tsho Chug mo (*gNam mTsho Phyug Mo*) or Tengri nor, Ya drog Yu tsho (*Ya a'Brog gYu mTsho*) or Pal ti, Thri shor Gyal mo (*Khri Shor rGyal Mo*) or mTsho sNgon or Koko nor, and Tsho Ma pham (*mTsho Ma Pham*) or Manasarowar.

197 Ten ma (*bsTan Ma*). Twelve local female spirits of Tibet who have taken the vow from Guru Padmasambhava to protect the Dharma and its followers: the Four Ten mas of the Dud mo (*bDud Mo*) type: 1) Tshe ring ma (*Tshe Ring Ma or Kun Grags Ma*), 2) Dor je Ya ma kyong (*rDo rJe gYa Ma sKyong*), 3) Kun zang mo (*Kun bZang Mo*) and

4) Geg gyi tso (*bGegs Kyi gTso*); The Four Ten mas of the Nod jin mo (S. *Yakṣasi*, T. *gNod sByin Mo*) type: 1) Chen chig ma (*sPyan gChig Ma*), 2) Kha ding Lu mo gyal (*mKha' lDing Klu Mo rGyal*), 3) Dor je Khyung tsun ma (*rDo rJe Khyung bTsun Ma*), and 4) Trag mo gyal (*Drag Mo rGyal*); The Four Men mo (*sMan Mo*): 1) Pod kham kyong (*Bod Khams sKyong*), 2) Men chig ma (*sMan gChig Ma*), 3) Yar mo sil (*gYar Mo bSil*), and 4) Dor je Zu le men (*rDo rJe Zu Le sMan*).

198 Pal tul Rinpoche (*dPal sPrul Rin Po Ch'e*, 1808–1887). One of the greatest Nyingma masters. His full name is O gyen Jig med Chö kyi Wang po (*O rGyan a'Jigs Med Ch'os Kyi dBang Po*), given by the First Dodrup Chen Rinpoche (1745–1821). He studied and taught at Dzog chen monastery, becoming a well known Bodhisattva, teacher and writer. Among his pupils were Ju Mi pham Nam gyal (*a'Ju Mi Pham rNam rGyal*, 1846–1912) and the Third Dodrup Chen Rinpoche (1865–1926).

199 Jambu continent, S. Jambudvīpa, T. Dzam bu ling (*a'Dzam Bu Gling*). In Indian cosmology our world consists of four continents and eight sub-continents around a huge mountain called Mt. Meru. All of them are surrounded by a great wall. The southern continent of that system is called Jambu continent and seems to represent Asia.

200 Monkey month. The twelfth month of the Tibetan calendar, or the sixth, which occurs in summer, according to the system which is followed here.

201 S. Atīśa, T. Jo wo je (*Jo Bo rJe*). A great scholar from Vikramaśīla, one of the most famous seats of Buddhist learning in India. He lived in Tibet in the eleventh century and wrote *The Lamp of the Path to Enlightenment*, S. *Bodhipathapradīpa*, T. *Chang chub Lam gyi Dron ma* (*Byang Ch'ub Lam Gyi sGron Ma*), a gradual way of practice to attain Englightenment. His disciples founded the Ka dam pa (*bKa' gDams Pa*) school, but later his teachings merged into or were accepted by other schools and no separate school remains.

202 Drub thob Ngö drub (*Grub Thob dNgos Grub*, twelfth century ad). An early Terton. Among his Termas are the *Ma ṇi Ka bum* (*Ma Ni bKa' a' Bum*) and *Gyal Po Ka chem*

(*rGyal Po bKa' Ch'em*), texts attributed to King Srong tsen Gam po (617–698) on historical events of ancient Tibet and teachings on Avalokiteśvara. It is said that those works of the Dharma King were concealed in an image in the Tshug lag khang (*sTsug Lag Khang*), the main temple in Lhasa built by King Srong tsen Gam po and discovered by Guru Padmasambhava. After showing them to King Thri srong Deu tsen, he reconcealed them, and later Drub thob ngö drub discovered them.

203 The Buddha entrusted Tibet to Avalokiteśvara. According to the sūtra, S. *Vimalaprabhaparipṛcchā*, T. *Dri ma med pa'i od kyi zhu pa* (*Dri Ma Med Pa'i Od Kyis Zhus Pa*) (*De ge Kajur, mDo sDe*, Volume Ba, page 211–259) the Buddha instructed Avalokiteśvara to discipline, serve and preach Dharma in Tibet at the appropriate future time.

204 Noble monkey meditator, Phag pa Trel gom (*a'Phags Pa sPrel bsGom*). According to Tibetan historical texts, the human race orginated in Tibet from the union of a monkey, who was an incarnation of Avalokiteśvara, and a mountain ogress.

205 Seven kinds of crops: After the human race appeared in Tibet, the descendants of the monkey and the mountain ogress increased and there was severe hunger. As requested by the monkey, Avalokiteśvara scattered the seeds of seven crops with aspirational blessings after which grains started to grow for the first time. The seven crops are: barley, wheat, black peas, corn, beans, buckwheat and mustard.

206 S. *Potala*, T. *Ri wo Tru dzin* (*Ri Bo Gru a'Dzin*). The pure land of Avalokiteśvara. There is an island associated with Avalokiteśvara's Potala pure land in the China sea off the coast of Shanghai, known as Pu to. The famous palace of the Dalai Lamas in Lhasa, also is named after this pure land.

207 S. *Karaṇḍavyūha sūtra*, T. *Do de Za ma tog* (*mDo sDe Za Ma Tog*). A scripture on Avalokiteśvara spoken by the Buddha. This was the first Buddhist scripture to reach Tibet.

208 Ka dam Leg pam (*bKa' gDams Gleg Bam*). An important scripture of the Kadampa (*bKa' gDams Pa*) tradition.

209 Image of Lord Śākyamuni. King Srong tsen Gam po, an

incarnation of Avalokiteśvara, married Princess Bhṛkuṭi, daughter of King Aṃsuvarma of Nepāl and Princess Wen Ch'en, a daughter of the Emperor T'ang T'ai Tsung of China. Both devout Buddhists, they brought two important images of the Lord Buddha to Tibet. The image of the Buddha from Nepāl, the Cho wo Mi kyod Dor je (*Jo Bo Mi bsKyod rDo rJe*), was installed in the Ra sa Thrul nang or Cho khang (*Ra Sa a'Phrul sNang or Jo Khang*) temple. The image brought by the Chinese princess, the Cho wo Yid zhin Nor bu (*Jo Bo Yid bZhin Nor Bu*), the Wish-fulfilling Gem, was installed in the Ra mo che (*Ra Mo Ch'e*) temple. Later, for reasons of safety, the images were exchanged with one another. The image of Cho wo Yid zhin Nor bu is the most important religious object of Tibet and the Cho khang is the most revered temple. They exist in Lhasa to this day. Cho wo Mi kyod Dor je and Ra mo che temple were the second most important image and temple in Tibet.

210 Ra sa'i Tsug lag Khang (*Ra Sa'i gTsug Lag Khang*). Another name for the Cho khang (*Jo Khang*).

211 Self-arisen image of Avalokiteśvara, Rang chung Phag pa (Rang Byung a'Phags Pa). An image of Avalokiteśvara which remained in the Cho khang temple until the 1960s. King Srong tsen Gam po is said to have assembled materials for building an image, including an image which had been brought from India. The next day when he went to look at the materials, the statue had already been completed as a self-arisen image. When the King and his two wives died, they each dissolved into the image to become objects of homage for the people. The image became known as Cho wo Rang chung Nga den (*Jo Bo Rang Byung lNga lDan*), the Self-arisen Image of Five: the sacred image brought from India, the self-arisen image itself, the king, the princess of Nepāl and the princess of China. When the King with his Nepāli queen began to build the Ra sa Temple over a lake in Lhasa, in response to prayers made by the King, rays came from the self-arisen image and the problem of filling the lake was solved miraculously.

212 Thon mi Sambhoṭa. A minister in the court of King Srong tsen Gam po. Until the seventh century a.d. there

was no script or grammar for the Tibetan language. The King sent Thon mi Sambhoṭa to India to learn Indian languages. On his return, as commanded, Thon mi devised the Tibetan script by adapting the Brāhmi and Gupta scripts. He also wrote eight texts on grammar for the Tibetan language based on Sanskrit grammatical structures. Now only two texts are available, which are the root grammar texts for Tibetan to this day.

213 Law of Ten Virtues. S. Daśakuśalakarma, T. Ge wa Chu (*dGe Ba bChu*). King Srong tsen Gam po proclaimed three codes of law based on Buddhist teachings. One is the Law of Ten Virtues:

Three Laws of the Body
1. Refraining from destroying life
2. Refraining from taking what is not given
3. Refraining from sexual misconduct

Four Laws of Speech
1. Refraining from false speech
2. Refraining from slanderous speech
3. Refraining from harsh speech
4. Refraining from foolish chatter

Three Laws of the Mind
1. Refraining from covetousness
2. Refraining from ill will
3. Refraining from wrong views

214 Thrul nang, Tha dul, Yang dul and Ru non (*a'Phrul sNang* or *Ra sa, mTha' a'Dul, Yang a'Dul* and *Ru gNon*) temples. When King Srong tsen Gam po and others examined the geographical significance of Tibet, they found it to be in the shape of an ogress lying on her back. He built the Ra sa or Thrul nang temple at the point of her heart and one hundred and eight temples at the joints and sub-joints of the ogress-shaped land.

215 Mani mantra: OM MA ṆI PADME HŪṀ. The six-syllable mantra of Avalokiteśvara, the most popular prayer of Tibetans.

216 Ka gyed kyi drub zhung. The main text of Long chen nying thig on the practice of Ka gyed (*bKa' brGyad*), the Eight Great Maṇḍalas, entitled *Pal chen dü pa* (*dPal Ch'en*

a'Dus Pa).

217 Primordial Wisdom, S. Jñāna, T. Ye shey (*Ye Shes*). The Buddha nature, transcendental wisdom of the Buddha. It has two qualities: Chi ta wa Khyen pa (*Ji lTa Ba mKhyen Pa*), the wisdom of knowing the absolute nature of all, and Chi nyed pa Khyen pa (*Ji sNyed Pa mKhyen Pa*), the wisdom of discriminating all the details of phenomena simultaneously without confusion.

218 Rest. This refers to secondary symbolic scripts (*brDa gZhan*), which help in discovering the branch texts. They are not the symbolic script which had been used in the Mind-mandate Transmission.

219 Lañca and Vartu. Ancient Indian scripts. Most Buddhist scriptures translated into Tibetan were in these two Sanskrit scripts. To this day many traditional scholars in Nepāl read Sanskrit literature in Lañca. Vartu seems to be the old Bengali script, or is closely related to it.

220 Trag mar Tsho mo gul (*Brag dMar mTsho Mo mGul*). A pilgrimage place near Sam ye monastery. Birth place of King Thri srong Deu tsen. Also known as Trag mar Drin zang (*Brag dMar mGrin bZang*).

221 Do chang (*mDo Byang*). Text discovered by Terton Le rab Ling pa (*Las Rab Gling Pa*, 1856–1926). The full title is Ter gyi Do chang Chen mo (*gTer Gyi mDo Byang Ch'en Mo*). Le rab Ling pa, also known as Nyag la Sod gyal (*Nyag Bla bSod rGyal*), was a teacher, disciple and spiritual brother of the Third Dodrup Chen.

222 Ter sar (*gTer gSar*). New Terma, here referring to the Termas of Le rab Ling pa.

223 Matted Hemp. The Tibetan reads; Bal Ba Dza lTar a'Dzings Pa. Bal Ba (Pa) Dza is a synonym for rTsa Dres Ma, which means 'hemp'.

224 Long sal Nying po (*Klong gSal sNying Po*, 1625–1692). A great Terton and disciple of the great Terton Dud dul Dor je (*bDud a'Dul rDo rJe*, 1615–1672). Long sal Nying po made Ka thog monastery in Kham his main seat.

225 Lo drö Tha ye (Blo Gros mTha' Yas, 1813–1899), popularly known as Jam gon Kong tul (*a'Jam mGon Kong sPrul*). A great writer and Terton. He compiled major Termas of the great Tertons in sixty volumes (the new edition published by Dil go Khyen tse Rinpoche is in 135

volumes) under the title *Rin chen Ter dzod* (*Rin Ch'en gTer mDzod*) or *Rin po che Ter gyi dzod* (*Rin Po Ch'e gTer Gyi mDzod*). Lo drö Tha ye belonged to the Kagyud school but his works are on Kagyud and Nyingma teachings and include studies of Bon.

226 Psychic visions or experiences, Nyam cho (*Nyams Ch'os*), *Nyam* means psychic, *Chö* means doctrine. Because of their clarity or intelligence some people write wonderful books without having had much education. They are the result of their past good karma, the fine system of channels and circulation of energy in their bodies. These writings are not the result of accomplishment, insight or inner wisdom. They are vastly different from Mind Termas, yet people mistake them for Mind Terma or Pure Vision teachings.

227 Demonic teachings discovered through the power of worldly gods and demons, Lha dre'i Cho thrul (*Lha a'Dre'i Ch'o a'Phrul*). Some people, although they do not have education or spiritual accomplishment, are able to write wonderful works by the power of gods or demons who fulfill their wishes. Sometimes gods or demons appear before them, in person or in dreams, in the form of enlightened sages and saints, and give teachings, which the hearer transcribes. They may be mistaken for Pure Visions or Mind Termas. Although some appear to be powerful and beneficial teachings, they lead not along the path of enlightenment but to worldly achievements. In Tibet, newly discovered teachings, even if they seem to have been found miraculously, must be authenticated by an undisputed spiritual authority.

228 Transcribing, Per Beb pa (*dPer a'Bebs Pa*). Tertons usually dictate their texts to others. For example, my teacher Tulku Kun zang Nyi ma (*Kun bZang Nyi Ma*, d. 1958?), the speech incarnation of Dud jom Ling pa (*bDud a'Joms Gling Pa*, 1835–1903) sometimes had five scribes working at the same time. He would dictate a line of each text to a transcriber, never omitting or mixing lines of the different texts, and never having to ask for the last line of one of the texts to be read to him.

229 Permission, Nang wa (*gNang Ba*). There were exceptional cases in which some great Terton who possessed

power and Mind-mandate Transmission discovered many Termas without the permission of the actual Terton. Rig dzin Nyi ma Trag pa (*Rig a'Dzin Nyi Ma Grags Pa*), a contemporary of the Fifth Dalai Lama (1617–1682), was well known for discovering Termas of others.

230 Lung ten Ka gya ma (*Lung bsTan bKa' rGya Ma*). A famous prophetic text of La ma Gong dü (*Bla Ma dGongs a'Dus*) discovered by Sang gye Ling pa (1340–1396). It is the same text referred to as *The Great Prophecy of Gong dü* (*dGongs a'Dus Lung bsTan Ch'en Mo*).

231 Mu rum Tsen po (Mu Rum bTsan Po) also known as Lha se Dam dzin (Lha Sras Dam a'Dzin). The second of three sons of King Thri srong Deu tsen and a disciple of Guru Padmasambhava. The Dodrup Chens are incarnations of Mu rum Tsen po.

232 Ba yo Chö kyi Lo drö (*Ba Yo Ch'os Kyi Blo Gros*). A teacher of Sang gye Ling pa who became one of the twenty-one doctrine-holders of La ma Gong dü, a Terma of Sang gye Ling pa. He was an incarnation of Vairocana but not a Terton in that lifetime. Since he did not take birth to decode or discover Terma, he was unable to read symbolic scripts.

233 Long po Chang chub Ling pa (*Long Po Byang Ch'ub Gling Pa*). An incarnation of Nam kha'i Nying po and a contemporary of Sang gye Ling pa. He is an example of someone who can decode symbolic scripts because he has received the Mind-mandate Transmission and who is a Terton in his present life.

234 Nam kha'i Nyingpo (*Nam mKha'i sNying Po*) or Nam nying (*Nam sNying*). A member of the Nub (*gNubs*) family and one of the twenty-five chief disciples of Guru Padmasambhava. He was a great translator, monk (*dGe Slong*), siddha (*Grub Thob*). He made Lho trag Khar chu (*Lho Brag mKhar Ch'u*) in southern Tibet his main seat. He departed in the body for the pure land.

235 Dud jom or Dor je Dud jom (*rDo rJe bDud a'Joms*). A member of the Na nam (*sNa Nam*) family and one of the twenty-five chief disciples of Guru Padmasambhava. He was a great siddha.

236 Omniscient Guru Vajradhara refers to Khyen tse'i Wang po (1820–1892).

237 Guru Mañjughoṣa refers to Khyen tse'i Wang po.

238 Consecrating wisdom deity. When a tantrik confers an empowerment or blessing he invites the wisdom, or absolute, deity, merges the deity in the mind of the disciple and establishes the deity there. The text reads: *Ye Shes Pa Phab Nas sNying dBus Kyi Thig Ler brTan Par Byas.*

239 Mirror divination, Tra phab pa (*Bra Phab Pa*). Observing the appearance of signs or letters in a blessed mirror. Sometimes one is able to see clearly something which will occur or has occurred, and sometimes the image is in symbolic form. The message may appear in ordinary writing, code, or an unknown language. The power does not always result from esoteric accomplishment but from prior recitations and the right circumstances.

240 Substitute for Ter, Ter tshab (*gTer Tshab*). Whenever a Terton makes a discovery, he conceals religious objects, which may be specified in the Prophetic Guide, in place of the Ter and closes the door of concealment.

241 Grave consequences, Nyey mig (*Nyes dMigs*). To discover and practice Terma teachings according to the vision of Guru Padmasambhava is highly effective and beneficial; but if the Terton acts improperly in discovering or practicing the teachings, equally grave negative results such as illness and death are inevitable.

242 Instruct instantly, Thral nyid du De tar Ka go wa (*a'Phral Nyid Du De lTar bKa' bsGos Pa*). Guru Padmasambhava has the wisdom and power at any time to command from his pure land that Termas be concealed and handed over to the appropriate Tertons.

243 Feast Offering, or Assemblage of Offerings, S. Gaṇacakrapūjā, T. Tshog kyi Khor lo or Tshog (*Tshogs Kyi a'Khor Lo* or *Tshogs*). Assemblages of Offerings. A tantric offering ritual consisting of three assemblages: devotees, offerings and objects of offering (deities).

244 Gods and nāgas, S. Deva, T. Lha. In Buḍdhism gods are the beings of the upper realms or births and spirits who are powerful because of their past good deeds and are

supporters of the virtuous. They are not enlightened but ordinary beings. S. Nāga, T. Lu (*Klu*). Beings, half-human and half-serpent, who live in water. They have limited miraculous powers and are usually invisible to ordinary human beings.

245 Recollection, S. Dhāraṇī, T. Zung (*gZungs*). Some highly realized beings have achieved the power of remembering whatever they have known. The Third Dodrup Chen wrote a famous text, *The Recollection of Bodhisattvas*, in which he distinguished four types of memory.

246 Teleportational reconcealment, Thod gal du Ba wa (*Thod rGal Du rBa Ba*). A method of reconcealing Ter from a great distance without the Terton's going to the place.

247 O kar trag (*O dKar Brag*). The place where Ter dag Ling pa discovered the text on the practice of Vajrasattva. Here the author refers to the Prophetic Guide (*Kha Byang*) of this text, entitled *rDor Sems Thugs Kyi sGrub Pa Las Zab gTer Kha Byang*.

248 Ten powers, S. Daśabala, T. Tob chu (*sTobs bChu*). The ten powers of knowledge of the enlightened ones, who know all correctly and totally:

1. The power of knowledge of what is and is not real. S. Sthānāsthānajñānabala, T. Ne dang Ne ma yin pa Khyen pa'i Tob (*gNas Dang gNas Ma Yin Pa mKhyen Pa'i sTobs*).
2. The power of knowledge of the causal relationship between actions and their consequences. S. Karmavipākajñānabala, T. Le kyi Nam par min pa Khyen pa'i Tob (*Las Kyi rNam Par sMin Pa mKhyen Pa'i sTobs*).
3. The power of knowledge of the varieties of complex types and natures of beings. S. Nānadhātujñānabala, T. Rig dang kham Chi nyed pa Khyen pa'i Tob (*Rigs Dang Khams Ji sNyed Pa mKhyen Pa'i sTobs*).
4. The power of knowledge of the complex varieties of individual inclinations of beings. S. Nānādhimuktijñānabala, T. Dro wa'i mö pa na tshog Khyen pa (*a'Gro Ba'i Mos Pa sNa Tshogs mKhyen Pa*).
5. The power of knowledge of the limit of mental

capacities of beings. S. Indriyaparāparajñānabala, T. Wang po chog men Khyen pa (*dBang Po mCh'og dMan mKhyen Pa*).

6. The power of knowledge of the various paths leading to liberation and enlightenment. S. Vimuktisarvajñānagāmipratipathajñānabala, T. Thar pa dang Tham ched khyen pa'i lam na tshog Khyen pa'i Tob (*Thar Pa Dang Tham Chad mKhyen Pa'i Lam sNa Tshogs mKhyen Pa'i sTobs*).
7. The power of knowledge of various samādhis (absorptions) both with and without emotions. S. Āśravanashravasarvadhyānajñānabala, T. Zag che dang Zag med kyee dü pa'i sam ten Chi nyed Khyen pa'i Tob (*Zag bChas Dang Zag Med Kyis bsDus Pa'i bSam gTan Ji sNyed mKhyen Pa'i sTobs*).
8. The power of knowledge of all past events (lives) of oneself and others. S. Pūrvanivāsānusmṛtijñānabala, T. Rang zhen kyi ngon kyi ne jey su Tren pa (*Rang gZan Gyi sNgon Gyi gNas rJes Su Dran Pa*).
9. The power of the knowledge of the deaths and births of beings, S. Cyūtyupapattijñānabala, T. Dro wa'i ch'i pho key wa Dren pa'i Tob (*a'Gro Ba'i a'Ch'i a'Pho sKye Ba Dran Pa'i sTobs*).
10. The power of knowledge of the path and result of freedom from emotions, S. Āśravakṣyapathaphalajñānabala, T. Zag pa zed pa'i lam dang dre bu Khyen pa'i Tob (*Zag Pa Zad Pa'i Lam Dang a'Bras Bu mKhyen Pa'i sTobs*).

249 Nada. Here it refers to the ultimate essence, enlightened state, absolute nature, most subtle point, freedom from elaborations and changes.

250 Triple vajra. S. Vajra, T. Dor je (*rDo rJe*). The triple vajra is three sacred aspects of the enlightened ones: vajra body, vajra speech and vajra mind. Here it refers to the triple vajra of Guru Padmasambhava.

251 Periods. The author speaks of the power and effect of the Termas as varying in different periods of time. In general the duration of the Buddhist doctrine in the world is divided into four periods, from the Buddha's time till the future total extinction of Buddhism. The exoteric

teachings of Śākyamuni Buddha will remain in the world for five thousand years. The first 1500 years is called 'the fruition period' (*a'Bras Bu'i Dus*), when many achieved the highest result of the path of practice. The second 1500 year period is called 'The practice period' (*sGrub Pa'i Dus*) when many devote themselves to practicing the path. The third 1500 years is called 'the scripture or precept period' (*Lung Gi Dus*) since many emphasize the study of scriptures. The fourth period of 500 years is called 'the merely symbolic period' (*rTags Tsam a'Dzin Pa*) since the followers of the Buddha's doctrine merely hold on to the signs or external characteristics of wearing robes, etc. Many believe that we are now in the third hundred years of 'the practice period', while others think we are in the first or second hundred years of 'the scripture period.' That is the general division into four periods of the doctrine. This text speaks of two systems of four periods which apply to the teachings of Guru Padmasambhava. They make clear, among other things, the need for new Termas. The first system is the four periods of esoteric teachings beginning at the time of Guru Padmasambhava. The second is the four periods of Termas beginning at the time of their earliest discovery. Each of these systems presumes varying degrees of spiritual effectiveness at different periods of time.

252 Early Dharma Treasure, Ter kha Kong ma (*gTer Kha Gong Ma*). The Termas discovered by Nyang Nyi ma Od zer (1124–1192).

253 Later Dharma Treasure, Ter Kha Og ma (*gTer Kha A'og Ma*). The Termas of Guru Chö wang (1212–1270).

254 Trol thig (*Grol Thig*). A Terma (OWC) of Threng po Shey rab Od zer (*a'Phreng Po Shes Rab A'od Zer*, 1517–?). The text referred to is an explanation by Jig med Ling pa of the empowerment of Trol thig.

255 Fulfilling Offering, Kang wa (*bsKang Ba*). A practice of specific offerings for fulfilling the wishes of deities in order to accumulate merits for living beings and to fulfill the obligations of one's esoteric practice.

256 Confession, Shag pa (*bShags Pa*). Ritual for purifying the misdeeds of oneself and others.

257 Path of spirits. Gong po'i Gyu lam (*a'Gong Po'i rGyu Lam*). Places thought to be frequented by harmful spirits.

258 Terma objects, Ter dze (*gTer rDzas*). Some of the discovered objects are made of unimaginable materials, sometimes eight or sixteen precious materials formed into an image with wonderful artistry. Guru Padmasambhava made many of them miraculously and instructed gods, nāgas and yakṣas to make others. Some are simple in nature and design, and many were made by human beings.

259 Nectar, S. Amṛta, T. Dud tsi (*bDud rTsi*). Nectars in liquid, powder or pill forms prepared with esoteric rituals. It is believed that special attainments can come just by tasting them with faith.

260 Evil ministers, Dud lon (*bDud Blon*). While Guru Padmasambhava was establishing Buddhism in Tibet until it reached its peak, many esoteric teachings were concealed for the future. Powerful but wrongly inspired ministers, people and spirits made evil aspirations to corrupt the Terma teachings by discovering false Termas in the future. That is why false Termas are discovered in Tibet from time to time as counterparts to the positively effective and precious Termas.

261 The ring (*Theu Ring*). Spirits in one-legged form.

262 Padma Le drel tsal (*Pad Ma Las a'Brel rTsal*, 1291?–1315?). A great Terton who discovered the Kha dro Nying thig. Because he could not follow the prophetic instructions properly, he died. Sum Tshog discovered a famous sādhana text called Yang Sang (*Yang gSang*) on S. Hyagrīva, T. Ta drin (*rTa mGrin*).

263 Won ton Kye gang pa (*dBon sTon sKye sGang Pa*). His given name was Chö kyi Seng ge (*Ch'os Kyi Seng Ge*). In a dream he visited Guru Padmasambhava at his pure land, the Copper Colored Mountain. He received the empowerment and teachings on the Hyagrīva deity called Ta drin Sang drub (*rTa mGrin gSang sGrub*). He was instructed by Guru Padmasambhava to receive the same teachings from Nye mo wa Sang gye Wang chen (*sNye Mo Ba Sangs rGyas dBang Ch'en*), who had discovered that scripture on Hyagrīva as a Terma. It became known as the Kye gang Ta drin or the teachings on

Hyagrīva of the Kye gang pa tradition. Nye mo wa Sang gye Wang chen was a contemporary of Nyang Nyi ma Od zer (1124–1192).

264 Ne dong ma (*sNe gDong Ma*), the one from Ne dong. According to *The Great History of Terma* (HSL) it refers to Dag po Chen po Jam yang pa (*bDag po Ch'en Po a'Jam dByangs Pa*), the successor of De sid Phag mo Tru pa (*sDe Srid Phag Mo Gru Pa*) or Tai Situ Chang chub Gyal tshen (*Byang Ch'ub rGyal mTshan,* 1302–1373) whose capital was Ne dong or Neu dong in the Yar lung (*Yar Klungs*) valley. De sid Phag mo Tru pa revolted against the Sa kya rulers, who ruled Tibet since 1253. He became the ruler of Tibet in 1349. He and his successors, the Phag mo Tru pas, ruled Tibet until 1435.

265 S. Prajñāpāramitā, T. Shey rab kyi Pha rol du Chin pa (*Shes Rab Kyi Pha Rol Tu Phyin Pa*). The texts which expound Transcendental Wisdom, the highest exoteric teaching of Mahāyāna Buddhism.

266 Non-returner, Chir mi Dog pa (*Phyir Mi lDog Pa*). Here it refers to the Bodhisattva who has attained the state of non-reversal of attainments and who is a non-returner to saṃsāra, or the world, because of his karma.

267 I have been told. Here the author is quoting Le rab Ling pa (*Las Rab Gling Pa,* 1856–1926), a Terton who was a teacher, colleague and disciple of the Third Dodrup Chen Rinpoche (1865–1926).

268 Ter sar Do chang (*gTer gSar mDo Byang*). Do chang is the name of a text by Le rab Ling pa. Ter sar means the new Terma here referring to the Termas of Le rab Ling pa.

269 New Tantra. Sang ngag Sar ma (*gSang sNgags gSar Ma*). The tantric scriptures which were translated into Tibetan in and after the eleventh century are known as New Tantras. All four major Buddhist schools except the Nyingmapa are followers of the New Tantras.

270 Nyal pa Nyi ma Shey rab (*gNyal Pa Nyi Ma Shes Rab*). A disciple of Zang kar Lo tsa wa (*Zangs sKar Lo Tsa Ba*), the translator from Zang kar and a great tantric scholar. He discovered texts of S. Vaiśravaṇa, T. Nam tho se (rNam Thos Sras). He was a contemporary of Sa kya Paṇḍita (1181–1251).

271 Nyen lo Dar ma trag (*gNyan Lo Dar Ma Grags*). Nyen is the name of his clan, Lo tsa wa means translator, and Dar ma trag was his name. He was a translator of Buddhist scriptures from Sanskrit to Tibetan. Among other texts he discovered the Terma on S. *Śrīnātha* in four-faced form, T. Pal Gon po (*dPal mGon Po*), and became known as Nyen gyi Gon po (*gNyan Gyi mGon Po*). He was a contemporary of the great yogi Milarepa (1040–1123).

272 Lord Tsang pa Gya re (*rJe gTsang Pa rGya Ras*, 1161–1211). Founder of the Drug pa Ka gyud (*a'Brug Pa bKa' brGyud*), one of the subschools of the Kagyud.

273 Gyud chen Sang gye Gya tsho (*rGyud Ch'en Sangs rGyas rGya mTsho*). A great Abbot of Srad Gyud pa Tra tshang (*Srad rGyud Pa Grva Tshang*). Gyud pa Tra tshang means a tantric college; Srad is the name of a valley in Tsang province in western Tibet. It was founded by Dul nag pa (*a'Dul Nag Pa*), a disciple of Je Shey rab Seng ge (*rJe Shes Rab Seng Ge*) a principal disciple of Je Tsong kha pa (1357–1419).

274 Other sources. Meaning Termas not connected with Guru Padmasambhava or the Nyingma.

275 Re chung Dor je Trag (*Ras Ch'ung rDo rJe Grags*, 1084–1161). One of the two major disciples of Milarepa the other being Gampopa (1079–1153).

276 Dro gon Chö gyal Phag pa (*a'Gro mGon Ch'os rGyal a'Phags Pa*, 1235–1280). A great master of the Sakya school who became ruler of Tibet in 1253. He was the preceptor of Kublai Khan, emperor of China.

277 Karmapa Rang chung Dor je (*Kar Ma Pa Rang Byung rDo rJe*, 1284–1334) was the Third Karmapa, the head of the Karma Kagyud sub-school of the Kagyud. He was a great scholar and accomplished one in Kagyud and Nyingma doctrine. He, among others, discovered teachings on Nying thig of the Nyingma.

278 Bu ton Rin chen trub (*Bu sTon Rin Ch'en Grub*, 1290–1364). One of the great writers of Tibet. He collected and edited into their present form the Kajur (*bKa' a'Gyur*) and Tenjur (*bsTan a'Gyur*), the canon and commentaries of Buddhism translated into Tibetan from Indian languages. He spent his last years at Zha lu (*Zhva

Lu) monastery.

279 Gyal wang Ge dun Gya tsho (*rGyal dBang dGe a'Dun rGya mTsho*, 1476–1542), the Second Dalai Lama. The Fifth Dalai Lama became the ruler of Tibet.

280 Lo drö Rin chen Seng ge (*Blo Gros Rin Ch'en Seng Ge*). Cham chen Cho je (*Byams Ch'en Ch'os rJe*), a principal disciple of Je Tsong kha pa, built Sera monastery near Lhasa in 1419. Lo drö Rin chen Seng ge was the fifth successor of Cham chen Chö je. He was also known as the Kun khyen (*Kun mKhyen*), the Omniscient One.

281 Transmission of seven streams, Ka bab Chu wo Dun (*dKa 'Babs Ch'u Bo bDun*), Khyen tse'i Wang po was one of the few masters of esoteric teachings who was a recipient, holder and transmitter of the whole transmission system of seven categories, one of Canonical teachings and six of Terma.

1. He received the transmission of both Old and New Canonical Tantras from the masters and deities in person and in visions.
2. He discovered many concealed esoteric teachings as Earth Terma (*Sa gTer*).
3. He rediscovered many earlier discovered Earth Terma.
4. He discovered many Mind Terma (*dGongs gTer*).
5. He rediscovered many earlier discovered Mind Terma.
6. He discovered many Pure Vision teachings.
7. He received many oral transmissions in pure vision and discovered them.

282 Dor je Zi jid (*rDo rJe gZi brJid*) is one of the many names of Khyen tse'i Wang po (1820–1892).

Glossary

English	*Sanskrit*	*Tibetan*
absolute nature	svabhava	gNas Lugs, gShis
absolute truth	paramārthasatya	Don Dam bDen Pa
absolute universal ground		Don Gyi Kun gZhi
aconite		Bong Nga
actions	karma, krīya	Las Tshogs
Actual Indication (symbolic script)		rTen Tsam dNgos
actual transmission		Don brGyud
adamantine	vajra	rDo rJe
all-pervading		Kun Khyab
alphabet		Ka dPe
nectar, ambrosia	amṛta	bDud rTsi
Ancient Tantras		sNgags rNying Ma
answers to questions		Zhus Lan
appearances		a'Ch'ar Ch'a
arise		sKye Ba
arm-spread		a'Dom
aspect of awareness		Rig Ch'a
aspect of wisdom		Shes Rab Kyi Ch'a
Aspirational Empowerment		sMon Lam dBang bsKur
Attainment of control over life		Tshe dBang Rig a 'Dzin
auspicious circumstances	pratītyasa-mutpāda	rTen a'Brel

English	*Sanskrit*	*Tibetan*
awareness state		Rig Ngor
Baskets: scriptures	piṭakas	sDe sNod
a being on the path of enlightment	bodhisattva	Byang Ch'ub Sems dPa'
beings, half-human and half-serpent, who live in the ocean	nāga	Klu
body of Great Transformation		a'Pho Ba Ch'en Po'i Lus
brief sādhana		sGrub gZhung bsDus Pa
Buddha nature	tathāgatagarbha	bDe gShegs sNying Po
Buddhism	dharma	Ch'os
canon of Hinayāna scriptures: "the three baskets"	tripiṭaka	sDe sNod gSum
canonical scriptures on mental contemplation and wisdom	prajñāpāramitā	Shes Rab Kyi Pha Rol Tu Phyin Pa
canonical teachings (category of Nyingma tantras)	vacana	bKa'Ma
casket		sGrom Bu
central deity		gTso Bo
cessation of suffering	nirvāṇa	Mya Ngan Las a'Das Pa
channels	nāḍī	rTsa
charm wheel		a'Khor Lo
circumstantial influences		rKhyen
clarifications		Zhal Shes
clarity		gSal Ba
classes		Rigs
code of moral discipline	vinaya	a'Dul Ba

English	*Sanskrit*	*Tibetan*
collection of mantras		sNgags a'Bum
compassion		Thugs rJe
compiled		bKa' bsDus
Complete Text (symbolic script)		mThar Ch'ags
concentration of mind		dGongs Pa gTad
conception		dMigs Pa
confession		bShags Pa
confession and purification		sKong bShags
consecrate		Phab Pa
consort, sacred support	vajradūta	rDo rJe'i Pho Nya Mo, gSang Grogs, Phyag rGya, gZungs Ma
continuum	tantra	rGyud
conventional level		Tha sNyad
cross thread ceremony		mDos gTo
cyclic existence	saṃsāra	a'Khor Ba
dagger	kīla	Phur Pa
ḍākinī script		mKha' a'Gro'i brDa Yig
decode		brDa Khrol
decoding		Phab Pa
deity in the form of a sacred bird	garuḍa	Khyung
development stage	utpannakrama	bsKyed Rim
Dharma treasure discoverer		gTer sTon
diagram	cakra	a'Khor Lo
direct introduction		Rang Shes Pa
discourses on spiritual training; exoteric teachings	sūtra	mDo sDe
discovered Dharma treasures, hidden teachings		gTer Ma
discovery of Termas		gTer Len Pa

English	*Sanskrit*	*Tibetan*
divination		rNo mThong
division or category of Great Expanse	abhyantaravarga	Klong sDe
division or category on the mind	cittavarga	Sems sDe
division or category of instructions	upadeśavarga	Man Ngag sDe
Doctrine-holders		Ch'os bDag
earlier spread of Buddhism		bsTan Pa sNga Dar
early Dharma treasure		gTer Kha Gong Ma
Earth Terma		Sa gTer
Eight Great Accomplishments		Grub Ch'en brGyad
Eight Great Deities		bKa' brGyad
Eight Great Knowledge-holders		Rig a'Dzin Ch'en Po brGyad
Eight Great Orders of Maṇḍalas		sGrub Pa bKa' brGyad
elaborated sādhana		sGrub gZhung rGyas Pa
empowerment, initiation	abhiṣekha	dBang
empty	śūnya	sTong Pa
end-age		Dus mTha'
energy or air	Vāyu	rLung
enjoyment body	saṃbhogakāya	Longs sKu
enlightened attitude	bodhicitta	Byang Sems
entering		bChug Nas
entities		dNgos Po
Entrustment to ḍākinīs		mKha' a'Gro gTad rGya
esoteric instructions	upadeśa	Man ngag
esoteric practices of tantra	yoga	rNal a'Byor
esoteric teachings	āgama	Lung
esoteric or inner teachings of Mahāyāna	vajrayāna, tantrayāna, tantra	gSang sNgags Do rJe Theg Pa, rGyud

English	*Sanskrit*	*Tibetan*
Buddhism; Adamantine Vehicle		
essence		Ngo Bo, Thig Le
essential aspects		Lam gNad
evil ministers		bDud Blon
exceptional remains of fully enlightened beings		gDung
exhorting mantras		Drag sNgags
experiences		Nyams
explanations of deities		Lha Khrid
extraction of nutrients		bChud Len
false Termas		gTer rDzun
favorable circumstances		rTen a'Brel
feast offering	gaṇacakrapūjā	Tshogs, Tshogs Kyi a'Khor Lo
female yogi	yoginī	
form bodies	rūpakāya	gZugs sKu
four elements		a'Byung Ba bZhi
four inch		Sor bZhi
four ranges		Ru bZhi
free from extremes of elaboration		sPros Bral
Friend		Grogs
Fruition Period		a'Bras Bu'i Dus
Fulfilling Offering		bsKang ba
fully enlightened person in pure form of female body	jñāna ḍākinī	Ye Shes mKha' a'Gro Ma
fully ordained monk	bhikṣu	dGe Slong
fully ordained nun	bhikṣuni	dGe Slong Ma
general (prophetic) guide		Kha Byang
gods	deva	Lha

English	*Sanskrit*	*Tibetan*
grave consequences		Nyes dMigs
great master (Guru Padmasambhava)		Slob dPon Ch'en Po
Great Mistress of Desire Realm		a'Dod Khams dBang Mo
Great Perfection meditation	atiyoga, mahāsandhi	rDzogs Pa Ch'en Po
Great Tertons		gTer Ch'en
Greater Vehicle	mahāyāna	Theg Pa Ch'en Po
Hearing, Aural or Oral Transmission		sNyan brGyud
Hearing Transmission Between People		Gang Zag sNyan brGyud
Hearing Transmission Between Yogis		rNal a'Byor rNa brGyud
Heart sādhana		sGrub gZhung sNyig Po
hook		lChags Kyu
identity of things		Ngo Bo
impoverish		Phongs
ill-effects		rDzi Dug
Illusory Miraculous script		a'Phrul Yig sGya Ma Chan
Indestructible Essence		Mi Shigs Pa'i Thig Le
indestructible casket of the sphere of awareness		dByings Rig Mi Shigs Pa'i sGrom Bu
Indian fig tree	nyagrodha	
Indication Transmission		brDa brGyud
Indication Transmission of Knowledge-holders		Rig a'Dzin brDa brGyud
indivisibility of appearance and emptiness		sNang sTong dByer Med
innermost (prophetic guide)		Nying Byang, Ti Ka

English	*Sanskrit*	*Tibetan*
inner (prophetic guide)		Yang Byang, gNad Byang
Inner Tantra		Nang rGyud
insight widsom	vipaśyanā	Lhag mThong
instruct instantly		Phral Nyid Du De lTar bKa' bsGos Pa
instruction		Khrid
instructional teachings		gDams Khrid
Instructions of the Innermost Essence	cittatilaka upadeśa	Man Ngag sNying Thig
instructions on essential aspects		gNad Yig
instruments		Phyag mTshan
intellectual reasoning		Rig Pa
interdependent causation	pratītyasamut-pāda	rTen Ching a'Brel a'Byung
interdependent postulation		bTags Pa
(introduction through the agency of) indefinite circumstances of the external world or of beings		brTan a'Gro'i Yul rKyen
introduction		Ngo sProd
(introduction) through keys		lDe Mig Chan
(introduction) through various circumstances		rKyen Las Nges
Jambu Continent	jambudvīpa	a'Dzam Bu Gling
Just an Indication (symbolic script)		rTen Tsam
Just Visible (symbolic script)		sNang Tsam
karmic energy		Las rLung
Knolwledge-holders	vidyādhara	Rig a'Dzin

English	*Sanskrit*	*Tibetan*
later translation period		Phyi a'Gyur
Later Dharma Treasure		gTer Kha A'og Ma
(Law of) Ten Virutes		dGe Ba bChu
lead		Drang
Lesser Vehicle	hinayāna	Theg dMan
liberation by seeing		mThong Grol
local spirits	bhūmipāla	gZhi bDag
local female spirits of Tibet (twelve)		bsTan Ma
long sacred verbal formula	dhāraṇī	gZungs
long transmission of the canon		Ring brGyud bKa' Ma
Lord	nātha	rJe
Lord (who is the) Wish-fulfilling Gem		Jo Bo Yid bZhin Nor Bu
Lotus-born Guru	Guru Padma-sambhava	
luminescent nature		gNyug Ma'i A'od gSal
luminous natural awareness		A'od gSal gNyug Ma'i Rig Pa
luminous vision		A'od gSal Gyi dGongs Pa
magical display		Ch'o a'Phrul
main texts of Sādhana		sGrub gZhung
manifestative power of the ultimate mind		rTsal
manifesting body; manifestative expression of the form-body	nirmāṇakāya	sPrul sKu
meaning		mTshon Bya Don
means of accomplishment	sādhana	sGrub Thabs

English	*Sanskrit*	*Tibetan*
medicine and treatment		sMan Dang mKhyud dPyad
meditational instructions		sGom Khog
meditation on the luminescent wisdom of self-discriminating awareness		So So Rang Gi Rig Pa'i Ye Shes A'od gSal Ba'i Don
meditation on transferring the consciousness		a'Pho Ba
meditative concentration of mind		dGongs Pa gTad
member of the priestly caste of Hinduism	brāhmin	Bram Ze
merely symbolic period		rTags Tsam a'Dzin Pa
middle length sādhana		sGrub gZhung a'Bring
mind	citta	Sems
mind-mandate transmission		gTad rGya
mind-mandate transmission of aspirational empowerment		sMon Lam dBang bsKur Gyi gTad rGya
mind-sādhana		Thugs sGrub
mind Termas		dGongs gTer
mind-transmission		dGongs brGyud
mind-transmission of the Buddhas		rGyal Ba dGongs brGyud
minor Tertons		gTer Phran
Miraculous (Discovered Dharma Treasure)		'Phurl Yig Chan
miraculous illusory script		a'Phrul Yig sGyu Ma Chan

English	*Sanskrit*	*Tibetan*
mirror divination		Bra Phab Pa
name or prophetic empowerment		Ming dBang
natural sphere of the luminous state		A'od gSal Gyi Khams
nature, reality identity		Rang bZhin
natural state		Ch'os Nyid gNyug Ma
nature of things		Ch'os Nyid
New Tantras (new Tantric system of Tibet)		sNgags gSar Ma
New Terma		gTer gSar
Nine Heart-sons		Thugs Sras dGu
Noble Monkey Meditator		d'Phags Pa sPrel bsGom
non-entities		dNgos Med
non-returner		Phyir Mi lDog Pa
not existing in any form		Gang Du ang Ma Grub Pa
obligations	samaya	Dam Tshig
Old School, The Ancient One		rNying Ma Pa, gSang sNgags sNgags rNying Ma Pa
one and a half feet		sKum Khru Gang
path of spirits		a'Gong Po'i rGyu Lam
Peaceful and Wrathful Deities		Zhi Khro
perfect stage	sampannakrama	rDzogs Rim
permanently staying		gTan 'Khyil
permission		gNang Ba
pliant, flowing		mNyen lChug
possessor of spiritual power in female form	ḍākinī	mKha' a'Gro Ma
possessor of spiritual power in male form	ḍaka	mKha' a'Gro

English	*Sanskrit*	*Tibetan*
power of awareness		Rig Pa'i rTsal
power of gods and demons		Lha a'Dre'i Ch'o a'Phrul
power of teachings		Ch'os Kyi dNgos Grub
Practice on the Spiritual Master	guru sādhana	Bla Ma'i sGrub Pa
practice period		sGrub Pa'i Dus
practitioner of yoga	yogin	rNal a'Byor Pa
preparatory practices, Effectuation of the Ter		gTer sGrub
Primordial Buddha	samantabhadra	Kun tu bZang Po
Profound Mind Dharma Treasure		Zab Pa dGongs gTer
Prophetic Authorization, Prophetic Empowerment		bKa' Babs Lung bsTan
Prophetic Guide, Prophetic Introduction		Kha Byang
Prophetic Mind-mandate Transmission		gTad rGya Lung bsTan
Prophetic Terma text		gTer Lung
prospering of wealth		Nor sGrub
Provoking the Memory (symbolic script)		rJes Dran bsKul Byed
psychic vision teachings, "Ordinary Experiential Vision or Psychic Vision"		Nyams sNang, Nyams Ch'os
publicly discovered Terma		Khrom gTer
Pure Vision		Dag sNang
radiance		A'od Zer

English	*Sanskrit*	*Tibetan*
realization of the Perfection Stage		rDzogs Rim Las Su Rung Ba
Recitation Transmission		bKa' Lung
recollection	dhāraṇī	gZungs; Bag Ch'ag, Dran Pa
reconcealment and rediscovery of Termas; rediscovered Ter		Yang gTer
red sand		Bye Ma A Grong
relative truth	samvṛtisatya	Kun rDzob bDen Pa
relics		Ring bSrel
Renunciate	pravrajita	Rab Byung
representative		sKu Tshab
right to their depths		Klong Tu Kyur
Root Doctrine-holder		rTsa Ba'i Ch'os bDag
rubrics		Phyag bZhes, Lag Len
sacred diagram	maṇḍala	dkyil a'Khor
sage	vajradhara	rDo rJe a'Ch'ang
School of the Elders	theravāda	gNas bsTan sDe
scripture on wisdom, philosophy and psychology	abhidharma	mNgon Pa
Scripture or Precept Period		Lung Gi Dus
scrolls of paper		Shog Dril
secondary symbolic script		brDa gZhan
secrecy		gSang rGya
secretly discovered Terma		gSang gTer
self-appearances		Rang sNang
self-arisen image of Avalokitésvara		Rang Byung a'Phags Pa
self-arisen image of five		Jo Bo Rang Byung lNga lDan
semen, essence		Khams
shaking forth		gYo Ba

English	*Sanskrit*	*Tibetan*
short transmission of Termas		Nye brGyud gTer Ma
specific textual categories		So Sor Phye Ba'i sKor
sphere of primordial wisdom		Ye Shes dByings
spirit	yakṣa	gNod sBying
spiritual community	saṅgha	dGe a'Dun
spiritual master	guru	Bla Ma
spontaneously arisen bliss		Lhan sKyes Kyi dGa' Ba
stabilize		brTan Par Byas
sub-concealed Ter, reconcealment of Termas		a'Dab gTer
Subjects		a'Bangs
substitute for Terma		gTer Tshab
Supreme Attainment		mCh'og Gi dNgos Grub
syllable		Grong Khyer
syllables of esoteric meaning and power	mantra	Rig sNgags
symbolic		mTshan Ma
symbolic script		brDa Yig
symbolic substances, mantras and gestures		rDzas sNgags phyag rGya
symbolic text		mTshon Byed brDa'i dPe
tantric (esoteric or ultimate) essence		sNgags Kyi sNying Po
tantriks, community of ascetic esoteric trainees		sNgags Pa
tantric teacher	vajrācārya	rDo rJe Slob dPon
teleportational reconcealment		Thod rGal
ten powers	daśabala	sTobs bChu
Ter casket		gTer sGrom

English	*Sanskrit*	*Tibetan*
Terma objects		gTer rDzas
Terma Protectors		gTer Srung
theoretical dialectics		rTog Ge'i Rig Pa
three categories of Worldly Deities		a'Jigs rTen Pa'i sDe gSum
three realms	tribhūmi	Sa gSum
traditions, schools or lineages of Buddhism		Ch'os Lugs
tranquillity	śamatha	Zhi gNas
transcribed		gTan La Phebs Zin Pa
transcribing		dPer a'Bebs Pa
transcription of teachings		gTan La Pheb Pa
transcription of Terma scripts		Phabs Pa
transmission		Babs So
Trânsmission of Aspirational Empowerment		sMon Lam dBang bsKur
transmission of blessing		Byin rLabs
Transmission of Compassionate Blessing		Thugs rJe Byin rLabs
transmission of seven streams		bKa' Babs Ch'u Bo bDun
Triple Gem	triratna	dKon mChog gSum
tutelary deity	iṣṭadevatā	Yi Dam
Two stages		Rim gNyis
two superior truths		Lhag Pa'i bDen Pa gNyis
two aspects		Zur gNyis
two truths	satyadvaya	bDen Pa gNyis
type of spirit	rākṣasa	Srin Po
ultimate body or state, formless body, absolute, empty aspect of Buddhahood	dharmakāya	Ch'os sKu

English	*Sanskrit*	*Tibetan*
ultimate, indestructible essence, Great Emptiness	nada	
ultimate nature of the mind, mindness		Sems Nyid
ultimate sphere	dharmadhātu	Ch'os dByings
understand		brDa a'Phrod
unforgetting memory	dhāraṇī	Mi brJed Pa'i gZungs
various (minor) actions		Las sNa Tshogs
various miraculous actions		sNa Tshogs rDzu a'Phrul
various protective means		Srung Ba sNa Tshogs
Vast Earth Terma		rGya Ch'e Ba Sa'i gTer
vehicle	yāna	Theg Pa
Vehicle of Hearers or Disciples	śravakayāna	Nyan Thos Kyi Theg Pa
Vehicle of Seekers of Enlightenment	bodhisattvayāna	Byang Ch'ub Sems dPa'i Theg Pa
Vehicle of Silent Buddhas	pratyekabud-dhayāna	Rang rGyal Gyi Theg Pa
verbal transmission of the yellow scroll		Shog Ser Tshig brGyud
vision		sNang Ch'a
vow-holders		Dam Chan
vows		Dam Tshig
welfare of crops		Lo Tog Phan Byed
wisdom of discriminating all details of phenomena simultaneously without confusion		Ji sNyed Pa mKhyen Pa
wisdom of knowing the absolute nature of all		Ji lTa Ba mKhyen Pa

English	*Sanskrit*	*Tibetan*
Wisdom, Primordial Wisdom	jñāna	Ye Shes
wisdom deity		Ye Shes Pa
wisdom of the luminous state		A'od gSal Gyi mKhyen Ch'a
yellow scrolls of paper		Shog Ser

Index

1. TECHNICAL TERMS IN ENGLISH

2. TECHNICAL TERMS IN TIBETAN AND SANSKRIT

3. NAMES OF PERSONS, PLACES AND WRITINGS